T0334541

BEHAVIORAL ECONOMICS
THE BASICS

The second edition of *Behavioral Economics: The Basics* summarizes behavioral economics, which uses insights from the social sciences, especially psychology, to explain real-world economic behavior. Behavioral economic insights are routinely used not only to understand the choices people make but also to influence them, whether the aim is to enable citizens to lead healthier and wealthier lives, or to turn browsers into buyers.

Revised and updated throughout with fresh current-event examples, *Behavioral Economics: The Basics* provides a rigorous yet accessible overview of the field that attempts to uncover the psychological processes which mediate all the economic judgments and decisions we make. The book showcases how behavioral economics is rooted in some now-old (philosophical, political, and moral) ideas surrounding economics, and in an important sense is a modern expression of some long-standing criticisms of mainstream economics. It contrasts the neoclassical economic perspective (ECON) with a more realistic perspective (HUMAN – the flesh-and-blood economic agent who is not perfect in all respects but who manages to do the best under limitations and constraints).

This is a comprehensive overview of the whole field, covering all the main areas, presented in a rigorous yet accessible form. It should especially appeal to students, those with an interest in applying behavioral economic knowledge in their professional life, and anyone who wants to know how they are being influenced every day of their lives by (usually unseen) behavioral insights.

Philip Corr is Professor of Psychology at City, University of London, UK, and Honorary Professor at Brunel University, UK, where he specializes in behavioral economics. Reflecting his broader personality neuroscience focus, he is most interested in how individual differences in fundamental systems of motivation and emotion relate to economic behavior.

Anke Plagnol is Senior Lecturer in Psychology (Behavioral Economics) at City, University of London, UK. Her research focuses on the economic choices individuals make and how these affect their subjective well-being.

The Basics Series

The Basics is a highly successful series of accessible guidebooks which provide an overview of the fundamental principles of a subject area in a jargon-free and undaunting format.

Intended for students approaching a subject for the first time, the books both introduce the essentials of a subject and provide an ideal springboard for further study. With over 50 titles spanning subjects from artificial intelligence (AI) to women's studies, *The Basics* are an ideal starting point for students seeking to understand a subject area.

Each text comes with recommendations for further study and gradually introduces the complexities and nuances within a subject.

For a full list of titles in this series, please visit www.routledge.com/The-Basics/book-series/B

BEHAVIORAL ECONOMICS

THE BASICS

SECOND EDITION

Philip Corr and Anke Plagnol

Routledge
Taylor & Francis Group

LONDON AND NEW YORK

Designed cover image: © Getty Images

Second edition published 2023
by Routledge
4 Park Square, Milton Park, Abingdon, Oxon, OX14 4RN

and by Routledge
605 Third Avenue, New York, NY 10158

Routledge is an imprint of the Taylor & Francis Group, an informa business

First edition published by Routledge 2018

British Library Cataloguing-in-Publication Data
A catalogue record for this book is available from the British Library

ISBN: 978-0-367-76434-0 (hbk)
ISBN: 978-0-367-76432-6 (pbk)
ISBN: 978-1-003-16690-0 (ebk)

DOI: 10.4324/9781003166900

Typeset in Bembo
by codeMantra

CONTENTS

PREFACE

This is the second edition of the book. In the first edition, published in 2018, we noted that behavioral economics is a relatively new and exciting branch of the social sciences with considerable real-world applications. Since that time, we have had no reason to doubt the veracity of this statement. Indeed, quite the opposite: behavioral economic principles and practices are now even more widespread, especially in the commercial world. As also noted, the field is important but it can be complex and, even, confusing. In line with the aims of the first edition and in response to the developments since, we provide an updated introduction to the basic issues that continue to define the field, including theoretical, historical, and practical aspects. Our new edition also reflects the helpful comments of several reviewers, who suggested changes to some of the chapters – we were pleased (and relieved) that they thought favorably of the overall structure, content, and clarity of the first edition. Especially, we appreciated their affirmation of our belief that although behavioral economics may be a new branch of the social sciences, its roots go very deep in economic theory and history – all the way back to the first economist in the modern sense, Adam Smith. Indeed, as we claimed in the first edition, behavioral economics can be seen as the modern form of several much older traditions in economics and political thought. We also appreciated the reviewers' observation that we managed to avoid sterile Straw

(Wo)man arguments and presented a balanced view of the different sides of the debates.

In planning this revised edition, we continued to do something different to other books on behavioral economics. Like the first, the second edition of the book has an interested reader in mind who wants to get a real – and academically credible – understanding of this complex field. It is intended to be suitable for students, too, and has been informed by our experience of teaching on the MSc Behavioural Economics at City, University of London. More generally, it should be a good starting point for the professional who wants to apply behavioral economics to their own field.

Although our book continues to be concerned with the basics, it is not intended to be basic in content and discussion. We provide a sufficiently detailed, yet accessible, introduction to the whole field of behavioral economics. This is no easy feat to achieve. We hope our account continues in its lively, stimulating, and, even, provocative fashion. This is reflected in the new front cover image which alludes to the greater utility that can be derived from the application of behavioral economic principles, across all sectors of the economy, as well as the relevance of subjective well-being as an index of economic success. After all, citizens' well-being is (or at least should be) the central goal of governments and more of them are now employing the services of dedicated behavioral insights teams to achieve this goal.

To reiterate what we said in the first edition, we continue to believe that a book of this kind is needed. First, most behavioral economics books aimed at students are rich in mathematics and technical terms and are largely inaccessible to the non-economist; ours is not. Second, our book differs from other popular books in being more systematic in the presentation of material – in particular, we include a discussion of the history of economics (and some moral philosophy and politics) to let the reader gain an appreciation of the wider intellectual landscape that defines the field. Third, some of the more accessible books on behavioral economics do not cover in sufficient detail what, we believe, the interested reader needs to know. We continue to present the 'big picture', with the aim of giving a bird's eye view. We especially avoid mathematics, and we do our best to explain the technical terms which must be included if we are to do justice to the field. Students who wish to consult the primary sources of the studies summarized can refer to the bibliography at the end of each chapter. Most of the classic theories and concepts – including utility functions and opportunity costs (from economics), and social influence and priming (from psychology) – are covered in textbooks such as *Microeconomics and Behaviour* by Frank and Cartwright, or *An Introduction to Social Psychology* by Hewstone, Stroebe and Jonas.

As should be expected, the updated content includes reference to the Covid-19 pandemic – this has been a testing time for all, including the application of behavioral economics principles by governments and companies around the world (e.g., effective framing and communication of health-related measures). We have, however, avoided the temptation to increase the word count substantially by including more and more studies – to aid the reader, we have added relevant citations and references to recent research studies and theoretical issues, including a number of controversies that have arisen since the publication of the first edition.

As an economist (Anke Plagnol) and a psychologist (Philip Corr), we have tried to present both sides of behavioral economics. We continue to believe that it is at the intersection of these fields where behavioral economics was born, and where its creative synergies are located.

Further online resources may be found at:
https://www.ankeplagnol.com/behavioraleconomics

WHAT IS BEHAVIORAL ECONOMICS AND WHY IS IT IMPORTANT?

Behavioral economics applies psychological insights into economic judgment and decision making. It aims to describe how real people make decisions in their private and public lives under various constraints, such as time, knowledge, cognitive processing limitations, or social pressure. From both field studies and experiments, behavioral economists now know that humans often seem not to behave in a fully rational manner in everyday life: their behavior is affected by heuristics (mental shortcuts) and biases. This is in stark contrast to the assumptions that neoclassical (mainstream) economists make about economic behavior. In this sense, behavioral economics is about *misbehaving*: how real humans deviate from traditional economic model predictions. We will see why behavioral economics developed and how it has become more widely accepted following the 2008 global financial crisis. We will also briefly discuss in this chapter, and more in later chapters, how behavioral economics principles were applied during the Covid-19 pandemic. Some researchers have declared that "We're all behavioral economists now" (Angner, 2019), suggesting that the field is slowly becoming more accepted by mainstream economists. This introductory chapter provides a road map for this relatively new, exciting, but potentially confusing field.

DOI: 10.4324/9781003166900-1

INTRODUCTION

What is 'behavioral economics', and why has it become so prominent in the worlds of business, finance, and government? Why do
you need to know about it? What does it tell us about how people
form judgments and make decisions in their private and public lives?
How does it help us understand the psychological foibles that shape
our economic behavior? And what does it tell us about the periodic
nature of the financial catastrophes that afflict our economic system
(e.g., the stock market crash of 1929 and the global financial collapse
of 2007/2008)? Can we use insights gained from behavioral economics research to influence people's behavior during a global health crisis,
such as the Covid-19 pandemic? What are the implications of behavioral economics for mainstream economics that touches upon so many
areas of everyday life? By the end of this book, you will have answers
to these and many more questions; also, you should have your own
questions to ask about the world of economics as well as your own
behavioral insights to answer them.

In this introductory chapter, we see why there is such a need for
behavioral economics. We will understand why two pioneers received
the Nobel Memorial Prize in Economic Sciences – Daniel Kahneman
in 2002, even though he is a psychologist, and, more recently, Richard
Thaler in 2017, whose background is in economics.

In contrast to the presumptions of mainstream economics (which
we will discuss in detail in Chapter 3), we will see just how and
why we are so often *misbehaving* in everyday economic life – to borrow the title of Richard Thaler's 2015 book by the same name. In
particular, we will learn how economic judgments and decisions are
made by flesh-and-blood human beings, not disembodied calculating machines, and how apparent *mis*behavior may not be so irrational
after all. Once we have this basic knowledge under our intellectual belts, we will be in a better position to put to work what we
know. For example, what behavioral economics has to say about the
design and implementation of effective public policy interventions
(Chapter 6).

Applications in public policy are seen most clearly in the work of
the Behavioural Insights Team (the BIT, also known as the 'Nudge
Unit'[1]), the first of its kind, which informs UK government public

policy intervention. It was established in 2010 and later privatized in the form of a social purpose company, which allowed the BIT to provide advice to companies and foreign governments. Behavioral units have also been recognized by the US government – as the former US President, Barack Obama, said in 2015:

> A growing body of evidence demonstrates that behavioral science insights – research findings from fields such as behavioral economics and psychology about how people make decisions and act on them – can be used to design government policies to better serve the American people ....
>
> (Obama, 2015)

BEHAVIORAL INSIGHTS AROUND THE WORLD

Since then, the number of teams that apply behavioral insights to public policy has exploded around the world. The Organization for Economic Co-operation and Development (OECD) counted 202 such teams in 2018,[2] a number which is sure to increase as governments and citizens become more familiar with the benefits of their work.

The World Bank launched its Global Insights Initiative (GINI) in 2015 to incorporate behavioral insights into project design and development interventions. The 2015 World Development Report, appropriately titled, *Mind, Society, and Behavior*, gives examples of considering the social context in which decisions in developing countries are made. For example, it is better to approach poor farmers about enrolling their children in school when their seasonal income is high.

The United Nations (UN) appointed its first Behavioral Science Advisor in January 2016. UN Secretary General Ban Ki-moon noted the value of using behavioral insights for policy formulation and to ensure the success of the UN's Agenda 2030:

> Our organization, our global agenda – and most importantly the people worldwide they are intended to serve – deserve nothing less than the best science available. A human-centered agenda requires a rigorous, research-based understanding of people.
>
> (United Nations Development Programme, 2016)

Agenda 2030, which was adopted in 2015, includes 17 sustainable development goals, such as achieving zero hunger, good health and well-being, quality education, gender equality, and the elimination of poverty (United Nations, 2015). Behavioral insights will play a key role in reaching these objectives by 2030.

We will also discuss how the applications of behavioral insights inform the commercial, and even political, world (Chapter 7). These applications have implications for daily life – indeed, few of us are left untouched by them. We will also see that, although in the past much reliance was placed on folklore and faddish psychological speculation, commercial applications are increasingly turning to hard scientific evidence in an attempt to influence consumers, often in ways that are not made obvious. Crucially, we will see that behavioral economics *really* is about the world in which we live. It is not an Ivory Tower academic discipline accessible only to the initiated few and intellectually nerdy. In this way, knowledge of behavioral economics can be seen as a liberating force, by putting back some of the power in the hands of citizens and consumers. As a result, we should be better able to defend against the darker applications.

This is a 'Basics' book, intended for the newcomer to behavioral economics; yet, we hope, it is not a watered-down account of the subject – it is intended to be a clear and informative account, even a lively one. The content is sufficiently detailed to provide a necessary overview of the foundational knowledge that defines the field – of course, it cannot be exhaustive, but it needs to be sufficient for its stated purpose. In particular, we believe, it should provide a good 'feel' for the subject, which must include discussion of some contentious issues.

WHAT IS BEHAVIORAL ECONOMICS?

Let us get straight down to business. At its most general level, behavioral economics uses insights from the social sciences (e.g., sociology) in general, and psychology in particular, to inform economic thinking and theorizing. It takes knowledge from judgment and decision-making (JDM) research to develop *realistic* assumptions about how people typically think, feel, and act – social psychology plays a large part, too. It makes predictions that can be tested, either in the laboratory (where controlled studies with experimental manipulations are possible) or in the field (where either observational or experimental studies can be conducted). 'Field experiments' are especially popular where controlled research is conducted in a real-life context; for example, researchers may observe farming communities to examine the factors underlying cooperative behavior, quite literally 'in the field'. Increasingly, behavioral economics research is incorporating knowledge gained from neuroscience – the direct study of the brain in relation to psychological processes. In these ways, behavioral economics shares much in common with 'experimental economics', which also uses empirical (e.g., experimental) methods to test theories, but not necessarily ones that contain 'behavioral' aspects derived from psychology and related academic disciplines. However, a more cynical view is that behavioral economics is little more than repackaged psychology couched in terms more amenable to economists; and there is also the suspicion that it is used to impress those in business and government who hold economics, but much less so psychology, in high regard – there is some truth to these claims, but it is very far from being the whole story. In any event, as Schwartz (2008) aptly notes, economic theory without the best theories and findings from psychology is akin to dealing with quantitative relationships without recourse to the most appropriate techniques in mathematics – itself an example of misbehaving.

It is appropriate here to note the distinction between 'behavioral economics' and 'behavioral science' as this can lead to confusion. Behavioral economics can be defined as behavioral science applied to the problems of economics: choice under uncertainty aimed at maximizing some benefit by the optimal allocation of scarce resources. Although potentially any aspect of behavioral science can be applied to economic matters, in practice not all of behavioral science is used – behavioral science is vast, including not only psychology but also communications science and related academic fields, so some of it is more useful than others. Behavioral economics can 'dip into' behavioral science when and where needed (e.g., using personality science to help explain the variability observed in behavior, as in individual differences to reactions to various forms of incentives; see Chapter 5). To give a salient example, the Covid-19 pandemic motivated people to change their behavior in reaction to changed incentives (i.e., risk of infection and illness): people wanted to maximize their utility (i.e., to live a longer, healthier life). People had to make choices under considerable uncertainty, for example, to wear a face covering or not. There was talk in government about the possibility of 'behavioral fatigue' and people adopting less healthy life choices. The Covid-19 pandemic is just one example of how utility is not just about money – it can be, quite literally, about life and death. As we will see in Chapter 5, differences in the major traits of personality influence adherence to stay-safe behaviors – by understanding the psychological nature of these traits, we can start to get a behavioral science perspective on what is underpinning economic choice behavior.

We also need to know what we mean by *behavioral* in the context of economics. Charlie Munger, the partner of Warren Buffett of Berkshire Hathaway said: "If economics is not behavioral, then what is it?" We might agree with him in a general sense, but what do we really mean? There are two opposing views on this matter. The first goes back to the founding father of economics, Adam Smith, who showed how economics could be seen to represent a *system* with various, often 'hidden', components – we learn more about Smith in Chapter 2. It is to Smith we look when the Bank of England in the United Kingdom or the Federal Reserve in the United States uses the lever of interest rates to curb inflation. In this tradition, people are affected by the system's activity – that is, the system exists independently of people's behavior. For example, the government may increase taxation on sugar to discourage its consumption. In this way, people are rather passive, influenced by the pulls and pushes of the economic system. The second, opposing view is that the economic system reflects the collective decisions of people – it is influenced and defined by their *behavior*. In this way, if we can change people's behavior, then the system's dynamics can be changed. This view sees people as active agents, and the economic system, to the extent that it exists in some independent form, is always playing catch-up. Of course, with any such apparent dichotomy, we might prefer to see both views as valid, depending on the specific actions of the system and people. Whatever view we prefer, behavioral economics is very much of the opinion that people's behavior heavily influences the economic system; therefore, the economic system *can* be altered by affecting a change in people's behavior, as, for example, by a nudge intervention (see Chapter 6).

Still, we might argue about the best label or terminology for this relatively new field, and theorists have done so and still do. But, the main aim of behavioral economics is reasonably clear: it strives to provide a *scientific* account of *real* economic behavior, broadly defined and not restricted to money-defined choices. An important point to bear in mind is that, generally speaking, behavioral economics attempts to build on the existing foundations of mainstream economics, and in this way, it is quite different from more dissident approaches that deny the value of much of the standard analysis of economic phenomena. However, as we see throughout this book, protagonists differ in their respect for mainstream economic thinking, with some contending that it is so fundamentally flawed that it cannot be salvaged by behavioral economics. For those economists who do not perceive the need to abandon the central principles of mainstream economics, findings from behavioral studies are seen as contributing to the basic toolkit of economic analysis – perhaps, some argue, to such an extent that a new unified economics will emerge which will dissolve the need to have a specifically separate 'behavioral' variety.

Whatever view is taken, behavioral economics develops theories, generates hypotheses, makes predictions, and tests them against the world of actual judgment and decision making – that is, against the behavior of real people in the real world. It is less reliant than mainstream economics on a small number of foundational assumptions/axioms upon which theories and their predictions are based. To achieve its scientific aims, behavioral economics uses the latest knowledge from the social sciences. It is not static and is continually in development. As such, it is something of a moving target and, therefore, not altogether easy to define or understand. This is only to be expected because as an academic field it is at the interface of economics and the wider social sciences, especially psychology. More generally, when thinking about these issues, it is as well to view the power of behavioral economics as the potential to transform anomalies and (apparent) inconsistencies seen in the actual economic life into regularities that can be measured, understood, and incorporated into standard economic theory.

There is something else we need to know. Behavioral economics reflects the combined work of psychologists and economists – although both belong to the wider social sciences, typically they think, theorize, and research in very different ways. This poses a problem when we talk about behavioral *economics* because often we are talking about the extension of psychological ideas to matters of economics – some mainstream economists claim that such ideas have little to do with 'real' economics. Nonetheless, psychologists have made major contributions to economics, as shown by the Nobel Prize-winning work of Daniel Kahneman. But, it is not only psychologists who are challenging mainstream economics. Many behavioral economists come from a mainstream economics background (e.g., George Loewenstein and Richard Thaler), but they have grown disillusioned with it. They are far from satisfied with the standard assumptions and models and, instead, apply insights from behavioral science to *improve* economics on its own terms. As we shall see, some behavioral economists (e.g., Dan Ariely) are psychologists who are less wedded to the belief that central economics principles need to be retained.

Whatever our perspective, behavioral economics was wrought into existence by the increasing weight of evidence of strange observations, anomalies, and odd facts that the mainstream economic approach struggled to explain – or even comprehend: *mis*behaviors. Such aberrant judgments and decisions are reflected in the fact that, too often, we do not follow through with our best intentions. New Year's resolutions are one annual example – they are now something of a ritualized illustration of the failure of willpower. And even when we appear to have a definite preference for something (e.g., saving for retirement), we do not always act in a way that maximizes the desired outcome. We procrastinate, misjudge probabilities (e.g., we think we may not live to enjoy the benefits), and fall prey to a number of biases that serve only to illustrate our inability to conform to the image of the idealized rational economic agent (defined in Chapter 3). We often live for today – so often it seems that 'tomorrow's another day' that can be neglected. Sometimes, we just seem to do things all wrong – and, importantly, *systematically* so. Now, none of this is especially newsworthy, but it does perplex mainstream economists and strains the credibility of standard economic models.

Getting a proper grasp on behavioral economics is not helped by the fact that there is not one official account of it, nor even one that the majority of researchers and practitioners in the field would readily accept. *Our* account in this book is only one possible version. In our defense, we believe that it does contain most of the elements that make up other accounts – and expert book reviewers agree with us. In any event, one of the best summaries of the history of behavioral economics is provided by Colin Camerer and George Loewenstein (2003), who are two of the leading lights and advocates in behavioral economics. In their paper, 'Behavioral Economics: Past, Present, Future', they trace the problems encountered by mainstream economics and the solutions that come from more psychologically realistic thinking. Their paper is well worth a read.

On closer scrutiny, what is intriguing is that many of the ideas that fall within behavioral economics are themselves old, but too often have been forgotten. Our account tries to uncover these deeper roots and for this reason Chapter 2 spends some time on the history of economics and long-standing criticisms of today's mainstream approach (neoclassical economics, as we will learn in Chapters 2 and 3) – some people may think this historical account is unnecessary, but, we believe, it is *really* needed to understand current-day behavioral economics. In an important sense, the behavioral economics of today gives scientific and professional respectability to earlier criticisms of the mainstream approach. Certainly, behavioral economics offers a more viable account of a wider range of behaviors, including those that are prone to baffle the mainstream theorist who expects people to behave in a consistent, rational, and optimizing fashion – important themes we explore as we travel through the pages of this book.

ECON OR HUMAN?

But for now, to begin to understand the different conceptions of mainstream and behavioral economics, it is convenient to contrast the depictions of ECON (or *homo economicus*) and HUMAN (or *homo psychologicus*) (see text box). Both are concerned with the fundamental problem in economics: how to allocate scarce resources to maximize some benefit (called 'utility' in economics). This can relate to *anything* in life, for example, where to live, who to marry, where to invest, or how to act during a global health pandemic.

So, we see that behavioral economics is about how people *actually* behave (in academic jargon, this is called 'descriptive' or 'positive' economics). It is clearly concerned with flesh–and–blood humans who often do not *seem* to know what they want or how to get things done in the most logical and efficient fashion. The other, more mainstream, economics perspective focuses on how people *should* behave ('normative' economics, in academic jargon). These economic agents

ECON AND HUMAN

These are depictions – some would say caricatures – of the two types of mind thought to be important in behavioral economics. Mainstream economics emphasizes ECON (*homo economicus*): the cold, rational, calculating, self-interested; psychology focuses on HUMAN (*homo psychologicus*): the flesh-and-blood being who is limited in processing capacity and prone to a number of biases, errors, and influences, and who is emotionally warm, and sometimes hot, in how they make decisions. HUMAN is more Homer Simpson than Mr Spock-like ECON.

conform to something approximating a perfectly rational model – the fact that few people are perfect need not concern us, so long as we assume that they aspire to this optimal state and try to achieve it to the best of their (often limited) ability and circumstances (e.g., time availability). In its purest form, ECON makes rational decisions that conform to logic, is self-interested, and finely weighs costs against benefits in order to maximize the benefit *to themselves*. Unlike the seemingly wayward HUMAN, ECON is analytical, intelligent, disinterested, and not influenced by states of the body, mood, emotion, and such like. According to some behavioral economists' way of thinking, ECON is little more than a figment of the imagination of mainstream economics – and a theoretically misleading one at that, even possibly a dangerous one. As Richard Thaler stated in an interview: "I believe that for the last 50 or 60 years, economists have devoted themselves to studying fictional creatures … They may as well be studying unicorns" (as quoted in The Psychologist, 2017). This is a quite remarkable observation from a classically trained economist who has a Nobel Prize to his name.

At this point, you may well be asking: if we know that humans are not really like ECON then why does this notion still retain such a powerful hold on mainstream economics? This is a good question which is easier to ask than answer. One possible reason is that science often works by holding simplifying assumptions: reducing the complexity of the *manifest* world by creating constructs of a more abstract and *latent* (i.e., hidden) nature. If this set of constructs can be used to understand the complex world, then something important has been achieved. This scientific model can then be used to predict ('forecast') new phenomena in other contexts. But there is perhaps another, more HUMAN, reason.

During the twentieth century, mainstream economics increasingly adopted a mathematically inspired conception of the world. In this, certain assumptions had to be made in order for the equations to work – they had to be *tractable*. This permitted formal theorizing expressed in the language and logical machinery of mathematics. Mathematical notation charmed and impressed the profession and, at the same time, intimidated those who challenged its basic tenets and general worldview (e.g., the 'free market'). Such mathematics is the way economic theory is conceptualized and constructed – it is how economists *think* about economic problems. Mathematical prowess has become something of a badge of respectability in the economics profession and serves an important career-enhancing function. It is a good way to get ahead – very HUMAN!

Well, knowing this, the big question remains: does ECON exist *in some form*? Does the idealized depiction of the rational economic agent predict the way things work in the *real* world? If ECON does exist – and we should be careful not to dismiss it too readily – then there really would be little need for *behavioral* economics: it could be relegated to the conscientious study of psychological trivia with few real-world applications. To the extent that mainstream economics does accept the existence of HUMAN, it assumes that it aspires to be an ECON in all important respects, *especially* when the stakes are high and important decisions are being made. It must also assume that HUMAN manages a good enough approximation to ECON to make mainstream economic models work.

But if ECON does not exist in a pure form, then at what stage does it segue into HUMAN? Some behavioral economists – from both psychology (e.g., Daniel Kahneman) and economics (e.g., George Loewenstein) backgrounds – believe that the ECON model is simply unrealistic, containing an imaginary fictional creature only to be found between the dust covers of an economics textbook where typical forms of HUMAN thinking, feeling, and behaving are largely ignored and, when not ignored, disparaged as 'irrational'. However, even in economic terms, there might well be an economic advantage to avoiding striving for analytical perfection. As John Maynard Keynes noted: "It is better to be roughly right than precisely wrong".

Although caricatures, HUMAN/ECON depictions highlight the salient features of each approach. But, we need to be careful here as this sharp distinction is prone to lead, itself, to a certain level of confusion. For example, it encourages binary thinking: ECON *or* HUMAN. This may conceal the similarities between them. It is possible that people move between these two states, and these simple depictions do not do justice to the true variety and complexity of behavior. In addition, the HUMAN depiction is more concerned with descriptive and positive aspects: not what *ought to* be, but what *is* – as first expressed by David Hume (1711–1776), who formulated the idea: "you cannot deduce ought from is" in his most important work *A Treatise of Human Nature* (1738). Hume meant that what we *choose* to do with knowledge is different from the ways things are – think of cancer ('is') and what we 'ought' to do about it (i.e., oppose and destroy it, not support it because it follows a natural law of cell proliferation). One of the problems of understanding behavioral economics is to keep these two perspectives in mind at the same time because both have their merits.

In fact, it is a little too easy to be critical of the assumptions of mainstream economics and to get carried away with all the excitement of the weird-and-wonderful world of behavioral economics. In this book, we do our best to eschew this temptation – probably not succeeding to everyone's satisfaction. In particular, we try to show that not all apparent examples of 'misbehaving' are opposed to the ECON model: on closer inspection, they may well be more rational they might appear.

MISBEHAVING

We really do not have to look too far for examples of how in everyday life people *seem* to deviate from the cherished assumptions of mainstream economics (rationality, logical decision making, and so on – these are defined in Chapter 3). Whether these misbehaviors are 'noise' in an otherwise rational/logical system and everything turns out ECON in the end is an open question. In any event, some behavioral economists think such deviations are normal – the stuff of everyday economic life, *even when making important decisions*. For example, Richard Thaler, in his 2015 book of the same name, contends that behavioral economics is all about *misbehaving* – an expression we have already employed above – by which he describes how HUMAN economic agents deviate from ECON model predictions: "I mean that their behavior was inconsistent with the idealized model of behavior that is at the heart of what we call economic theory". Trained in economics, Thaler spent much of his early career cataloging such misbehaviors, what he calls 'supposedly irrelevant factors' (SIFs), which turn out to be very relevant in practice.

As Thaler (2015) says: "For four decades, since my time as a graduate student, I have always been preoccupied by these kinds of stories about the myriad ways in which people depart from the fictional creatures that populate economic models". He lists many forms of misbehaving in his lively book, which recounts his journey from ignored economist (who seemed interested only in the trivia of behavior) to professional respectability as the 2015 President of the American Economic Association and 2017 Nobel Prize winner. Thaler characterizes his early days as responding to "one-line putdowns" from economists who "had their own way of doing things".

The fact that we so often misbehave should not come as too much of a surprise, at least not to most of us. Consider one of the central assumptions of economic theory. People make choices by *optimizing*; that is, they are said to make the best choices, based on what is available (e.g., information and incentives) and what they can afford (choices are subject to their *budget constraints* – to you and me, what we can afford). This is fair enough. But, as Thaler notes in his 2015 book: "There is, however, a problem: the premises on which economic theory rests are flawed. First, optimization problems that ordinary people confront are often too hard for them to solve, or even come close to solving". Thaler goes on to say: "Second, the beliefs upon which people make their choices are not unbiased. Overconfidence may not be in the economists' dictionary, but it is a well-established feature of human nature, and there are countless other biases that have been documented by psychologists". Thaler then notes an additional issue that reflects the complexity of actual economic life: "Third, there are many factors that the optimization model leaves out … there is a long list of things that are supposedly irrelevant". Thaler gives many examples of misbehaving and the influence of SIFs.

Let us consider one SIF: a student essay marked out of a total 100 or 137 marks. Thaler found that his students would often grumble if they received a 72 (out of 100 possible marks), but they would be quite content to receive 96 (out of a possible 137) – and these were economics students who are otherwise thought to be rational! Well, which mark would you prefer? In the second case, students are getting 70%, which is lower than the 72% in the first case. There are several biases here: 96 is *bigger* than 72; it is easy to see that 72/100 is 72%, but what about 96/137? Many of us would need a calculator. You can probably think of other things going on, too. From a strictly rational point of view, this is all nonsense – *misbehaving* – as 72% is always better than 70% but it is not the way students see things. In an important way, behavioral economics is characterized by taking seriously such SIFs, that is factors that should not matter in theory, but do in practice. This can be *very* annoying because it makes the world of mainstream economics, which contains simple assumptions and elegant mathematical models, very messy, even *intractable* – and, worst of all, mathematically

---

SIFS: SAVING $10

Suppose David is shopping for a clock radio. He finds a model he likes and his search has uncovered that it is available for $45 in a local shop. As David is about to buy it, the sales assistant mentions that that same clock radio can be bought at their new store, a ten-minute drive away, for a special offer price of $35 (we assume the cost of the additional travel is minor). Do you think David will drive to the new score for this bargain? Would you?

On another occasion, David is shopping for a flat-screen TV and finds one at a good price of $495 at the same local store. As luck would have it, when he is about to buy it, the sales assistant once again mentions that he can buy the same TV for $485 at another of their newly opened stores which is also a ten-minute drive away. What does David do in this case, and is it different from his decision with the clock radio?

When posed with these choices, many people say they would drive to the new store to save $10 on the clock radio, but they would not drive there to save the same amount of money on the TV. Mainstream economic madness! This is because from a mainstream economic perspective, there is an identical (absolute) saving is made in both cases: $10. What seems to be influencing these different decisions is the *percentage* of the total price that can be saved by driving to the other store – but this is a SIF and it should not influence David's buying decision.

---

unworkable. Whether the payoff in terms of realistic theorizing and prediction is a price worth paying for disrupting this internally consistent worldview of mainstream economics is a moot point: behavioral economics thinks it is.

Throughout this book, we see many more examples of well-established *misbehaviors* which characterize how typical humans come to form judgments and make decisions. In the text box below, we see one well-known puzzle that has most people scratching their heads – and then kicking themselves for being so silly when they learn of the right solution.

Thaler goes on to make a good point about how we should interpret the foibles of everyday human judgment and decision making: "It has never been my point to say that there is something wrong with people; we are all just human beings – homo sapiens. Rather, the problem is with the model used by economists". This statement comes from an economist steeped in mainstream economic thinking who has reached the top of his profession and who is regularly consulted by national governments (e.g., the UK government 'Nudge Unit'). The abstract ECON, which is at the core of mainstream economic models, is apparently a very poor substitute for a realistic HUMAN.

MISBEHAVING: BAT AND BALL PROBLEM

Think about this seemingly simple calculation. "A bat and a ball cost $1.10 in total. The bat costs $1.00 more than the ball. How much does the ball cost?" What is your answer? Most people are confident that the ball must cost 10 cents. This feels like the right answer, but it is not. Think about it this way. If the ball costs 10 cents and the bat costs $1.00 more than the ball, then the bat would cost $1.10 giving a total of $1.20. The correct answer is that the ball costs 5 cents and the bat costs – at a dollar more – $1.05 giving a total of $1.10. This is an example of how we typically replace a difficult problem with a simpler one. One explanation of this puzzle is that we seem nonconsciously to substitute the 'more than' statement in the problem (i.e., the bat costs $1.00 *more than* the ball) with an absolute statement (the bat costs $1.00). (This puzzle can be found in Kahneman, 2011, and other sources.)

BEHAVIORAL ECONOMICS:
SUPPLANT OR SUPPLEMENT?

At this point in our discussion, it is appropriate to enquire about the ultimate aim of behavioral economics. One view is that it is a natural development of mainstream economics which it merely aims to improve. As Camerer and Loewenstein (2003) state: "Behavioral economics increases the explanatory power of economics by providing it with more realistic psychological foundations". They also state that their belief in the power of realistic psychological models "does not imply a wholesale rejection of the neoclassical approach ...." (In the following chapters, we will discuss 'neoclassical' economics, which for the time being we are calling 'mainstream' economics.)

However, other notable behavioral economists are less optimistic. For example, Dan Ariely in his highly popular 2008 book, *Predictably Irrational*, says in relation to trying to convince mainstream economists of the importance of what he calls 'irrational' behavior:

> Of course, I ran into the biggest difficulties when arguing for irrationality with card-carrying rational economists, whose disregard of my experimental data was almost as intense as their nearly religious belief in rationality (if Adam Smith's 'invisible hand' doesn't sound like God, I don't know what does). (Adam Smith's ideas are discussed in Chapter 2.)

As Ariely was not trained in economics – he is a psychologist and behavioral scientist – along with scientists like Daniel Kahneman, he is far less sympathetic to the general aims of mainstream economics than those coming from this intellectual tradition. Ariely further says:

> I have been acutely aware that humans engage in actions and make decisions that are often divorced from rationality, and sometimes very far from ideal. Over the years I've tried to understand the silly, dumb, amusing, and sometimes dangerous mistakes we all make, in the hope that by understanding our irrational quirks, we can retrain ourselves to make better decisions.

Mainstream economists have not taken these criticisms entirely with a sense of equanimity. They retort: findings from (artificial and contrived) laboratory studies, often based on small samples of psychology students, may not generalize to the real, competitive world (the 'market') where participants are truly incentivized and motivated to behave as rationally as possible. Surely, they say, people would be fools not to behave as rationally, and self-optimizing, as possible, *especially when it really matters*. The assumption is that, when truly put to the test, HUMAN quickly becomes ECON: people behave rationally when motivated to do so (e.g., choosing a mortgage or marriage partner). Economists of this more traditional mindset also probably have little time for anecdotes of the kind favored by Dan Ariely and Richard Thaler about their personal observations of the foibles of others – instead, they prefer axiomatic assumptions and what they believe to be tried-and-tested principles.

Still, other, some very notable, economists are pragmatic about the whole business. As the leading economist Larry Summers, former Secretary of the US Treasury and past President of Harvard University, said: "And if you are worldly and empirical, you are drawn to behavioral approaches" (Quoted in Harvard Magazine, Lambert, 2006).

However, mainstream economists' belief in the inherent rationality of humans is sometimes put to the test not by small-scale, student-focused lab studies but by global events that profoundly shock economies around the world.

THE 2007–2008 GLOBAL FINANCIAL CRASH

Few events are more likely to focus the minds of economists and the general public than the loss of many billions of dollars. The 2007–2008 global financial crash marked a truly critical turning point in the recognition and, increasingly, acceptance of behavioral economics. It also reminded economists of Karl Marx's prediction that the capitalistic system was not only prone to periodic crises but to eventual collapse due to its internal contradictions. Before the crash, few mainstream economists worried about this dismal Marxian forecast – after it, they had more cause not to dismiss it entirely. The unpredictability of the 2007–2008 crash came as much as a surprise to them as to nonexperts.

Indeed, as Thaler (2015) highlighted: "Virtually no economist saw the financial crisis of 2007–2008 coming, and worse, many thought that both the crash and its aftermath were things that simply could not happen". One exception was Robert Shiller, who went on to win the Nobel Prize for Economic Sciences in 2013. Shiller warned in his 2000 book, *Irrational Exuberance*, that the stock market had already, by 2000, become a bubble and was bound to burst at some point. (During the inflation of such a bubble, jumping on the speculative bandwagon is not, of course, irrational, but the trick is to know when to jump off before it crashes!) Shiller's academic work challenged the 'efficient market hypothesis', which assumes that stock market investors base stock prices on the expected future dividends, discounted to present value. Analysis of data going back to the nineteenth century convinced Shiller that this theory simply cannot explain the large variation observed in stock market prices – prices fluctuate, often wildly, for reasons other than a 'rational' valuation of companies. His subsequent work confirmed that traders are influenced by their emotions and not a rational calculation of the market.

The policy decisions of economists, such as Alan Greenspan (Chairman of the Federal Reserve of the United States, 1987–2006), contributed to the 2007–2008 financial crash. In what must be one of the most honest admissions of all time, Greenspan said before the Congressional Committee on October 23, 2008: "Those of us who have looked to the self-interest of lending institutions to protect shareholder's equity – myself especially – are in a state of shocked disbelief". And referring to his free-market ideology, Greenspan added: "I have found a flaw. I don't know how significant or permanent it is. But I have been very distressed by that fact". Pressed by Representative Henry Waxman, who asked Greenspan: "In other words, you found that your view of the world, your ideology, was not right, it was not working". Greenspan replied candidly: "Absolutely, precisely. You know, that's precisely the reason I was shocked, because I have been going for 40 years or more with very considerable evidence that it was working exceptionally well" (Clark & Treanor, 2008). Greenspan's disbelief in what happened seems to have been conditioned, in some part, by his adherence to the philosophy of free markets and personal responsibility (which included favoring Ayn Rand's extreme form of philosophical individualism called *Objectivism*) – the latter assumption is rather HUMAN.

Dan Ariely (2008) recorded the views of *The New York Times* columnist David Brooks that Greenspan's Congressional confession:

> ... amounted to a coming-out party for behavioral economists and others who are bringing sophisticated psychology to the realm of public

policy. At least these folks have plausible explanations for why so many people could have been so gigantically wrong about the risks they were taking.

The 2007–2008 time period was, indeed, critical for the world economy and crucial for behavioral economics. It was not the first, of course. Just think of the US stock market crash of 1929 and the resulting deep depression of the early 1930s. It is unlikely to be the last – history has a habit of making fools of those who claim "it can't happen again". This was seen with another notable economist, Ben Bernanke (formerly Chairman of the Central Reserve, the 'central bank' of the United States and chairman of President George W. Bush's Council of Economic Advisers), who espoused the theory of 'the Great Moderation', which stated that traditional 'business cycles' are less volatile and the economic world is a more stable place (e.g., Bernanke, 2004). Like many others, this theory had good cause to be revised after 2008.

Such is the appeal – or shock – of the 2007–2008 financial crash, popular films have chronicled it, for example, *Margin Call* in 2011. In 2015, *The Big Short* did a superb job of explaining how highly complex financial derivatives based on bundles of mortgages obscured the fragility of the market, especially as many of the mortgages were high-risk sub-prime – Richard Thaler had a cameo role in the film. Appropriately, the film opens with an apt (if misattributed to Mark Twain) quote: "It ain't what you don't know that gets you into trouble. It's what you know for sure that just ain't so".

As noted earlier, the Nobel Laureate in Economic Sciences, Robert Shiller, predicted the 2007/2008 financial crisis, and some other economists pointed to the flaws in the economic system. One notable person was J. K. Galbraith who we will encounter again in this chapter and in the next – he has been an academic thorn in the side of mainstream economics since the 1940s.

HISTORY REPEATS ITSELF

Economic history is not (now) typically taught in university economics courses, which is to be regretted because it contains important lessons. History issued one notable lesson to Irving Fisher (1867–1947), who was one of the foremost mainstream economists of his day. Shortly before the 1929 stock market crash, he confidently pronounced "a permanently high plateau" in the US stock market. Fisher's family (mis)fortune provided an instructive lesson of the power of reality over presumption. Rival forecaster Roger Babson wryly observed that Fisher "thinks the world is ruled by figures instead of feelings" (as quoted in Harford, 2014) – throughout this book, we will see the power of feelings, emotion, and the like in economic judgment, decision making, and behavior.

As the above examples attest, history has no respect for reputation or status – indeed, it so often shows disdain. This is periodically shown by finance ministers who are sometimes prone to declare the end of 'boom and bust' due to their self-declared prudent fiscal administration. For example, before the 2007/8 financial crash, the then UK Chancellor of the Exchequer (equivalent to a finance minister in other countries), Gordon Brown, asserted: the "British economy of the future must be built not on the shifting sands of boom and bust, but on the bedrock of prudent and wise economic management for the long term" (as quoted in Summers, 2008). We might well think that the fable of King Canute should be in the minds of those who have a fondness for fortune telling, especially in economic matters. (J. K. Galbraith cruelly joked: economic forecasting was invented to make astrology look respectable!).

Jokes aside, critics of mainstream economics continue to point to its inability to predict and explain financial crashes – they also accuse their opponents of being in denial of the magnitude of their predictive failures. This even comes from true insiders. Mervyn King, former Governor of the Bank of England, and a foremost academic economist who has been at the heart of central government policy making for many years, makes this clear in his 2016 book, *The End of Alchemy: Banking, the Global Economy and the Future of Money.* His argument is that economic decisions always occur under conditions of, what he calls, 'radical uncertainty' – that is, true ignorance about the future. This cannot be remedied by the quantification of probabilities and, as such, optimizing behavior is not possible. To deal with this uncertain state, King contends that people use 'narratives' to make sense of the world. In the felicitous phrase of J. K. Galbraith (1958), we are much reassured by the "conventional wisdom" which "accommodates itself not to the world that it is meant to interpret, but to the audience's view of the world". King believes that mainstream economics misunderstood the world before the 2007–2008 financial crisis, and, most worryingly, it has not learned its lessons since. King makes another good point: "History is what happened before you were born. That is why it is so hard to learn lessons from recent history: the mistakes were made by the previous generation". Surely, *we* might think, we would not be as stupid as them?

As a consequence of the fallout from the 2007–2008 financial crash in academic circles, especially regarding the perceived inadequacies of mainstream economic theories, some students of economics have been in revolt, demanding a change to the standard curriculum. The narrow and uncritical focus of mainstream economics is addressed in the student-led 2016 book by Earle, Moran, and Ward-Perkins, *The Econocracy: The Perils of Leaving Economics to the Experts*. They note that students can (and often do) go through three years of a university economics degree course without ever being asked to write an essay, let alone a critical one of the discipline. (We know this from our own teaching of students from the Economics Department.) As a consequence, critics of mainstream economics have been assisted by the establishment of new professional bodies which challenge orthodoxy and encourage, what they see as, more enlightened forms of economic thinking – for example, in the United Kingdom, the *New Economics Foundation*, and in the United States, the *Institute for New Economic Thinking*.

In all of this, the major challenge faced by behavioral economics is to make models more psychologically realistic without sacrificing the parsimony and wide-ranging applications enjoyed by the mainstream approach. This is no small challenge – it is often more comforting to stick with the tried-and-failed than the new-and-unknown: perhaps another example of *misbehaving*!

MONEY, MONEY, MONEY

To understand mainstream and behavioral economics a little better it is worth thinking about the concept of money – it may not be a 'concept' when in your purse/wallet, but it is in economic theory. The pop group ABBA had a smash hit in 1976 with *Money, Money, Money*, in which they sang about money being funny; they were right – but in economics, not quite in the way they meant.

As noted by Mervyn King in his 2016 book, money often seems to be the main focus of economics, and, somewhat surprisingly to the noneconomist, there is no consensus as to what it is and how it is created – strange perhaps, but true! There is something else about money that we need to appreciate in relation to behavioral economics – in fact, as discussed below and elsewhere in this book, money can confuse what we mean by self-interested behavior and rationality.

Mention of economics in the Fashion or Lifestyle sections of the national press is rarely seen; it is to be found in the Money, Business, or Financial pages. This tells us something important, namely, the central role assigned to money (it is so obvious, we rarely have cause to think about it). Indeed, it can seem that economics is interested in little else, but this is quite untrue. For a start, we may give away money in an apparently unselfish act, but in return, we derive *psychological* benefit (value or utility). Formulating economic behavior purely in terms of money is unhelpful at best and misleading at worst. ABBA was right: money is a funny thing.

Money certainly has a psychological dimension – it conveys meaning and interpersonal value. Mainstream economics tells us that values we attach to all things in life can be expressed in monetary form; this is reflected in the 'willingness to pay' concept, which is used in economic research. 'Willingness to pay' reflects the maximum amount of money someone is willing to give up in order to obtain a good or service or to avoid a bad outcome. It can be used to evaluate outcomes that are inherently nonmonetary, for example, the benefits resulting from healthcare programs. The idea that 'goods' and 'bads' can be measured in monetary terms makes it possible to compare the satisfaction, happiness, or whatever (i.e., value/utility) of one thing with another. It is for this reason that economics is so focused on money – it really is the common currency of everyday life. Therefore, money can be used as a convenient metric to measure, what often seem, intangible things vis-à-vis other goods and services we might want to 'consume'. Behavioral economics is very much about such apparent intangibles (e.g., cooperation and the subjective utility we get from helping other people).

What this discussion suggests is that once we move away from a strictly money-based interpretation of value or utility, we enter the social realm populated by behavioral ideas – and while this realm is not necessarily antithetical to mainstream economics, it is far more tolerant of alternative perspectives. Indeed, as we see in the next section, focusing on money can seriously confuse matters.

'ONE DAY AT A TIME': NEW YORK CITY TAXI DRIVERS

One of the most vivid field studies in behavioral economics focused on the working patterns of taxi drivers in New York City. Reported by Camerer, Babcock, Loewenstein, and Thaler (1997), this study found that taxi drivers (especially inexperienced ones) tended to set themselves a daily target and then stopped work once this target had been met – this occurred irrespective of the hourly earnings potential which varied day-by-day depending on weather conditions. Taxi driving is ideal for such a study because drivers decide their own working hours – typically, they hire their taxis for 12 hours per day. This study raises many issues of relevance to economics and, for us, is a convenient way to think about the assumptions and principles discussed throughout this book.

This field study is notable for several reasons. First, the findings contradict one major mainstream economic theory of labor supply – called the 'life-cycle model' (e.g., Lucas & Rapping, 1969). The 'life-cycle' part of the theory relates to the fact that people should allocate their labor resources (i.e., time spent working) efficiently over time (weeks, months, years, and even lifetime), and not based on just one day at a time. Central to the model is the idea that people should work more when wages are high and consume more leisure time when its price (i.e., the foregone wage) is low. What this means is that taxi drivers should spend more time working when business is good (i.e., on rainy days), and they should take it easy on bad business days (i.e., when the sun is out and people want to stretch their legs and are less likely to hail a taxi). As Camerer et al. (1997) put it more formally: "workers [should] intertemporally substitute labor and leisure" – that is, they should not work 'one day at a time' but think about how they can trade off their labor with their leisure over time. However, their study showed just the opposite. In addition, taxi drivers set loose income targets and quit working once these targets had been reached. We will see more clearly in subsequent chapters why such behavior *seems* to violate mainstream economic thinking. It clearly violates the 'life-cycle' assumption that our labor supply decisions should take into account how best to optimize the trade-off between work and other preferences (e.g., for leisure, social, and family) over time.

By not conforming to life-cycle labor supply theory, are New York City taxi drivers really *misbehaving*? Well, according to this theory, clearly they are. But what is wrong: the theory or the taxi drivers' choices? In this case, is there *really* greater utility per hour on a rainy day than there is on a sunny day? In purely monetary terms, there is, unquestionably, greater utility. This question is especially pertinent when we consider that if taxi drivers had worked longer hours on a bad weather day, they could 'sun themselves' on days when the weather is good but the taxi business is bad: over the 'life cycle' of their labor supply (which they decide), they could work less and have more leisure time – they would maximize their utility.

Well, *should* taxi drivers decide to work longer on rainy days? This question returns us to the issue of money in defining personal utility. An important point here is that utility is not just about acquiring money – indeed, it can be the opposite. We may decide to give money to charity (making us financially worse off), but we thereby gain utility from the 'warm glow' derived from this donation – we may also get further psychological utility from letting the world know of our good nature (something called 'virtue signaling'; e.g., Bartholomew, 2015). Therefore, money and psychological utility are independent (i.e., knowing something about one tells us little or nothing about the other), although this is true only once a certain level of wealth is reached (we are unlikely to give to charity if it means we go hungry). In all of this, it is important to know that mainstream economics does not insist on defining utility in purely monetary terms, yet it can often seem so.

Here, we come across something of importance regarding what is meant by utility (i.e., benefit/value/well-being). It could be concerned purely with money (e.g., income from taxi fares), but there are other ways to view matters. In place of pure monetary income, the taxi drivers' benefit (utility) may be defined in terms of income plus an assessment of risk and convenience (and the 'opportunity cost' – foregone pleasure – of lost time with family and friends, and so on). We need to remember that it is what the selfish rational person considers to be important *to themselves* that defines *their* utility – this need not be money – and this determines how they decide to allocate their scarce resources (e.g., time and effort). For this reason, viewing the total utility of taxi drivers purely in financial terms is inappropriate, and, surely, it would not be the way even the most hard-headed mainstream economist would conduct their own personal affairs. Broadening utility from pure income renders the judgments and decisions of taxi drivers not so irrational after all.

Putting this discussion into context shows us the reality of driving a taxi on a rainy New York City street. There are several things of some psychological interest here. First, working on a bad weather day is harder work and the chances of accidents must be higher – both should be expected to reduce the broader notion of utility described above (in other words, working longer hours entails *dis*utility, i.e., negative value). In addition, many drivers want a regular working day that is predictable and to disrupt this may reduce their overall quality of life (which is another way of defining utility) – they may be missing out on family, social or leisure pursuits that have a higher level of utility (we need to consider their opportunity costs; the costs/benefits of their best foregone alternative). The loss of valued time with family, friends, etc., can never be recovered.

In addition, it is important to realize that most economic models are based on the *all else being equal* assumption (which is known to economics students and Latin speakers as *ceteris paribus*). The trouble with this assumption is that things are rarely equal. In the case of taxi drivers, it may simply not be possible for them to work longer hours on a rainy day because they may have other commitments (e.g., picking up children from school); or, more psychologically, they may have made plans which, although they could be changed at the last minute, have their own costs attached in terms of consistency of behavior – chopping-and-changing on a daily basis is unpleasant for many people who place value on stability and predictability.

On a more mundane but not irrelevant note, we should expect that money-focused economists – assuming they exist – who argue that taxi drivers are not behaving rationally, have probably never driven a taxi in New York City when the weather is bad. But, observing the behavior of taxi drivers from an air-conditioned office in an ivory academic tower, it may well seem so – indeed, they may well be there writing an academic article for which they can expect very little, or no, utility in monetary terms and they may even have to pay to get the article published – in their own terms, it may be the economist who is the one *misbehaving*! So, we can see that, if we interpret this example differently, taxi drivers in New York City may well be maximizing their utility and behaving rationally. Indeed, the authors of this seminal study acknowledge that such alternative explanations exist. For instance, they discuss that busy, high-wage days imply that drivers pick up more or longer fares and, thus, may quit earlier because they are tired.

Our discussion of the working patterns of taxi drivers attests to the fact that mainstream economic approaches can accommodate what may seem on the face of it a gross violation of rationality. This example goes to show that we need to be careful not to fall into the trap of the Straw (Wo)Man argument when pitting ECON and HUMAN models against each other – to do so would only be another example of *misbehaving.*

GROSS NATIONAL PRODUCT OR GROSS NATIONAL HAPPINESS?

As the New York City taxi driver example shows, economics is not all about money, although it can appear that governments are concerned with little else. For example, Gross Domestic Product (GDP) is used as an important indicator of a nation's prosperity and progress over time; it comprises the monetary value of goods and services produced in an economy. But as Robert Kennedy noted in 1968:

> The Gross National Product counts air pollution and cigarette advertising, and ... the destruction of the redwood and the loss of our natural wonder in chaotic sprawl ... Yet [it] does not allow for the health of our children, the quality of their education, or the joy of their play ... the beauty of our poetry or the strength of our marriages ... it measures everything, in short, except that which makes life worthwhile.
>
> (As quoted in nef (new economics foundation), 2009)

The calculation of GDP in the United Kingdom now includes illegal drug sales and prostitution, which helped it to overtake France in 2014 to become the fifth largest economy in the world (e.g., Cusick, 2014). As these sources of GDP show, not all prosperity is necessarily desirable, and there are many more positive aspects of an economy that are not captured by GDP at all despite their effects on people's quality of life. These include unpaid work in households (e.g., care for children or elderly relatives) and voluntary work – which means that the work of a large proportion of the population (often women) is not considered valuable. Most economies still fail to account fully for other negative outcomes, including how resources are distributed in a society (income inequality); the depletion of resources (often economic 'externalities', which we will discuss later in the book); and criminal activities. Some people have argued that not only is the notion of GDP incomplete but it is misaligned with what people consider to benefit society (e.g., Diener & Seligman, 2004).

Following decade-long appeals from researchers, governments have only fairly recently begun to consider people's *subjective well-being* in policy decisions. This encompasses individuals' *own* evaluations of their well-being. In survey research, this is usually assessed with measures of happiness, life satisfaction, quality of life, and, less frequently, eudaimonic well-being, which encompasses fulfillment, self-actualization, and finding meaning and purpose in life – of course, these are only possible in those who are not hungry, thirsty, and under threat to life.

The then French President Nicholas Sarkozy commissioned a 25-member group of mostly economists, led by Joseph Stiglitz, Amartya Sen (both Nobel Prize winners), and Jean-Paul Fitoussi, to consider better ways of measuring societal well-being than GDP. The result was the *Report by the Commission on the Measurement of Economic Performance and Social Progress* (2009), which advocated the use of measures of subjective well-being for designing policies and assessing social progress, denoting a shift away from a 'production-oriented' measurement system. Shortly after the publication of the Sarkozy report, the then Prime Minister, David Cameron, announced in November 2010 that the UK Office for National Statistics (ONS) would start measuring subjective well-being to help guide national policy. Around the same time, the United Nations encouraged member countries to measure and use the happiness of their citizens to guide public policies, in July 2011; and in 2013, the OECD published guidelines to assess well-being, in which it defined subjective well-being as:

> Good mental states, including all of the various evaluations, positive and negative, that people make of their lives, and the affective reactions of people to their experiences.

The OECD definition covered three elements. First, life *evaluation* (reflective assessment, evaluation), which is sometimes referred to as hedonic well-being. Second, *affect* (a person's feelings). Third, *eudaimonia* (a feeling of sense and purpose in life), sometimes called psychological well-being or 'flourishing'.

According to this perspective, policies that aim to increase subjective well-being in society should, therefore, target life domains in which long-term improvements in well-being can be achieved and sustained, and these might be the best candidates for the type of 'nudging' we discuss in Chapter 6. For example, policies that aim to improve health or try to enhance social ties in communities to increase social capital may be better placed to increase societal well-being in the long run. The initiatives of several European governments systematically to collect data on and consider their citizens' subjective well-being are seen by many to be a step in the right direction. Global data on subjective

THE WORLD HAPPINESS REPORT

First published in 2012, the World Happiness Report is published annually on or close to the International Day of Happiness by the Sustainable Solutions Network (it is freely available at https://worldhappiness.report/). The report usually attracts considerable media attention as it provides country rankings based on average happiness (life evaluation) in the previous two years. The report (Helliwell et al., 2022), based on surveys collected between 2019–2021, declared Finland to be the happiest country out of 146 countries, ahead of Denmark (2), Iceland (3), Switzerland (4), the Netherlands (5), Luxembourg (6), the United States (16), and the United Kingdom (17). As in previous years, countries with high levels of GDP per capita and good social safety nets tend to rank highly, while countries that suffer from high levels of poverty and conflicts can be found at the bottom of the ranking (Zimbabwe, Lebanon, and Afghanistan occupy the last three spots). These rankings tend to be fairly stable over time.

According to the 2022 World Happiness Report, worry, sadness, and stress increased during the Covid-19 pandemic, but average life evaluations remained fairly constant. However, compared to prepandemic levels, younger people reported somewhat lower life satisfaction during the pandemic, while people over 60 reported increased life satisfaction. Encouragingly, prosocial behavior, such as donating, volunteering, and helping strangers, all increased in 2021 compared to earlier time periods.

well-being has been available for more than a decade now (see textbox above) and can be used to evaluate which macro-economic factors might place a country higher in World Happiness rankings.

Starting in 2019, the government of New Zealand went even further than merely collecting happiness data by declaring that from now on the annual Budget, which outlines the country's fiscal decisions, would be guided by the Government's well-being objectives. Prime Minister Jacinda Ardern pointed out in the preamble of the 2020 Wellbeing Budget, which was released during the Covid-19 pandemic, that the Budget reflects a "focus on the things we know matter" and was created "through a wellbeing lens that considers the needs of New Zealand's people and environment alongside our economy" (The Treasury of New Zealand, 2020). This remarkable change in focus on the well-being of current and future generations rather than economic growth has not yet been copied by many countries.

CONCLUSIONS

In this introductory chapter, we have seen why *behavioral* economics developed and how its views on human economic judgment and decision making have become more widely accepted, especially in the aftermath of the 2007–2008 global financial crisis, which came as a shock to most mainstream economists, and is still (in different ways) shocking today. We have also seen the tensions between the traditional view of ECON and the flesh-and-blood HUMAN, which is prone to misbehave in all areas of life. The chapters to follow build upon these foundations.

The next chapter charts the fascinating history of economics and how it evolved over the past 300 years. In this regard, it is important to appreciate that many of the current concerns of behavioral economics have been voiced for a very long time, albeit in somewhat different tones. As we shall see, it would be a mistake to think behavioral economics is new in terms of the kinds of problems it is addressing. What is new, though, is the application of psychological models to economic problems and the empirical–experimental approach it adopts – for this reason, Daniel Kahneman shared the 2002 Nobel Prize in Economic Sciences with Vernon Smith, who pioneered experimental approaches to understanding economic phenomena. These positive scientific developments stand in contrast to the reply to earlier criticisms of mainstream economics, claiming that they were no more than ill-aimed philosophical, moral, and political dissent, often coming from opponents of capitalism and the market system. This position allowed mainstream economists to ignore, dismiss, or sideline their critics – and they kept their students well away from the heretical iconoclasts. Here as elsewhere, professional tensions play a role – in this respect, even hard-headed mainstream economists are HUMAN.

FURTHER READING

Ariely, D. (2008). *Predictably irrational: The hidden forces that shape our decisions.* Harper Collins.

Ariely, D. (2015). *Behavioural economics saved my dog: Life advice for the imperfect human.* Oneworld.

Thaler, R. (2015). *Misbehaving: The making of behavioural economics.* Allen Lane.

REFERENCES

Angner, E. (2019). *We're all behavioral economists now.* https://doi.org/10.1080/1350178X.2019.1625210

Ariely, D. (2008). *Predictably irrational: The hidden forces that shape our decisions.* Harper Collins.

Bartholomew, J. (2015, October 10). I invented 'virtue signalling'. Now it's taking over the world. *The Spectator.* https://www.spectator.co.uk/article/i-invented-virtue-signalling-now-it-s-taking-over-the-world/

Bernanke, B. S. (2004). The great moderation. *At the Meetings of the Eastern Economic Association, Washington, DC February 20, 2004.* https://www.federalreserve.gov/boarddocs/speeches/2004/20040220/

Camerer, C., Babcock, L., Loewenstein, G., & Thaler, R. (1997). Labor supply of New York City cabdrivers: One day at a time. *The Quarterly Journal of Economics, 112*(2), 407–441. https://doi.org/10.1162/003355397555244

Camerer, C. F., & Loewenstein, G. (2003). Behavioral economics: Past, present, future. In C. F. Camerer, G. Loewenstein, & M. Rabin (Eds.), *Advances in behavioral economics.* Princeton University Press.

Clark, A., & Treanor, J. (2008, October 24). Greenspan – I was wrong about the economy. Sort of. *The Guardian.* https://www.theguardian.com/business/2008/oct/24/economics-creditcrunch-federal-reserve-greenspan

Cusick, J. (2014, December 26). Prostitution and illegal drugs help UK overtake France in global wealth league. *The Independent.* http://www.independent.co.uk/news/business/news/prostitution-and-illegal-drugs-help-uk-overtake-france-in-global-wealth-league-9945007.html

Diener, E., & Seligman, M. E. P. (2004). Beyond money: Towards an economy of well-being. *Psychological Science in the Public Interest, 5*, 1–31.

Earle, J., Moran, C., & Ward-Perkins, Z. (2016). *The econocracy: The perils of leaving economics to the experts.* Manchester University Press.

Galbraith, J. K. (1958). *The affluent society.* Houghton Mifflin Harcourt.

Harford, T. (2014, September 5). How to see into the future. *Financial Times – FT Magazine.* https://www.ft.com/content/3950604a-33bc-11e4-ba62-00144feabdc0

Helliwell, J. F., Layard, R., Sachs, J. D., De Neve, J.-E., Aknin, L. B., & Wang, S. (Eds.). (2022). *World Happiness Report 2022.* Sustainable Development Solutions Network.

Hume, D. (1738). *A treatise of human nature.* John Noon.

Kahneman, D. (2011). *Thinking, fast and slow.* Farrar, Straus and Giroux.

King, M. (2016). *The end of alchemy: Money, banking, and the future of the global economy.* Hachette.

Lambert, C. (2006). The marketplace of perceptions. *Harvard Magazine*, 50–95. http://people.hbs.edu/nashraf/marketplaceofperceptions.pdf

Lucas, R. E., & Rapping, L. A. (1969). Real wages, employment, and inflation. *Journal of Political Economy, 77*, 721–754. https://doi.org/10.1086/259559

nef (new economics foundation). (2009). *National Accounts of Well-being: Bringing real wealth onto the balance sheet.* http://www.nationalaccountsofwellbeing.org/public-data/files/national-accounts-of-well-being-report.pdf

Obama, B. (2015). *Executive order – Using behavioral science insights to better serve the American people.* https://obamawhitehouse.archives.gov/the-press-office/2015/09/15/executive-order-using-behavioral-science-insights-better-serve-american

OECD. (2013). *OECD guidelines on measuring subjective well-being.* OECD Publishing. https://www.oecd.org/statistics/oecd-guidelines-on-measuring-subjective-well-being-9789264191655-en.htm

Schwartz, H. (2008). *A guide to behavioral economics.* Higher Education Publication.

Shiller, R. J. (2000). *Irrational exuberance.* Princeton University Press.

Stiglitz, J. E., Sen, A., & Fitoussi, J. P. (2009). *Report of the Commission on the Measurement of Economic Performance and Social Progress (CMEPSP).* http://ec.europa.eu/eurostat/documents/8131721/8131772/Stiglitz-Sen-Fitoussi-Commission-report.pdf

Summers, D. (2008, September 11). No return to boom and bust: What Brown said when he was chancellor. *The Guardian.* https://www.theguardian.com/politics/2008/sep/11/gordonbrown.economy

Thaler, R. (2015). *Misbehaving: The making of behavioural economics.* Allen Lane.

The Psychologist. (2017). A Nobel nudge. Award for Professor Richard Thaler. *The Psychologist, 30*, 13. https://www.bps.org.uk/psychologist/nobel-nudge

The Treasury of New Zealand. (2020). *Wellbeing Budget 2020: Rebuilding together.* https://www.treasury.govt.nz/publications/wellbeing-budget/wellbeing-budget-2020-html

The World Bank. (2015). *World development report 2015: Mind, society, and behavior.* https://doi.org/10.1596/978-1-4648-0342-0

United Nations. (2015). *Transforming our world: The 2030 agenda for sustainable development.* United Nations. https://sustainabledevelopment.un.org/post2015/transformingourworld/publication

United Nations Development Programme. (2016). *Behavioural Insights at the United Nations – Achieving Agenda 2030.* http://www.undp.org/content/undp/en/home/librarypage/development-impact/behavioural-insights-at-the-united-nations--achieving-agenda-203.html

NOTES

1   Reference to behavioral insight teams as 'nudge units' attests to something important – it stresses nudge theory and somewhat downplays those aspects of behavioral economics that do not entail nudging. Although, as government use of behavioral insights often results in a nudge in one form or another this shorthand name is understandable.

2   https://www.oecd.org/gov/regulatory-policy/behavioural-insights.htm.

BEHAVIORAL ECONOMICS IN RETROSPECT
HOW AND WHY IT STARTED

It may come as something of a surprise to learn that the roots of modern-day behavioral economics can be found in the origins of neoclassical (mainstream) economics. As the prefix suggests, *neo*classical economics grew out of *classical* economics (sometimes referred to as the 'dismal science', and, as we will discuss below, this term has questionable roots). Many behavioral economic principles are, in fact, a rediscovery of ideas that were first formulated in the work of classical economic thinkers, notably Adam Smith, who is considered to be the first economist in the modern sense, and who is best known for his principles of the free market but he contributed much more.

This history and concepts-based chapter describes the work of these classical thinkers, including David Ricardo, Jeremy Bentham, and John Stuart Mill, as well as later critics of the assumptions of neoclassical economics, notably, Thorstein Veblen and John Kenneth Galbraith. What is important for behavioral economics is how these early theorists shaped classical and, then, neoclassical economics, and how the assumptions they held still inform economic thinking today. The dawning of more sophisticated ideas in psychology in the twentieth century, and the work of Tversky and Kahneman in particular, contributed greatly to the synthesis of psychology and economics in the emerging field of behavioral economics.

DOI: 10.4324/9781003166900-2

INTRODUCTION

Behavioral economics as we know it today may not have been around much before the 1970s, but the issues it tackles have been around for a very long time. In fact, this relatively new discipline is steeped in the past of economic thinking. It is for this reason that viewing behavioral economics against the larger historical and conceptual backdrop is crucial not only for understanding the past but also the present – importantly, it exposes some long-standing concerns that are fundamental to both mainstream and behavioral economics. There is another reason for taking this perspective. This relates to the very nature of economics: are the phenomena it tries to explain cast in 'iron laws' (along the lines of physics), or are they more malleable, subject to the economic, and even political, conditions of the time?

In this book, we show that the applicability of the theories of economics is, indeed, reflective of their times. What may work in the preindustrial and industrial ages may not work in the information age of today. This is important to know because current-day mainstream economics remains heavily influenced by past theorizing. In this way, *truly* to understand the present, we have no other option than to know about the past.

In addition to the 'conditions of the times' validity of economic theorizing, we see something else of relevance: the psychological ('behavioral') assumptions lurking in the *origins* of mainstream economics. In this way, behavioral economics is far from being entirely a recent development with few antecedents – if anything, the opposite is the case. There are moral and political themes shaping the 'political economy' of any single country as well as internationally. For good reason, the term 'political economy' was the preferred name for economics until the adoption of a seemingly more detached, scientific approach, which occurred around the turn of the twentieth century and which became to define current-day mainstream (neoclassical) economics, detailed in Chapter 3.

These and related issues are the focus of this chapter.

THE CLASSICAL ECONOMIC TRADITION

Looking back over the past few centuries, it is fascinating that within a relatively short period of time, moral, philosophical, political, and economic ideas were developed to such an extent that they sustain the intellectual life of society today – nationally and internationally.

As summarized below, several notable figures are remembered for their lasting contributions. Before discussing their specific ideas, it is as well to know that classical thinkers believed that they had discovered natural laws and processes. Behavioral economics has reason to challenge this very notion – it especially challenges the idea that economics embodies 'iron laws' that operate throughout all time and in all circumstances.

However, this is not to say that the theories of the classic economic tradition are no longer of relevance and deserve to occupy our time out of historical curiosity only. Even if we despair at the thought of a world depicted by classical economics, it would not be prudent to ignore the potential consequences – if true, they are highly important. A case in point is the notion of the 'iron law' of wages which states that labor wage rates could never rise above a mere subsistence level because, if they were to, the resulting increase in births and hungry mouths to feed would force down wages – as this example attests, there were certain presumptions about how the working class would react to an increased wage rate. (The term was coined by Ferdinand Lassalle, but the origin of the concept is less clear and could be attributed to several economists, among them David Ricardo.) It was also assumed that labor would need to be paid above the mere subsistence level to allow them – most often, him – to raise a family in order to supply the next generation of workers. With just cause, in 1849, Thomas Carlyle dubbed economics the 'dismal science' (see text box) – but as few readers might know, this term is steeped in racism as it was used to denote British political economy in the 1840s to emphasize its role in the emancipation of West Indian slaves (see Levy, 2001).

Fortunately, for the wealth and health of these classical thinkers, this 'iron law' seemed not to apply to their economic activities – this was one of the reasons for Marx's class-based economics, which made a clear distinction between 'wage slaves' and their capitalistic masters (e.g., Marx, 1932; based on notes written in 1844, but not published during his lifetime). (Along with other historical and contemporary resources, many of the classic works discussed in this section are freely available at: www.econlib.org)

We now take a closer look at the development of the main ideas that characterize classical economics by discussing the most prominent thinkers and luminaries. This allows us to understand better the origins of the *neo*classical economics that followed and to what extent behavioral economics represents a return to some of these older ideas.

ADAM SMITH (1723–1790)

Without much doubt, the towering figure in classical thought is Adam Smith. He is rightly considered to be the first economist in the modern sense – he introduced the notion of the 'imaginary machine' that entails the coordination of all economic activities in cause-and-effect relationships: the economic *system*. When we hear that the Bank of England is increasing the interest rate to curb inflation, it is Adam Smith's 'machine' to which they refer. Smith was enlightened, and although he is most known for his principles of the free market – one of the main ideas of classical economics – he believed this to be a means to an end, not an end in itself. His view was that the greatest happiness in life comes not from the accumulation of money (or, more generally, 'materialism') but from the companionship of fellow men and women. His social views of economics were contained in his important 1759 book, *The Theory Of Moral Sentiments,* which has

CLASSICAL ECONOMICS: THE DISMAL SCIENCE

A number of seminal ideas developed out of the classical tradition, although individual thinkers quibbled about details and interpretation – this is not surprising because as George Bernard Shaw supposedly once quipped: if you laid all economists end-to-end, they would not reach a conclusion! These important ideas included the following.

1   Prudent self-interest benefits the whole of society by allocating scarce resources in the most efficient manner – this is discussed below in relation to Adam Smith;
2   Individual liberty is fundamental: no one knows better what is good for them than the individual concerned;
3   There are invisible forces at work (Adam Smith's 'invisible hand') that guide the economy along productive lines – interference by the government with such invisible forces leads to inevitable inefficiencies;

4   Free trade (both nationally and internationally) benefits the whole economy – for example, by the law of 'comparative cost advantage' (i.e., different countries can supply commodities and goods at lower relative cost);

5   Efficient production comes from the 'division of labor' (something that, much earlier, the Greek philosopher Plato spoke about); that is, the production process is broken down into specialized tasks, each of which is performed by a dedicated worker (see below);

6   The accumulation of profit and the allocation of capital are necessary to facilitate efficient production processes;

7   Private capital(ism) is for the public good – and deprivations (e.g., subsistence wages of workers) are the necessary price that must be paid – much earlier, the Greek philosopher Aristotle also extolled the virtues of private ownership on efficient economic affairs;

8   Natural scarce resources (especially land, but also coal, oil, etc.) potentially limit increasing productivity, so international trade is essential as may well be 'imperialism' to secure the necessary factors of production;

9   Laws (e.g., of contract) and punishment (jurisprudence) are necessary to regulate the 'free' economic system in order for it not to be corrupted by immoral economic behavior that erodes trust and thus the general efficiency of trade.

been overshadowed by his much more famous 1776 book, *An Inquiry into the Nature and Causes of the Wealth of Nations* (often abbreviated as *The Wealth of Nations*). Smith's earlier book placed feelings, emotions, virtues, and such like center-stage in economic life. The compatibility of these two views has long been debated, but they are not mutually exclusive. This is because there is so much that classical (and neoclassical) economics *does not* consider – 'social' preferences can always work their way into 'utility functions' (see text box) to maintain the elegance of neoclassical mathematical formalism.

Such psychological notions were rediscovered by behavioral economists, but they were there all along in Smith's classical work. As Thaler noted in 2015: "The famous Chicago economist George Stigler was fond of saying that there was nothing new in economics; Adam Smith had said it all". The same may be said of much of behavioral economics.

UTILITY FUNCTIONS

A utility function orders and measures preferences over a set of goods and services. Utility, which can be measured in a common metric, 'utils', represents the happiness, welfare, or satisfaction resulting from the consumption of goods and services (broadly defined). As it is not possible to measure utility directly, it is typically measured in terms of 'revealed preferences': the decision made among an array of choices. In other words, an individual's actions/decisions *reveal* their true *preferences* (and these maximize their utility). The utility function is widely used in rational choice theory, which neoclassical economists use to analyze choice behavior.

SMITH'S SENTIMENTS

When seen in the light of what we now know, remarkably, Smith argued that social psychology tells us more about moral action than reason alone, let alone pure logic. Smith identifies the rules of 'prudence' and 'justice' and explains how these are required for society to survive and thrive.

PRUDENCE

Smith noted that individuals have, what he considers to be, a natural tendency to look after themselves. This he called 'prudence'. He also noted, though, that we have sympathy (today, 'empathy') toward others. For example, if we see people distressed or happy, we experience something of the same ourselves, and other people react in the same way to us. This allows us to regulate our feelings and behaviors toward others, and as we grow up, we learn what is right and wrong. According to Smith, this moral impulse stems from our social nature. In this view, we are far from the stereotypical selfish, 'rational' creature often depicted in economics: our actions are influenced by the emotions of other people. This social view is a central idea today in behavioral economics.

JUSTICE

In addition to Smith's notion of prudence, he said we have 'justice'. We may well be prudently self-interested – 'charity begins at home' – but we have to live in a community, and this requires shared values and mutually beneficial behavior. A productive society needs people who are willing and able to do good, but this raises the prospect of free-loaders, who take all and give nothing back. It is for this reason that society needs a 'justice' system: primarily to deter wrong-doing and to punish those who violate social rules. As this account of Smith's work shows, there has always been a close connection between eco-nomics and the law. Today, lawless societies are the very ones that are economically impoverished, and international organizations, such as the World Bank, are much interested in establishing the 'rule of law' in order to foster economic productivity and the 'wealth of nations' – they even conduct carefully controlled empirical studies (often exper-iments) to try to find out how best to motivate judges to be more efficient and fairer, and less corrupt.

In order to regulate individual behavior to achieve social harmony, Smith tells us that something else is required: the 'impartial spectator', who is conceived as an ideal person who would completely empathize with our emotions and actions. The thought of such an observer helps to regulate our behavior because, according to Smith, we want to meet their expectations. This notion is bound up with the concept of con-science and seems not entirely divorced from the notion of an all-seeing God who is continuously observing and judging us. (See Dan Ariely's observation in Chapter 1.) Now, all of this requires self-control – Smith called this 'virtue'. In contrast to Smith's notion of justice, this is a form of morality that requires active deliberation (in the classical tradition, it is also about what we 'ought' to try to achieve) – it may also be thought of as a personality characteristic, with those lacking in this quality being seen as feckless and irresponsible, and deserving of the negative conse-quences that are sure to follow. (This distinction of nature vs. nurture of virtue was put to good comic effect in the 1983 film, *Trading Places*, starring Dan Aykroyd and Eddie Murphy.)

Now, none of Smith's presumptions demand much in the way of a conscious calculating (human) machine. It is said to be part-and-parcel of our social nature: we are sensitive to other people's feelings, and we get pleasure when the things we do are praised, and we feel psychological pain when the things we do are criticized. We have a tendency to curb our excessive emotions (e.g., anger) because we know it would distress the other person. According to Smith, we aim to modulate our emotions to a point where the 'impartial spectator' would sympathize and approve of us, and we take pleasure in this knowledge. In this way, we 'socialize' to the society in which we live. The idea that we are seeking the approval of others – even the imaginary 'impartial spectator' – leads to the development of morality and socially approved behavior.

All of the above is in the spirit of modern-day behavioral economics and it is essentially *psychological*.

SMITH'S 'INVISIBLE HAND'

More related to the conventional view of economics, in his 1776 book, *The Wealth of Nations*, Smith gave us the concept of an 'invisible hand', which serves to guide the efficient allocation of scarce resources in the capitalistic (laissez faire) economy. To understand the development of economics, it will repay us to summarize Smith's arguments.

We need to know that Smith's 1776 book has several themes. First, he argued that the nation's wealth consists of the store of goods and services it creates – today's gross *domestic* product (GPD), which we briefly discussed in Chapter 1, is based on the same idea. (When we focus on only the goods and services produced and owned by a country's citizens, whether domestic or abroad, we have gross *national* product, GNP.) According to Smith, the way to increase wealth is to release the productive forces of society – to allow free spirit and human ingenuity to flourish. Here, we see the forces of industry, creativity, and innovation of the population. Smith was adamant that government regulation of commerce, however well intentioned, is counter-productive and prone to do more harm than good.

Second, the major components of how the 'market' system works come from the 'laws' of supply and demand. Scarcity of supply of a good or service means its price will rise because scarcity implies that more people want the goods/services than are available and many are willing to pay a higher price to obtain them. But, when there is a 'surplus' – fewer people wanting the goods/services than are available – the price must fall to attract more buyers. These assumptions lead to the notion of 'equilibrium': the idea that prices will always adjust to reach a 'market clearing' level where all goods and services are traded.

Third, Smith argued that when a profit is made (the sale price is higher than the cost of production), this will attract new entrants into the market, especially if the level of profit is higher than that achieved in other markets. If this happens, the supply of the good or service is increased, the price will fall, and so will the profit – a self-regulating economic machine. A seemingly perfect mechanism for matching buyers and sellers, and all regulated by the 'invisible hand', achieving efficient production and the resulting equilibrium that leads to economic stability – and to boot, no need for political coordination or interfering regulators.

The important point to note is that, although in all of this we may be acting in our own 'prudent' self-interest, the genius – if that is what it is – of the economic system described by Adam Smith is that this self-interest serves to benefit the whole nation. As Smith said:

> It is not from the benevolence of the butcher, the brewer, or the baker, that we expect our dinner, but from their regard to their own interest

In the next sentence, Smith goes on to say:

> We address ourselves, not to their humanity but to their self-love, and never talk to them of their own necessities but of their advantages.

So, we see how self-interest leads to, what Smiths calls, beneficial "unintended social outcomes". (Smith's theory is satirized in the 1987 film *Wall Street*, in which Gordon Gekko famously gives an extended speech to justify his belief that 'greed is good'.) Smith's theory is much more nuanced than popular depictions might lead us to believe – reading Smith's own works gives a real sense of his sophisticated thinking.

The effective operation of an invisible hand must rely on the assumption that market participants can compute complex information and behave according to Smith's principles. However, when thinking about the assumptions of mainstream economics, it is necessary to note that such a process need not be conscious, but it surely must mean that the human mind, in some way, is sensitive to these economic forces and is motivated to respond accordingly.

Smith was, indeed, one of the first thinkers to address the question of the *efficiency* of production – efficiency in the allocation of scarce resources is a recurring theme in neoclassical economics. Presaging the industrial age, Smith contended that the division of labor, and the accumulation of capital, are vital ingredients for a successful economy.

He noted that large efficiencies are achieved when the production process is broken down into many small tasks, each one performed by a skilled operative (his famous example is the pin factory; see text box). Such efficiency ensures that output is maximized for any set of inputs – resources are *optimally* allocated to maximize utility, in this case, profit. This profit can then be invested in new forms of production, exchanges with others, and so on, to fuel economic expansion and the 'wealth of nations'.

These were seminal ideas and sparked intellectual excitement in those notable philosopher-cum-economists who followed in Smith's footsteps.

The power of Adam Smith's thinking is seen in the modern market economy which, by and large, operates very much along the lines he articulated – even debates around the wisdom of market intervention

THE PIN FACTORY

The classic example of the beneficial effects of the division of labor was seen in the 'trifling manufacture' of the humble pin. Adam Smith visited a pin factory and observed that it required 18 separate production processes. He observed that the division of labor leads to greater 'dexterity' (skill) in workers, which along with avoiding the time-consuming act of moving workers from one production process to the other, as well as the use of capital-intensive machinery, creates great economic efficiency: whereas one operative could make between 1 and 20 pins a day, when labor was divided the rate of productivity rose to 4,800!

However, division of labor comes with a high price, as noted by Smith:

> His dexterity at his own particular trade seems ... to be acquired at the expense of his intellectual, social and martial virtues ... unless government takes some pains to prevent it.

Indeed, it may lead, through the narrowing of interests, to such 'mental mutilation' as to produce a breakdown of moral regulation by the Impartial Spectator to whom we aspire to please in our actions (see above). This mechanical process was brilliantly satirized by Charlie Chaplin in the film, *Modern Times*.

by well-intentioned governments (think Margaret Thatcher in the United Kingdom, Ronald Reagan in the United States, and the ongoing economic/political debates of today).

OTHER CLASSICAL THINKERS

Classical economics is certainly defined by the ideas of Adam Smith, but there were other seminal thinkers, too. What is important for our understanding of present-day behavioral economics is how these theorists shaped classical and, then, current mainstream (*neo*classical) economic thinking. Figure 2.1 provides a brief overview of the main players, discussed in detail below. Their ideas shape our thinking today, although some of them have only been 'rediscovered' recently by behavioral economists.

DAVID RICARDO (1772–1823)

David Ricardo is regarded as another of the outstanding economists of the classical age. His ideas permeate current-day economics. Trained as a stockbroker by his father, by the age of 27, Ricardo was very successful. However, his Jewish family disowned him when he married a Quaker. (During this time, Ricardo happened to read Smith's *The Wealth of Nations* and was excited by it.) He then set up his own stock brokerage company acting on his own account as a stockjobber, and by the age of 37, he was fabulously wealthy – although by means of what we would now call insider trading and market manipulation related to the Battle of Waterloo. From the age of 37 to his death at the young age of 51, he spent 14 years thinking and writing about economics and engaging in stimulating debates with his notable contemporaries (e.g., Jeremy Bentham, see below).

Like Adam Smith before him, Ricardo argued for free trade and the virtues of nongovernment intervention (e.g., Ricardo, 1817). In support of free trade, Ricardo is known for his principle of *comparative costs* (sometimes called 'comparative advantage'; see text box). The doctrine of comparative cost advantage is pleasing and an important justification of international trade. It contends that all countries have the potential to offer something of economic value to themselves and the rest of the world – just think of tea from China and call centers in India. The globalization of trade is a direct consequence of this idea.

Classical Economics
(late 18th to mid 19th century, mostly in Britain)

Thinkers (a selection)

Adam Smith (1723–1790) - the father of modern economics

- free market, invisible hand (which guides efficient allocation of scarce resources), people look after themselves (prudence) but also care about others (sympathy/empathy) and their communities (which need to be regulated by 'justice' systems; behavior is also regulated to please an 'impartial spectator'; this requires self-control/'virtue')

David Ricardo (1772–1823)

- free trade, comparative costs/advantage, law of diminishing marginal returns, iron law of wages

Jeremy Bentham (1748–1832)

- utilitarianism (the greatest happiness for the greatest number)

Thomas Robert Malthus (1766–1834)

- relationship between population growth and food production, people are sensitive to incentives

Jean-Baptiste Say (1767–1832)

- Say's Law (supply creates its own demand)

John Stuart Mill (1806–1873)

- opportunity costs, comparative cost advantage, freedom of speech, free choices

William Stanley Jevons (1835–1882)

- marginal view (decreasing marginal utility), productivity is limited by finite natural resources

Critics of classical and neo-classical economics
(a small selection)

Thorstein Veblen (1857–1929)

- conspicuous consumption (e.g., status goods)

- utility maximization and markets do not lead to successful societies

John Maynard Keynes (1983-1946)

-failure of market equilibrium

- economy is affected by 'animal spirits'

- business cycles should be smoothed through fiscal and monetary policies

John Kenneth Galbraith (1908–2006)

- challenged assumption of sovereignty of consumer

- economy suffers from periodic crises if left to market forces

- power structures in society shape economic activity (not invisible hand)

FIGURE 2.1 From classical to neoclassical economics: important thinkers, their theories, and critics

Ricardo advanced another important idea: the law of diminishing marginal returns. (We will see the importance of *marginalism* to neo-classical economics in the next chapter – it is central to the very notion of 'rationality'.) This 'law' states that as one input variable is increased while other input variables are held constant (fixed), *increments* to output (marginal returns) are bound to decline. In other words, the efficiency of the combination of inputs decreases which may lead to declining productivity. A classic example describes how adding more workers to a field or factory will eventually lead to less output per worker as they start disturbing each other's work or they have to wait their turn to access tools.

One input variable that is often described as fixed in these models is land – very little of it is added to the sum total each year, and some is lost to climate erosion. As a consequence, as good land is scarce and will become increasingly sought after with economic expansion, its value would increase to the joyful benefit of the landowner.

COMPARATIVE COST ADVANTAGE

Comparative cost advantage underpins the idea that each country has an advantage in the cost of producing certain goods (and today, services). The concept is often misunderstood because it is more intuitive to assume that the country which can produce a good at the lowest absolute cost should produce it. Thus, countries with low labor costs might be able to produce a number of goods at lower costs than countries with high labor costs. However, as Ricardo explained, using the example of producing cloth and wine in either England or Portugal, what really matters for international trade is the *comparative* cost advantage of producing these goods; that is, the country with the lowest opportunity costs (i.e., the cost of the best foregone alternative, see the text box below) of producing wine should produce it. In Ricardo's example: how many units of cloth must Portugal give up in order to produce one unit of wine? Portugal has the comparative advantage in the wine industry if it can produce wine at lower opportunity costs (production of fewer units of cloth) than England. With the international trade of these goods and services, there is a benefit to the whole world – this comes from the most efficient allocation of scarce resources (today in Britain, we see this with the importation of coal and steel).

In the spirit of free trade, Ricardo argued that the laws of economics should be allowed to play themselves out, which means, among other things, ensuring the poor are not supported beyond a level of subsistence as this would only erode their work motivation, encourage reproduction beyond what can be sustained by subsistence wages, foster fecklessness, and generally undermine the efficiency of the market system – this was his *Iron Law of Wages*, although others made essentially the same point before and since. (Critics have accused Ricardo of holding to this belief from the position of being a Gentleman of Leisure, secured from what would now be considered ill-gotten gains.) As confirmation of the reverberation of his ideas throughout the years, Ricardo popularized the notion that the road to economic hell is paved with good intentions – whenever one passes a beggar in the street, it is Ricardo's voice that is heard whispering that giving money to them will *really* do more harm than good.

In mitigation of Ricardo's position, he was interested only in respecting what he saw as natural laws of economics – in the case of wages, the 'iron law'. But, once we move away from this view of natural laws of economics to one based on psychological factors, Ricardo's approach loses much of its veracity – for it would then be possible to use behavioral insights to influence people to behave in ways that benefit society (e.g., using strategies to increase motivation for work and to limit excessive births through the prudent use of contraception; see Thomas Malthus, below). In addition, as with other supposed 'iron laws', Ricardo's ideas were very much part of his economic time – of limited resources, hard manual labor, and little technological innovation to boost productivity. This is why Karl Marx's labor theory of value had merit in a time when a product or service could be easily measured by the number of labor hours that went into its production. In relation to the classes that dominated Marx's political economy, the classical view contained psychological models of the motivation of the true working class at the time – motivation that was in no way noble but maintained by the prospect of poverty or worse (the workhouses and debtors' prisons of Dicken's literature, in which his own father resided for a period, were a constant threat to those who violated these 'iron laws' of nature). For Marx, there was class warfare in action – his mission was not to understand this world in some abstract intellectual sense but to change it by a revolution of ideas and action. Economic ideas changed the world.

Now, Ricardo's ideas may well seem somewhat distant from the concerns of modern-day behavioral economics. They should not be seen as such. Let us remind ourselves that behavioral economics challenges the central assumptions of mainstream economics. For example, it challenges the idea that there exist natural 'iron laws' that govern economic life independently of psychological and social factors. Also, as 'nudge' theory attests (see Chapter 6), behavioral economics does not see government interventions to influence people's decision making as inevitably a bad thing – indeed, it is argued that such nudging is needed to encourage people to make the right decisions (e.g., Thaler & Sunstein, 2008). All of this raises moral, ethical, and political issues that are still debated today.

JEREMY BENTHAM (1748–1832)

Another notable thinker in the classical tradition was the moral and political philosopher Jeremy Bentham. (You can see his body in a showcase at University College London, an institution he helped found.) He is best known for advocating *Utilitarianism*, which advances the idea that the greatest happiness of the greatest number should be the foundation of morals and legislation (e.g., Bentham, 1789). Bentham was interested in what regulates human behavior and the close connection between jurisprudence and the 'economic mind'. His work on the notion of utility had a major impact on the development of neoclassical economics.

Bentham's philosophy can be best described as a form of *consequentialism*, based on the idea that actions, policies, rules, and so on should be judged on the basis of their consequences, that is, the utility they yield. The continued relevance of these ideas can be seen in the public application of behavioral economics in nudge initiatives (see Chapter 6), where the criterion of successful policy intervention is whether it *works* to improve the welfare of society. It is also the general criterion used in wider public economic policy.

THOMAS ROBERT MALTHUS (1766–1834)

Thomas Malthus is best known for his work on the relationship between population and the production of food. His conclusions are often cited as testimony to the accuracy of economics being a 'dismal science'. Rather like a mathematical economist of today, Malthus was diligent in gathering information on births, marriages, deaths, longevity, and number of offspring. His most famous book, *An Essay on the Principles of Population* (1798), concluded that as the supply of food increases *arithmetically*, but the population increases at a much faster (*geometric*) rate, the destiny of mankind is to live on the edge of starvation. Adam Smith believed much the same; as he states in *The Wealth of Nations*: "As men, like all other animals, naturally multiply in proportion to the means of their subsistence, food is always, more or less, in demand".

If there is a positive message to be found in Malthus's work – and they are not so easy to find – it is that the dismal science predicts that, because populations do not always live on the edge of starvation, this must mean that they make decisions to avoid this outcome. For example, people may choose to marry late, use contraception, emigrate, tolerate poor living conditions, and even engage in infanticide and wage war – a somewhat dismal means to avoid a dismal outcome! The important thing to bear in mind is that we are not merely passive recipients of the terrible fate of economic nature and its immutable 'iron laws'. Although hope may spring eternal, reality can be jarring. Hundreds of years after Malthus, and with the development of a powerful set of economic principles and procedures, the nightmare he envisioned of populations living at the edge of starvation is not absent from all parts of the world: populations' demand for nutrition often outstrips the production and supply of food and water, especially in times of famine.

But, the Malthusian view of the world is not without hope, although it is often without expectation. In particular, his interest in the sensitivity of people to incentives is something that dominates neoclassical economics. From this tradition, we get the notion that people are capable of making the correct choices, if sufficiently incentivized to do so – nudging may help, too.

We can see that Malthus' work and those of other classical economists is still highly relevant to the economic concerns of today.

JEAN-BAPTISTE SAY (1767–1832)

An achievement of Jean-Baptiste Say is to have his name attached to an economic 'law'. 'Say's law' states that supply (or production) creates its own demand – "build it and they will come" – which happened to be the guiding spirit behind the project to build *The Titanic* ship (with much the same fate as Say's law). Say's law is a rather fine example of the operation of Adam Smith's invisible hand. As Say said in 1803: "It is worthwhile to remark that a product is no sooner created than it, from that instant, affords a market for other products to the full extent of its own value". In other words, workers receive wages for their labor which they will then use to purchase other goods. This increase in production thus creates demand for other goods in the economy, leading to economic growth – another example of Smith's economic machine in motion.

Say believed that his law holds for the short run as well as the long run. While it might be true that there cannot be a glut of goods in the long run, the famous twentieth-century economist, John Maynard Keynes, in particular, challenged the truth of this law for the short run: sometimes aggregate demand is too low to 'clear' the market at prices which entail no loss, such as during times of recession and depression. Ruefully reflecting back on the Great Depression in the early 1930s, J. K. Galbraith (1975) opined that Say's Law is "the most distinguished example of the stability of economic ideas, including when they are wrong".

JOHN STUART MILL (1806–1873)

One of the most famous moral philosophers of all time, John Stuart Mill, followed in the footsteps of his less well-known but still illustrative father, James Mill (1773–1836), who was a notable philosopher, historian, and political thinker. John Stuart Mill's views were expressed in his 1848 book, *Principles of Political Economy*, which was built upon the works of Smith and Ricardo. In the sphere of economics, Mill is especially remembered for developing the idea of 'opportunity cost' (see text box) and arguing for the Ricardian principle of comparative cost advantage (see above). Like David Hume (1711–1776) before him, Mill was also a believer in freedom of speech, and he is best known for his book, *On Liberty* (1859).

Mill argued for a free and liberal society, not only as a political ideal but as a means to achieve an efficient economy – again, we witness economic and political forces going hand-in-hand (the politicoeconomic machine at work). Central to Mill's position was the idea that the utility of society is maximized by allowing people to make their

---

OPPORTUNITY COSTS

The principle of opportunity costs is fundamental to economic thinking – it is seen in the guise of cost-benefit analysis. When faced with different courses of action, the opportunity cost refers to the utility (satisfaction, benefit, profit, and so on) of the best *foregone* alternative. For instance, if you decide to see a movie with your friends, what is your best alternative option? Maybe dinner with your family or watching TV at home? These foregone alternatives are the opportunity costs of your choice – they are real enough but usually not salient to us (for this reason, they take some thinking about to appreciate them). In the case of New York City taxi drivers (see Chapter 1), finishing work early incurs a cost in terms of foregone income, but working longer incurs a cost in terms of foregone leisure time – it is the costs and benefits assigned to these alternative choices that determine the decision made: this is how we maximize utility.

---

own *free* choices. According to this view, we should only interfere with the liberty of others for self-protection – this is one major role of government in establishing an effective national defense. This has been a dominant theme in mainstream economics and provides an intellectual and moral underpinning of the 'market economy'. Such is its power, nudge theory (see Chapter 6) goes to pains to stress that nudging does not take away the free choice of the individual.

WILLIAM STANLEY JEVONS (1835–1882)

Along with two other notable economists, Leon Walras (in Switzerland) and Carl Menger (in Vienna), and quite independently of their work, William Jevons (in Manchester) is best known for contributing significantly to the 'marginal' view of economic behavior which has come to exert a dominant pull on mainstream economic thinking. The marginal view, which was later formalized in Alfred Marshall's seminal *Principles of Economics* (1890; discussed in Chapter 3), contends that the utility ('value') of each additional unit of a commodity (i.e., its increment, extra, or *marginal* utility) decreases with further consumption. The principle of declining marginal utility says that the more we have of something, the less pleasure (utility) we get from each additional unit of consumption. Consider the declining marginal utility of money: the first million will always be sweeter than the second! To give an everyday example, the first bite of food has a high value (utility) for a hungry person, but after further consumption, each additional mouthful has a lower value until it reaches zero and may even become negative ('disutility').

Jevon's work serves well to illustrate the problems with an economic perspective that does not sufficiently consider the 'human capital' of skills, knowledge, innovation, and creativity – that is, a view that places immutable laws above psychological factors. This is seen in the 'dismal' conclusions of Jevons' consideration of the 'Coal Question' in Britain (Jevons, 1865), which said that industrial productivity would be increasingly limited by the finite supply of this vital natural resource. As history has shown, coal is not the only resource for power: technology and innovation have proved to be powerful economic forces in their own right. During its time, the coal problem was a real problem to be addressed, but it is no longer today (indeed, the desire is to burn less fossil fuel to help the environment and climate). This is another example of how apparent immutable laws were limited to their time, and not 'forever laws' – however, there is still a problem with the sourcing, securing, and price of fuel, so in one form or another Jevon's general 'coal problem' has not gone away, although it has been transformed in its specifics.

MORAL AND POLITICAL ASSUMPTIONS

As we have seen, the classical roots of economics run deep in modern-day economic thinking. Indeed, to such an extent that today's undergraduate economics students are still taught about comparative cost advantage, utility functions, opportunity costs, diminishing marginal utility, and some of the other economic concepts presented in this chapter. Not everyone agrees with the underlying assumptions. For example, Noam Chomsky, who is not only a famous linguist but also a political philosopher, certainly does not agree with the 'value' placed on competition and the 'winner takes all' of the free market espoused by much of mainstream economics, especially as it is expressed in the United States. If we believe that the market is not 'free' and 'the firm', as envisioned by classical economists, no longer exists in the modern world, these classical assumptions start to appear rather threadbare. For sure, they never appealed to the likes of J. K. Galbraith and other 'institutional' economists who have long argued that power structures in society shape economic activity and not Adam Smith's mysterious 'invisible hand'.

Still, the persistent appeal of Smith's guiding 'invisible hand' is that it does not require any form of deliberate or centralized planning – it happens all by itself, working best if left alone, unmolested by government interference and, even, well-intentioned, meddling. Through this conceptual lens, it is easy to see just how the capitalist system is seen by many to be a work of wonder! This was the view of one of the most famous economists of the mid-to-late twentieth century, Milton Friedman, who wrote the 1980 best-selling book whose name says it all, *Free to Choose*. The ideas it conveyed drove forward much of the economic policy of Reagan's and the Bushs' terms of office in the United States, as well as the Thatcher governments in the United Kingdom during the 1980s.

As the above discussion shows, in reality (though often not in the classroom), economics and politics are rarely separated. A few years before Adam Smith, the moral philosopher David Hume (1711–1776) popularized the view that still holds sway today that economic freedom is a precondition for freedom more generally. Essentially, the same point was made by Friedrich Hayek in his 1944 book, *The Road to Serfdom*. This contention seems to be one reason why so many people adhere to the notions developed by classical economists, especially in their objection to 'big government' – even when they may not embrace all of the underlying assumptions (e.g., the dubious motivations of the working class). Around the same time, in 1945, the philosopher Karl Popper published *The Open Society and its Enemies*. One of the 'enemies' was Marxist ideology that had already dominated Russia and China, and later Cuba. In this context, some claim that those who want to throw out the classical economic dirty water need to have a firm grip on the libertarian baby.

WHAT IS NEOCLASSICAL ECONOMICS?

It was in this intellectual fervor that *neo*classical economics was born – this is the brand that we have been referring to as current-day 'mainstream economics'. As the name suggests, this is the new form of 'classical' economics. It is noteworthy that 'classical' economics was christened by Karl Marx, and its revised form, 'neoclassical', by

Thorstein Veblen in a 1900 article 'The Preconceptions of Economic Science'. These terms were not intended to be complimentary.

Neoclassical economics is the dominant approach to economic thinking in the modern world – of course, in socialist countries (e.g., Cuba), Marxist economics rules. Neoclassical economics is now seen under a variety of other intellectual brands (e.g., 'mainstream', 'traditional', or the 'central tradition' – in 1936, John Maynard Keynes called it 'orthodox economics', referring to traditionally accepted rules or beliefs, which his *General Theory* of that year so famously challenged). We need to note, though, that neoclassical economics is not one thing but rather a general approach with a set of common assumptions and principles (see text box).

In any discussion of neoclassical economics, we need to be careful to avoid caricature, something that it rather readily invites. This is especially true for the claim that all human beings are perfect in all economic respects – most clearly, they are not, and it would be foolish to suggest otherwise. But, for the neoclassical model to have any truth and practical value, it must be assumed that the judgments and decision making of economic agents are *good enough*: we must be sufficiently ECON and not entirely HUMAN (these concepts are defined in Chapter 1).

The necessary thing to know is that the assumptions of ECON are important in neoclassical economic thinking/theorizing, and they are necessary for the success of mathematical models. However, in practice, there is quite a bit of wriggle room: the assumptions of neoclassical economics are often 'relaxed' (e.g., we do not behave selfishly all the time), and extra parameters can be added to formal mathematical models (risk aversion, social preferences, and so on) to make allowance for people's everyday behavior. However, assumptions cannot be relaxed to the point of collapse – the necessity of establishing a well-developed field of behavioral economics concerns this very *point*.

Behavioral economics is defined as much by what it is *not* than by what it *is*. It stands in contrast to neoclassical economics, which is a system of assumptions, concepts, principles, and (mathematical) procedures used to explain and predict 'economic phenomena', detailed in Chapter 3. As discussed in Chapter 1, it is important to know that neoclassical economics is largely 'normative' in orientation, concerning itself with prescriptions for how people *should* behave. Clearly, it also has moral, political, and ethical undertones which reflect the

NEOCLASSICAL ECONOMICS

The mainstream economics approach makes a number of assumptions. Although neoclassical economists may disagree on points of detail, they would adhere to some general principles:

1   People have a set of consistent preferences, which they 'reveal' through their choices;
2   People use logical forms of reasoning to arrive at judgments and decisions – although people may not know the formal rules and procedures of logical reasoning, they behave 'as if' they do;
3   People strive to maximize their 'utility' (i.e., happiness, satisfaction, well-being);
4   People process information in an unbiased way (at least, to the best of their ability);
5   Both individuals and firms strive to solve the 'optimization problem' – that is, to derive the most utility (pleasure or profit) from the allocation of scarce resources;
6   People are very sensitive and reactive to incentives, especially of a financial nature;
7   Individuals and firms are 'selfish' in that they place their own well-being and welfare above others';
8   The self-interest of individuals benefits society;
9   There are 'laws' of economics that are immutable, and interference (e.g., by the government) only thwarts the efficient allocation of scarce resources – of course, in a 'mixed economy', some government regulation and economic management are necessary, but this is seen as a problem in that its possible adverse side effects need to be monitored for inefficiencies (e.g., expenditure of socialized medical service, e.g., the NHS in the United Kingdom);
10 Economic principles are best expressed in mathematical form, allowing the construction of models built from basic assumptions/tenets/principles/axioms to arrive at logical conclusions (e.g., the consequences of increased taxation).

political economy of classical thinkers (discussed above). It is of no small interest that Adam Smith – the first economist in the modern sense – was Professor of Moral Philosophy at Glasgow University. As we have already seen, around the eighteenth and nineteenth centuries, the ideas of a number of moral and political philosophers shaped the economic thinking we have today.

In contrast to neoclassical economics, behavioral economics is much less constrained by these early classical influences, but it is not entirely free of them (e.g., it still emphasizes the importance of utility maximization and efficiency). In some important respects, behavioral economics has been inspired by them, especially Adam Smith's thinking on social factors.

DISSENTING ECONOMICS

Classical and neoclassical economics never had things all their own way – they were never the only game in town. This is important to know because many accounts of behavioral economics focus on the perceived problems of neoclassical economics and tend to ignore the wider realm of economic, social, and political dissent. People were challenging the conventions of neoclassical economics long before behavioral economics came onto the scene. For this reason, to best understand the position of behavioral economics in relation to neoclassical economics, we really need to know the position of neoclassical economics in relation to these broader voices. To this end, we will now discuss the work of two early critics of (mainstream) neoclassical economics.

THORSTEIN VEBLEN (1857–1929)

Notable pockets of resistance to the natural science approach to human behavior, and the specific assumptions of neoclassical economics, have always been heard around university corridors. One of the foremost came from the so-called 'American Marxist', Thorstein Veblen, who published in 1899 a remarkable little book, *The Theory of the Leisure Class*, in which he examined the fashions and foibles of social and economic life. Veblen is famous for coining the phrase 'conspicuous consumption' to denote the production of specific socially valued artifacts at the expense of the general welfare of society. In particular, he pointed to, as he saw things, wasteful patterns of production and consumption. Veblen's point was that economic life serves social ends (e.g., status, hence the 'conspicuous consumption' of works of art, and so on), and although people may be seen to be maximizing utility, it is very much a socially defined and constrained type with sociopolitical overtones. In Veblen's ways of viewing economic life, utility maximization, efficiency of the marketplace, and equilibrium (where it was established) did not equate to a productive and successful society. Indeed, he reasoned that these neoclassical economic principles may well lead to a socially divided society, with a concentration of utility, much like capital, in the hands of the few and not the many – in today's world, such ideas seem far from outdated and find resonance in the work of politically dissenting voices such as Noam Chomsky, and critics more widely.

JOHN KENNETH GALBRAITH (1908–2006)

Challenges to the foundations of neoclassical economics are the bread-and-butter of behavioral economics. Before its ascent to high academic office, others found reasons to challenge it. One notable economist, J. K. Galbraith, followed Veblen's critique – his views can be found in his numerous books and seen in his 1977 BBC television series on economic history, *The Age of Uncertainty* (this can be accessed via the internet). Galbraith achieved fame and fortune, and some degree of notoriety, for developing dissenting economic themes in his runaway best-sellers, *The Affluent Society* (1958) and the *New Industrial State* (1967). Both challenged the assumption of the *sovereignty* of the consumer. Adam Smith thought something similar when he entertained the possibility that firms might conspire among themselves to the detriment of the consumer – as he puts it: "conspiracy against the public or in some other contrivance to raise prices" and fixing a price "which can be squeezed out of the buyers". In addition, in relation to conspiring against workers, Adam Smith says (1776):

> We rarely hear, it has been said, of the combinations of masters, though frequently of those of workmen. But whoever imagines, upon this account, that masters rarely combine, is as ignorant of the world as of the subject. Masters are always and everywhere in a sort of tacit, but constant a uniform combination, not to raise the wages of labour above their actual rate.

Although to keep up the pretense, "These are always conducted with the utmost silence and secrecy". In marked contrast, when workers combine to raise the wages of their labor, "they are always abundantly heard of". It, thus, seems that the force of the 'iron law' of wages (see above) might, after all, need a little helping (non-invisible) hand!

These dangers are real enough; otherwise, why else would the UK government have established the Competition and Markets Authority (CMA) which scrutinizes business mergers and takeovers? The Financial Conduct Authority (FCA) is similarly charged with *protecting* financial consumers and regulating financial companies, as well as ensuring the integrity of the UK's financial markets. Neither regulatory organization is short of work.

Prescient, too, was Smith's warning that a business-dominated political system could lead to a conspiracy of businesses and industry against consumers, with business pulling the strings of government – politics being in the pockets of Big Business. This was the *military-industrial complex*, first noted by the former general and USA President Dwight Eisenhower in 1961 during his farewell address to warn the nation of a looming danger. Galbraith returned to the theme in one of his last books, *The Economics of Innocent Fraud* (2004), although he was inclined to believe that this 'fraud' was far from innocent, especially when war and its consequences are the inevitable outcomes. (His definition of 'innocent fraud' is: "what it is convenient to believe is greatly preferred" to what is true and the reality – it is his later expression of "the conventional wisdom".)

Reflecting on the experiences of his earlier years, and expressed through dry wit and elegant turn of phrase, Galbraith had cause to lament one major failure of neoclassical economics. As he wryly commented: "I was here during the years of the Great Depression, when nobody could say that the economic system was working with great precision and great compassionate effect" (Conversations with History: John Kenneth Galbraith, 1986). Galbraith also called attention to the fact that left to market forces, the economic system is prone to periodic crises.

John Maynard Keynes is justly famous for identifying the problem of the failure of equilibrium. In his ground-breaking 1936 book, *The General Theory of Employment, Interest, and Money*, he proposed the management of aggregate demand in the economy to smooth out the troughs and peaks of the 'business cycle' (as it was often called) by fiscal means (i.e., spending, taxation) and various forms of the control of the money supply (e.g., altering the central bank interest rate). According to Keynes, this could moderate recessions and stave off depressions. Central to Keynes's thinking is the notion that economic conditions are much influenced by 'animal spirits' and they do not reflect merely the evaluation of objective numerical facts. *Behavioral* economics writ large!

The essence of the complaint by the likes of Veblen and Galbraith – and, as we have seen, this has echoes in the classical work of Adam Smith – is that economics is not *at all* like the natural sciences, and certainly not physics. The variables that make up the economic system are not fixed; they are not immutable. Instead, variables are fluid, changing, and subject to influence from the political and social environment – and conditioned by individual and collective psychology. That is, the economic system is dynamic, not static, and people are *active* participants in it. This is what behavioral economics assumes and it was the challenge of those critics long before the emergence of this new discipline.

Establishment reactions to such dissenting voices led to the accusation that the likes of Galbraith were not *really* economists, but social and political commentators, or more accurately not the *right kind* of (neoclassical) economists – but this did not deter the American Economic Association from electing him President in 1972 (an honor bestowed on the behavioral economist Richard Thaler in 2015, who went on to win the Nobel Prize in 2017 – for decades before, Richard Thaler was marginalized by mainstream economists, but is now lauded by many of them).

PSYCHOLOGY: LOST AND FOUND

Given the importance attached to social factors and emotions by earlier classical thinkers, most notably Adam Smith, we might ask ourselves why economics came increasingly to side-line psychology in favor of 'axiomatic' assumptions. This turn of events could be seen as a form of *misbehaving* – clinging to older psychological ideas and willfully ignoring later developments in psychology. To be fair to economists, turn of the twentieth-century psychology had little to offer that was *tractable* – that is, concepts that are easy to incorporate into formal economic models. Freudian notions of repressed sexuality held little interest – at least in the professional lives of economists – and things were not much better in academic psychology where psychological ideas were many and varied, and it would be hard to distill them down to a set of assumptions/principles that could guide systematic, let alone rigorous, economic thinking (although the behaviorist's stress on the power of 'reinforcement' – incentives of various kinds – came very close). Along with this rejection of psychology, as the twentieth century dawned, academic economics increasingly followed the natural sciences in its pursuit of age-old laws and mathematical formulation – a fallback to the types of immutable laws favored by the classical economics of many years before. (If there is one immutable psychological law, then it might be "old habits die hard".)

The problems with this whole-scale rejection of psychology led one well-known psychologist, William McDougall, in 1908, and in a tone of frustration, to proclaim:

> Political economy suffered ... from the crude nature of the psychological assumptions from which it professed to deduce the explanations of its facts and its prescriptions for economic legislation. It would be a libel, not altogether devoid of truth, to say that classical political economy was a tissue of false conclusions drawn from false psychological assumptions.

Many academics who today lean toward behavioral economics would agree with McDougall's view – their new discipline is designed to remedy this failure.

CONCLUSIONS

We have seen the development of ideas from the classical moral and political philosophy of the eighteenth and nineteenth centuries, which made a serious attempt to understand the nature – and natural laws as they were seen – of economic life. The views expressed were imbued with political overtones, *conditioned by their time*. These ideas were of their time, even though they must have seemed ever-so-fixed and immutable when first formulated – and, during their time, they may have been much more relevant than they are today. As classical economic thought segued to neoclassical assumptions and principles, economics started to presume a more scientific status, but it never fully separated itself from its origins in political and moral matters. As we have been continuously reminded by its critics, not all was well, and reality provided a lesson in the form of periodic crises – the specter of Karl Marx's prediction of the inevitable collapse of capitalism gave food for thought to more intellectually sensitive theorists and public policy economists. The dawning of more sophisticated ideas in psychology provided new impetus to these developments leading to a greater synthesis of psychology and economics – to form the emerging field of behavioral economics.

The next chapter details the assumptions and principles of neoclassical economics, and the problems it encounters when trying to account for everyday economic life. It is against this background that behavioral economics is defined and tested.

FURTHER READING

Coyle, D. (Ed.). (2012). *What's the use of economics? Teaching the dismal science after the crisis.* London Publishing Partnership.

Galbraith, J. K. (2004). *The economics of innocent fraud: Truth for our time.* Houghton Mifflin.

King, M. (2016). *The end of alchemy: Money, banking, and the future of the global economy.* W. W. Norton & Co.

Samuelson, P. & Nordhaus, W. (2009). *Economics* (19th ed.). McGraw-Hill Education.

REFERENCES

Bentham, J. (1789). *An introduction to the principles of morals and legislation.* T. Payne and Son. http://www.koeblergerhard.de/Fontes/BenthamJere myMoralsandLegislation1789.pdf

Conversations with History: John Kenneth Galbraith. (1986). Institute of International Studies, UC Berkeley. http://globetrotter.berkeley.edu/conversations/Galbraith/galbraith1.html

Friedman, M. (1980). *Free to choose.* Harcourt.

Galbraith, J. K. (1958). *The affluent society.* Houghton Mifflin Harcourt.

Galbraith, J. K. (1967). *The new industrial state.* Houghton Mifflin.

Galbraith, J. K. (1975). *Money: Whence it came, where it went.* Houghton Mifflin.

Galbraith, J. K. (2004). *The economics of innocent fraud: Truth for our time.* Houghton Mifflin.

Hayek, F. (1944). *The road to serfdom.* Routledge Press.

Jevons, W. S. (1865). *The coal question: An inquiry concerning the progress of the nation, and the probable exhaustion of our coal mines.* Macmillan & Co,

Keynes, J. M. (1936). *The general theory of employment, interest and money.* Palgrave Macmillan.

Levy, D. M. (2001). How the dismal science got its name: Debating racial quackery. *Journal of the History of Economic Thought, 23*, 5–35. https://doi.org/10.1080/10427710120045628

Malthus, T. R. (1798). *An essay on the principle of population.* J. Johnson.

Marshall, A. (1890). *Principles of economics.* Macmillan.

Marx, K. (1932). *Ökonomisch-philosophische Manuskripte aus dem Jahre 1844 (Economic and philosophic manuscripts of 1844).* Progress Publishers.

Mill, J. S. (1848). *Principles of political economy.* John W. Parker.

Mill, J. S. (1859). *On liberty.* John W. Parker and Son.

Popper, K. (1945). *The open society and its enemies.* Routledge.

Say, J.-B. (1803). *Traité d'économie politique (A Treatise on Political Economy).* Crapelet.

Smith, A. (1759). *The theory of moral sentiments.* printed for Andrew Millar, in the Strand; and Alexander Kincaid and J. Bell, in Edinburgh.

Smith, A. (1776). *An inquiry into the nature and causes of the wealth of nations.* W. Strahan and T. Cadell.

Thaler, R. H. (2015). *Misbehaving: The making of behavioural economics.* Allen Lane.

Thaler, R. H., & Sunstein, C. R. (2008). *Nudge: Improving decisions about health, wealth, and happiness.* Yale University Press.

Veblen, T. (1899). *The theory of the leisure class.* Macmillan.

Veblen, T. (1900). The preconceptions of economic science. *The Quarterly Journal of Economics, 14*, 240–269.

ECON
HOMO ECONOMICUS

To gain a proper understanding of behavioral economics, we need to understand what came before. This chapter explores the assumptions and principles of neoclassical economics (today's mainstream view of economics) and its very definite view of rational human behavior, exemplified by *homo economicus* or ECON: a rational person with consistent preferences, making choices that serve to maximize their well-being (utility), given their budget constraints. Similarly, firms are said to seek to maximize profits. The rather abstract ECON depicted in neoclassical economics is characterized, among other things, by great mathematical skills, access to relevant, full information, and self-interest. However, these simplifying assumptions do not adequately reflect everyday economic life – as experiments and field studies show, people are often altruistic and their preferences dependent on context. Tversky and Kahneman, in particular, published highly influential research which described how humans (in stark contrast to *homo economicus*) are affected by distorting cognitive factors. They proposed that we use mental shortcuts – something they called 'heuristics' – when making judgments which can lead to biases. The neoclassical economic approach, therefore, seems in need of modification to include newer empirical findings and a more psychologically realistic understanding of them.

DOI: 10.4324/9781003166900-3

INTRODUCTION

Before we can appreciate what behavioral economics is about and trying to achieve, we need to know enough about the assumptions and principles of neoclassical economics – the theoretical tradition from which it developed. We see below that the mainstream, neoclassical economics approach has a very definite view of the 'economic agent': *homo economicus* or ECON. In contrast, behavioral economics adopts a different view, one based on flesh-and-blood HUMAN, detailed in the next chapter. Important to know is what behavioral economics is *not*, and this can only be understood by knowing what neoclassical economics *is*.

FUNDAMENTALS OF NEOCLASSICAL ECONOMICS

What do we mean when we talk of neoclassical economics? We have seen its outlines in Chapter 2 in its historical and conceptual *classical* origins. Neoclassical economics owes much to the highly influential 1890 book, *Principles of Economics*, by Alfred Marshall. This book came to represent what is meant by academically rigorous and acceptable economics – then and now. Not only did Marshall distill the major assumptions and principles of economics at that time, but he also illustrated them with captivating graphs which allowed visualization of complex mathematical relationships. This set the tone and provided the analytical template for the years to follow. Marshall's work centered economics around several major concepts, comprising rationality, preferences, and utility maximization. Efficiency has always been at the heart of these processes: getting the most (utility) out of the allocation of scarce resources. At its conceptual core, neoclassical economics assumes individuals act on consistent preferences, and it takes the maximization of *personal* (self-interested) satisfaction (utility) of these preferences as its *normative* criterion (i.e., the way things *should* work). It is the combination of these notions that comprise what is meant when we talk about neoclassical economics (see text box). There are clear links with the classical economics we summarized in Chapter 2: as pointed out by Keynes in his Preface to the German version of his highly influential *General Theory* (1936), Marshall "was at particular pains to emphasize the continuity of his thought with Ricardo's".

NEOCLASSICAL FUNDAMENTALS

The main tenets of neoclassical economics concern:

- Rationality, which is expressed in consistent preferences and although latent (hidden) they are revealed in choice behavior when the incentives are sufficient to motivate the individual.
- The individual aims to maximize their personal utility (satisfaction, beneficial outcomes, etc.) and they do this by allocating their limited (scarce) resources in the most efficient, optimizing manner possible, which they do by employing good enough mathematical (but not necessarily conscious) calculations.
- The individual acts on the basis of full and relevant information – or, at least, good enough information.
- The notion of *homo economicus* entails that the individual looks after themselves first and foremost, and to the extent that they help others to increase their utility, this is assumed to lead to an increase in their own utility (e.g., the 'warm glow' from giving to charity) – this is an example of a nonzero sum game.

These simplifying assumptions have the pleasing feature of allowing rigorous mathematical modeling of human behavior, something that is not possible when we allow for the complexity of real, often seemingly non-rational, behavior – in economics, mathematics is hard at the best of times, so to introduce psychologically realistic assumptions tends to make it unwieldy and intractable which would seem to violate the very outcome Alfred Marshall was trying to achieve.

Alfred Marshall may, indeed, be credited with instilling the desire to base economic theorizing on sound mathematical foundations, but he was sensitive to its limitations as well as its allure. As he stated in a letter to A. L. Bowley in 1906:

> (1) Use mathematics as shorthand language, rather than as an engine of inquiry. (2) Keep to them till you have done. (3) Translate into English. (4) Then illustrate by examples that are important in real life. (5) Burn the mathematics. (6) If you can't succeed in 4, burn 3. This I do often.
> (Cited in Sills & Merton, 2000)

Marshall's view was later reiterated by none other than John Maynard Keynes, who was not himself averse to complex equations. He said:

"Too large a proportion of recent 'mathematical' economics are mere concoctions, as imprecise as the initial assumptions they rest on, which allow the author to lose sight of the complexities and interdependencies of the real world in a maze of pretentious and unhelpful symbols".

(Keynes, 1936)

As then, more recently, the limitations of a too narrowly defined mathematical economics were highlighted by Mervyn King in his 2016 critique of the financial crisis of 2007–2008 – as the then Governor of the Bank of England he was in an excellent position to know. Yet, despite Marshall's warning, neoclassical economics developed along very specific mathematical lines, combining algebraic rigor with economic 'laws' to establish a powerful social science with considerable practical implications and applications. As the financial crash revealed, sometimes crucial factors (e.g., different types of debt and their levels) are left out of economic models to render them mathematically tenable. The predictive failures of these models even surprised those who held them most dearly (see Chapter 1).

ECONOMIC ENTITIES

When thinking about preferences and utility maximization, neoclassical economics assumes two entities: (1) the individual (also referred to as the *consumer* – the idea is that we are always consuming something, e.g., romance) and (2) the *firm*. Both the individual and the firm are said to seek to allocate their scarce resources in the most efficient manner in order to maximize their payoff: in the case of the individual,

MICROECONOMICS

As suggested by the name, the subfield of economics known as 'microeconomics' (*mikros* means small in Greek) is concerned with the behavior of individuals and firms in making decisions regarding the allocation of scarce resources, in their different (but analytically) similar domains. The other major subfield is 'macroeconomics' which is concerned with the aggregate economy – it examines general, economy-wide factors, such as economic growth, inflation, the unemployment rate, and the like. (Somewhat similar to small-scale quantum mechanics and large-scale general relativity in physics.)

some form of happiness (utility); and in the case of the firm, profit (or some other *value* measure; e.g., market share). It is, indeed, interesting to note that the same analytical machinery of neoclassical economics is applied to these, seemingly, very different economic entities – it may be for this reason that neoclassical economics appears to contain such a circumscribed vision of the individual human agent. In any event, to understand properly the neoclassical economic view of 'the consumer', we need to know something about 'the firm'.

THE FIRM

Central to Alfred Marshall's neoclassical economics work was the characterization of what is known as 'the firm' – this is the focus of the subfield of *microeconomics* (see text box). In its pure form, the theory of the firm contains several defining features. First, firms are assumed to sell standardized products so that the product from one firm is a perfect substitute for one sold by another firm – in the modern world, though, brand marketing is all about differentiating products (see Chapter 7). Second, firms are said to be price takers, not makers, which means they treat the 'market price' as given. Third, it is assumed there is free entry and exit in the market with perfectly mobile factors of production (e.g., labor, capital, land, as well as intellectual talent), at least in the long run – in many sectors of our modern economy, this is far from being the reality. Finally, both firms and consumers are assumed to have perfect information – no one is seriously hoodwinked about the nature of the economic transaction. These assumptions allow the construction of elegant mathematical models that can be used to describe, understand, and predict the future (e.g., what would be the consequence on consumer 'demand' of raising the price of petrol by 10% – the manner in which consumers react to a change in unit price is known as the 'price elasticity of demand'; see text box).

Marshall's work has been influential. For example, he is famous for introducing into economics the standard supply and demand graph, which is now contained in every economics textbook (also here, see Figure 3.1). The graph relates: (a) supply and demand curves, (b) market equilibrium, (c) how the quantity supplied/demanded is related to price, (d) the law of marginal utility, and (e) the law of diminishing returns. This has become the principal – and the principled – way economists communicate their ideas.

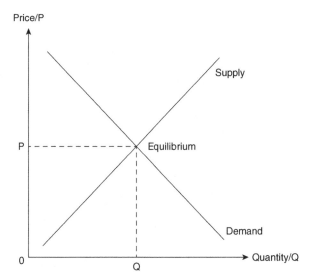

FIGURE 3.1 Supply and demand

Source: adapted from Marshall (1890), Figure 19

PRICE ELASTICITY OF DEMAND

The price elasticity of demand is a measure of how sensitive demand is to a change in the price of a good or service. It is calculated as follows: Price Elasticity of Demand = % Change in Quantity Demanded divided by % Change in Price. If a small change in price is followed by a large change in quantity demanded, the good/service is said to be elastic (i.e., responsive to a price change – this usually happens when substitutes exist, for example, consumers might switch from margarine to butter if the price of margarine increases); conversely, if the demand for the good/service is inelastic, then this means that a large price change is followed by only a small change in demand for the good/service. Demand for goods that are necessities and for which consumers cannot find suitable substitutes is usually price inelastic (for example, petrol – a 10% increase in prices will usually not lead to such a large decrease in demand).

All of the above assumptions, introduced by Marshall and elaborated by others, have been scrutinized and challenged, as already seen in examples in the previous chapters of this book and expanded further in this chapter. Nevertheless, these assumptions remain the workhorses of neoclassical economics: they are what behavioral economics challenges.

Now, before we dismiss the characterization of the firm as unrealistic, even silly, and out-of-step with the modern world, there remains an open question: do these assumptions contain a *good enough* representation of economic reality to make them viable and useful for practical purposes? Few people would say they are a perfect representation, not even neoclassical economists. (Here, as elsewhere, we must be careful to avoid the Straw (Wo)Man Argument.) This is what Milton Friedman had to say about Marshall's conception of the firm:

> Marshall's apparatus turned out to be most useful for problems in which a group of firms is affected by common stimuli, and in which the firms can be treated *as if* they were perfect competitors. This is the source of the misconception that Marshall 'assumed' perfect competition in some descriptive sense.
>
> (Reprinted in Friedman, 1953)

THE CONSUMER

The neoclassical conception of the individual consumer, *homo economicus* (ECON), has a set of definite characteristics that resemble those of the firm (see text box). However, instead of seeking to maximize profit, the individual consumer is said to seek to maximize their satisfaction, happiness, and welfare (i.e., utility). The individual consumer is assumed to have a set of consistent preferences, which means they can order their preferences for certain goods – do you prefer cream cakes over apples or apples over cream cakes? (Here, you might get a sense of the behavioral economists' critique: well, maybe it depends?)

As mentioned elsewhere and well worth repeating, these strict assumptions are often 'relaxed' to deal with reality, but for neoclassical economics to work, it must assume that, *to a sufficient extent*, people conform to these characterizations, especially when they behave in the market context with 'real money on the table' – this could be actual money or something else of importance to the individual consumer (e.g., romantic attachment). In this context, it may be said that

THE CONSUMER AND ALTRUISM

Homo economicus is assumed to be perfectly rational and selfishly motivated. In the same way, it would be irrational for a firm to assign its profit to another firm, the consumer cares only about maximizing their own utility in consumption and when they show regard for the utility of other people, this cannot be at the expense of their own. To the extent they do care about the utility of others without any corresponding increase in their own utility (e.g., as shown by altruistic behavior), they are said to be 'non-rational', even 'irrational'. (However, it can be argued that in some – maybe most cases – the mere act of behaving altruistically increases utility by evoking good feelings – and, maybe, longer-term favorable reciprocal relationships). The notion of the 'consumer' can be extended to all areas of life (e.g., friendships and romantic relationships) where resources are scarce and the allocation of them can lead to different levels of utility.

when people are properly incentivized to optimize choices and maximize their utility, their latent preferences will be 'revealed' in their choice behavior. While there will be gross failure by some individuals, the aggregate behavior of market participants is assumed to conform well to these characteristics, otherwise neoclassical economic models would be descriptively flawed and predictively hopeless, perhaps to a damaging degree.

The fact that these assumptions are not *really* a reflection of reality does not trouble much the neoclassical economist. They say that less-than-perfect models are better than no models at all – if nothing else, such rigorous mathematical models allow deviations from neoclassical predictions to be quickly spotted: behavioral economists have found this possibility positively inspiring.

MARSHALL AND MARGINALISM

As we dive deeper into what is meant when we talk about neoclassical assumptions and principles, and especially when we consider the notion of 'rational' behavior, we will quickly grasp the importance of *marginalism*, which applies equally to firms and individuals. Marginalism is especially important in economics because it shows that efficiency (an important part of rational decision making) is always obtained at the margins of activity. This is said to apply to all decision-making situations (e.g., relationships), and not just ones of an explicitly economic nature.

To illustrate the principle of marginalism, a firm producing a widget *should* (note the 'normative' tone) increase production to the point where the *marginal* cost of production (i.e., the cost of making one *extra* widget, e.g., $1.00) is equal to the *marginal* return from selling the additional widget (i.e., $1.00) – when the marginal return is $0.99, extra production should cease as a marginal unit loss of $0.01 is incurred. (Remember that in the jargon of economics, *marginal* refers to one additional/one extra unit.)

This reasoning provides a useful way to think about how many widgets a firm should produce, and it is a useful way to think of the decision making of the individual consumer: we should stop consuming when the (usually psychological) costs outweigh the benefits. We can even turn this around and say we should stop *producing* (e.g., investing in a relationship) when the marginal return has turned negative, where marginal cost is now greater than marginal benefit. In this way, it would be a mistake to average costs and benefits over a longer time frame, which we most certainly do in personal relationships – we forgive, but less often forget, marginal transgressions! (Obviously, there is a time frame over which marginal costs/benefits are considered, and this may well differ from person to person, and domain to domain.) Marginal utility is a fundamental concept in neoclassical economics, and it is a useful way of thinking about all economic activity – that is, the most efficient allocation of scarce resources (be it making widgets or allocating time to leisure pursuits – recall the example of the New York taxis drivers in Chapter 1).

The law of *diminishing* marginal utility says something especially important: the more we consume of something – for example, food or talking with friends – the less utility we are likely to derive from each extra (marginal) unit of consumption. There often comes a point where we have 'had enough' and each additional unit no longer brings pleasure (utility). That is, where we are better off stopping, or reducing, one behavior and switching to another that has a higher level of marginal utility. This makes good sense and we can easily relate it to everyday life.

To put things slightly differently, the doctrine of *diminishing* marginal utility states that we should continue eating cream cakes until the additional bite does not produce marginal (i.e., extra) utility (pleasure) – a point might even be reached when the marginal utility is negative (i.e., disutility: "no more, *please!*"). More formally, we should continue to consume until marginal utility equals marginal cost.

So compelling is the idea of *diminishing* marginal utility, when an individual violates it, we are inclined to say, "they have a problem". For example, excessive game playing, Twitter use, or pathological behavior (e.g., an addiction to gambling): these are almost defined as entailing the absence of normal declining marginal utility. However, things are not quite straightforward. We may have a very strong preference for something (e.g., cream cakes), and by consuming it, we are maximizing utility – "a problem" would be identified if we were neglecting other aspects of our life (e.g., job, family, etc.) in the exclusive pursuit of this one guilty pleasure (the opportunity cost of the chosen action comes into play here). Although few of us would think that eating cream cakes all day long was a desirable (and certainly not a healthy) thing to be doing, neoclassical economics tells us that it is the individual's preference and it is for them to decide how they want to maximize their utility – this attitude embodies the liberalism of John Stuart Mill, encountered in Chapter 2. Who is to say what is better, *in neoclassical terms*: a short, fat or long, thin life? (We may have other, and good, reasons for choosing one over the other, but do not bother looking at neoclassical economics for justification.)

CONSISTENT PREFERENCES (BETWEEN OUTCOMES)

There are a number of other assumptions (or 'axioms' – a word that adds a certain gravitas) regarding preferences – our wants and desires that motivate our choice behavior. These assumptions form an important part of *rational choice theory*, which underpins the behavior of the 'rational agent' in economic models. The major one relates to people knowing what they want, and, importantly, they must be *consistent* in their preferences for certain outcomes. These preferences should not jump around, for example, by being heavily influenced by how outcomes are communicated or 'framed' (see Chapter 4). This assumption implies that we all know, at some level (but not necessarily consciously, as preferences are said to be *latent*), what we want.

The first axiom, called *completeness*, states that a consistent set of preferences can be arranged in an ordering system. In other words: if given several options, we know which option we prefer. It is fine if people are indifferent to two or more options, but they are generally able to rank all available choices (preference ordering).

1 **Completeness:** the consumer is able to rank all possible combinations of goods and services. We might prefer Oranges (O) over Apples (A) over Lemons (L). To show this ordering of preference, we write:

O > A > L

So far, so good; next, we need to consider how these preferences relate to each other in a somewhat more complete way. A second important axiom in rational choice theory does just that.

2 **Transitivity:** for any three bundles O, A, and L, if we prefer Oranges to Apples and prefer Apples to Lemons, then we *must* always prefer Oranges to Lemons – not to adhere to this transitivity would seem plain silly and economists would label it irrational. However, it is relatively easy to see how this axiom is violated, for example, as in the 'Allais paradox' (see below) and the effects of framing (see Chapter 4) information in different ways.

Three other assumptions are less relevant for our discussion, but we need to know they exist: *More-Is-Better*: other things being equal, more of a good is preferable to less; *Continuity*: small changes in a bundle of goods should not lead to a jump in preferences; and *Convexity*: mixtures of goods (averages) are preferable to extremes.

RATIONALITY

Consistent behavior based on *consistent preferences* is a key aspect of neoclassical economists' definition of *rational behavior*. It is important for us to know what it means in neoclassical economics – for one, it does *not* refer to certain behaviors that we might otherwise label 'rational' (e.g., sensible behavior such as helping others at some cost to ourselves; i.e., true altruism). In neoclassical economics, rationality mainly refers to the utility-maximizing, consistent behavior of self-interested *homo economicus*

(ECON) who focuses on their own personal utility, and *now*. (As we see in Chapter 5, rationality can be defined in other ways; for example, it might well be 'rational' to cooperate with others in order to derive some future benefit, but this future-oriented form of rationality is *not* the definition in neoclassical economics and its notion of *homo economicus*.)

In addition to self-interested here-and-now choices, there are other elements of the neoclassically defined rational behavior of *homo economicus*, which reflect some of the assumptions and principles we have described above.

1   We should always think at the 'margins' of choices – that is, what changes will an additional action bring? In particular, weighing the costs and benefits of a choice at the margins is said to produce the maximum utility (also known as 'welfare').

2   This first principle is related to the idea of 'sunk costs', which neoclassical economics tells us we should not take into account when making choices at the margin – as the old saying tells us, it is no good 'crying over spilled milk'. This is simply because a sunk cost has already been incurred and cannot be recovered. *Prospective* costs are what really matter, as these have yet to be incurred, will depend on the choice made, and thus can still be avoided. But, as we will see in Chapter 4, people tend to consider sunk costs because they are *loss averse* – also, from a psychological perspective, sunk costs often tell us something about our mistakes, and this is important in modifying future behavior along more appropriate lines (i.e., utility maximizing in the medium to long-term – but, as seen above, this is *not* being rational in neoclassical terms).

3   Opportunity costs need to be considered when conducting a cost-benefit analysis in any given choice situation – what alternative courses of action, and associated utility, have we *foregone* in making *this* choice? (We have already encountered this concept in Chapter 2.)

4   We should respond appropriately to incentives that affect marginal costs and benefits. Increases in marginal benefits should mean more of the activity, whereas increases in marginal costs should mean less of the activity. This is consistent with the 'matching law' of behavioral psychology which shows that even simple animals allocate their behavior over different choice options in a way that maximizes their total reward, and thus their utility

(e.g., pigeons pecking at disks which have different reinforcement values attached). It is for this reason that government may tax products to lower consumption (e.g., the sugar tax).

PEOPLE ACT ON THE BASIS OF FULL AND RELEVANT INFORMATION

In addition to all of the above, something else is of importance in neoclassical economics. It is assumed for people to behave in a rational manner (as defined above), they must have access to full information, and they must process this information in an unbiased way. We will see in the following chapters the multiple ways people's use of information can be influenced by context, past experience, and *framing* (how information is presented). But for now, to appreciate this assumption, we do not need to assume that people are perfect computers because clearly, they are not (remember the bat and ball problem; see Chapter 1), and this, as with related assumptions, can be 'relaxed'. But such relaxation cannot go too far: the neoclassical muscles that do the hard-analytical lifting must stick to the claim that, *to the best of their ability*, people process relevant information in a rational way to satisfy their preferences and they manage to do so in a good enough fashion. What they cannot be is *systematically* biased in their processing (or, indeed, selection) of relevant information – to the neoclassical mind, this would be nothing less than a slippery conceptual slope into intractable and nonrational ideas of no value in formal economic modeling.

THE POINT OF IT ALL: UTILITY MAXIMIZATION

As we can now appreciate, all rational behavior is aimed at maximizing utility – satisfaction, happiness, benefit, pleasure, or welfare. Given the neoclassical definition of utility, any rational person would want to maximize their happiness. This seems straightforward enough and to want to do otherwise would seem foolishly self-defeating. To see what this is about, take the example of the total utility from a night out on the town with friends. Now, the first thing to note is that the possibilities for total utility are limited by budget constraints: you probably do not have all the money in the world to spend. Let us say you have $100. Given your preferences, how will you allocate your resources ($100) among the possible options open to you: buying drinks, having a meal, paying to enter a club, getting a taxi home? You would be foolish, indeed, not to try to maximize your happiness; after all that is the point of a night on the town. However, to achieve your desired end, you will want to allocate your resources most efficiently to maximize it (e.g., not having money for transport home and no other way to get there will most certainly impair the total utility of the night out on the town!). You will, of course, need to take heed of diminishing marginal utility, too, for any one good (see above – too much of a good thing, and all that). Well, if you are an example of *homo economicus* – and you may not be after a few drinks! – you will rely upon some formal logical system to compute the marginal utility associated with your choices. Your aim is to maximize your total utility and the way to do this is to apply the principles and procedures of *expected utility theory*, which is another major workhorse of neoclassical economics.

EXPECTED VALUE/UTILITY THEORY

The dominant (neoclassically defined) rational approach to calculating utility is *expected utility theory*. As we have already seen, it assumes the logically consistent (rational) person has definite preferences; however, it recognizes that decisions are made with an element of risk or uncertainty – the standard definition of the difference between risk and uncertainty is that the *probability* of a risky outcome occurring is known, which is not the case for uncertain outcomes (see text box). However, not all is lost in uncertain situations because we still may be able to assign (subjective) probability values to likely outcomes. For example, although it is sensible to save for retirement (who wants to be old *and* poor?), our future income is uncertain, and we may not even live long enough to enjoy our retirement savings (*note*: life expectancy is more of a risk because we can calculate the probability of reaching a given age – actuarial science is devoted to this very topic). Firms face a similar problem: in the face of uncertain demand, how should they decide which products to develop and which prices to charge? And how should governments set levels of taxation and expenditure when the growth of the economy, inflation, and so on are all uncertain?

In neoclassical economics, calculations are formalized in mathematical models, based on the von Neumann–Morgenstern utility theorem. This theorem demonstrates how rational *homo economicus* should calculate

RISK VS. UNCERTAINTY

In the standard theory, risk can be calculated from known probabilities. For example, what is the probability that if you tossed a fair coin it would come down heads; easy! This should happen half of the time (0.5), if the coin is indeed fair. (Whether it does or not is a different matter.) Therefore, risk relates to situations where it is possible to assign probabilities to each outcome occurring (and can be *insured* against). Uncertainty is a different thing, as it often concerns future events which are difficult to predict and we do not have a profile of probabilities: in this case, we simply do not know. Indeed, uncertainty relates to situations where assigning probabilities is little more than guesswork. Formal economic theory assumes that it is possible to assign probabilities, even if these are subjective – but sometimes, this is not possible (we may not be aware of all future outcomes; e.g., a pandemic). Such is the problem with the notion of risk vs. uncertainty, the mainstream economist and former Governor of the Bank of England, Mervyn King, in 2016 declared the whole economy is 'radically uncertain', which rather challenges the application of the concept of risk in neoclassical economic modeling.

how much utility is to be expected, on average, from each choice – an important step in choosing the option that maximizes utility.

VON NEUMANN–MORGENSTERN UTILITY THEOREM

We should probably start by saying that, although this is the gold standard of rational decision making in neoclassical economics, its merits are not intuitively obvious when applied to individual decision making. For this reason, the discussion in this chapter presents its benefits as well as its limitations.

The modern-day ideas of utility calculation are traced to the collaboration of an economist (Oskar Morgenstern) and a mathematician (John von Neumann) who published a remarkable book in 1944, *Theory of Games and Economic Behavior* – they considered their ideas on utility rather secondary to their game theory work (game theory is discussed in Chapter 5). Von Neumann and Morgenstern proposed expected utility theory as a form of precise mathematical reasoning for use in all strategic structures governing *rational* decision making – this applies to all spheres of life, including economic, political, and military (indeed, it can refer to anything, from optimal policy choices of presidential candidates, the arms race, public health policies, and competition between firms; and, even if one is so inclined, to romantic relationships).

In a nutshell, the von Neumann–Morgenstern utility theorem shows (in mathematical terms, 'proves') that, given a number of axioms (assumptions), a rational decision maker faced with risky or uncertain (i.e., probabilistic) outcomes of different choices should behave in a manner to maximize 'expected value', or utility. Put somewhat differently, expected utility theory (EUT) requires the decision maker to make a choice between risky or uncertain outcomes by comparing the expected utility values of different outcomes – formally, expected utility is calculated by adding the utility values of outcomes multiplied by their respective probabilities.

As this notion and its calculation are rather abstract, let us illustrate with an example. Consider yourself in the following position. You are presented with a gaming situation in which the probability of getting (A) $100 is 1 in 80 (0.0125, or 1.25%), and the other, more likely outcome (B) is to get nothing (0.9875, or 98.75%). The expected value of this gamble is $1.25 (we calculate this by multiplying the probability of outcome A occurring with the value of outcome A, and we then add the product of the probability of outcome B occurring with the value of outcome B).

We thus have:

For outcome A: ($100 × 0.0125) = $1.25

For outcome B: ($0 × 0.9875) = $0

Added up, we get the expected value: $1.25 + $0 = $1.25.

Now, if you are presented with a second situation, this time with a guaranteed payment of $1 – this is also the expected value – expected utility theory says that the rational person *should* choose the $100-or-nothing gamble (the first scenario) and not the second with the lower expected utility value. Which gamble would you take? Many people opt for the guaranteed ('sure thing') $1, which, according to expected utility theory, is *not* the rational choice. As we will see in Chapter 4, people who prefer the sure payoff of $1 are said to be risk averse.

CRITICISMS OF EXPECTED UTILITY THEORY (EUT)

EUT is not without its limitations or its critics. The first problem is that uncertainty is treated as an objective risk – we are 'given' the probabilities of different outcomes. But, most decision situations in real-life do not come with a defined risk (e.g., who will be the next Prime Minister of the United Kingdom?). (Recall that the election of President Donald Trump in 2016 defied the vast majority of pollsters, political analysts, and bookmakers.) Such situations demand that we come up with our *subjective* estimates of the possible outcomes – however, this is likely to be influenced by a range of factors, including how favorable or unfavorable the different outcomes appear (or *framed*; see Chapter 4) to us at any one time (even perhaps the mood we are in on that day; see Chapter 5). We might conclude, though, that this is better than nothing, which may sometimes be true; yet, it can be very misleading, producing over-confidence, especially when there is an unwarranted consensus among a group of people. (We tend to forget that the estimate was tentative to start with.)

Savage (1954) addressed the problem of real-world decision making. He argued that if we treat subjective probabilities as if they were *objective*, then the expected utility model holds true. To take an example, no one can know the true ('objective') probability of the political party that will form the next government. Still, we can make a guess of this ('subjective') probability – perhaps not much of a major problem if we remember that *it is* a guess. However, a limitation of this approach, which is often ignored in economic analysis, was noted by Savage himself, when he cautioned that his theory was intended only for 'small worlds' where all possible states are imaginable and knowable. But many important problems, for example, possible outcomes of global warming, belong to 'large worlds' where it seems improbable that the decision maker could delineate all possible states of the future world and, therefore, generate sensible probability values on which to base expected utility theory. For example, who would have guessed the impact of global events on the security, supply, and price of gas in 2022 and beyond?

Savage's subjective probability approach, itself, has another limitation. It applies to a single person. With two people, expected utility could be quite different because they have different subjective probabilities. But in economic modeling, it is standard practice to assume that if people have access to the same information then they will come to the same (even subjective) probabilities – this is known as the *common prior assumption* – but is this really likely when individual differences between people are likely to affect perceptions and judgments of the probability of outcomes (see Chapter 5)? In any event, the common prior assumption underlying expected utility theory assumes that differences in judgment, opinion, and so on reflect differences *only* in information: it is a big assumption to make, and to justify – empirical evidence challenges it regularly.

A related issue is Bayesian reasoning – it is based on Bayes's theorem, which is named after Reverend Thomas Bayes who published work on conditional probability in 1763 (it was discovered many years after his death). This is a powerful and widely used form of statistical reasoning (e.g., medical diagnostic techniques), in which probabilities of an outcome occurring are updated as more information is obtained. However, there are major problems with it. First, in general, people are quite bad at taking *base-rate* information (prior probability) into proper account, as they tend to be focused on certain salient information to the exclusion of other relevant information. Second, when that *state* of the world changes, and thus the probabilities of the outcomes, people fail to adequately update their judgments (see text box). It is as if, once we have come to a definite judgment, we find it very hard to change it, even when we know that the *probability state* of the world has changed. Such a cognitive limitation does not bode well for the effective application of expected utility theory.

Perhaps, a more obvious criticism of expected utility theory is that it is unrealistic to expect the average person – perhaps even the above average neoclassical economist – to engage in this form of computation, and indeed, it seems that to do so is the exception rather than the rule (e.g., see the Allais paradox, below).

Well, let us take another look at the expected utility problem. Returning to the games presented above, for a start, is the choice of accepting a gamble with an expected value of $1.25 *really* rational, preferable, or better than a sure amount of $1 *when* there is only a 1.25% chance of obtaining any money? Our tendency to avoid risk and prefer the 'sure thing' is disparaged as violating expected utility theory and not being 'rational'. Several aspects of this problem seem relevant here. A guaranteed $1 may be seen to be better (indeed, more 'rational', albeit not in a strict neoclassical sense) than a highly improbable $100, especially if $1 represents a large proportion of one's wealth (add zeros on to the number if this improves realism for you).

BAYESIAN UPDATING

Imagine the following. You are presented with three cups, and under one of them (let us make it interesting) there is $1,000. You have to guess which one. You make your choice. Now, imagine someone else (who has full information about the cups) chooses a cup and turns it over to reveal that the $1,000 is not under it. Now, the *state* of the world has changed: there are only two cups remaining. You are then asked: "do you want to change the cup you first chose"? You might say, "Not really, as I now have a 1 in 2 (50%) chance of being right". According to Bayesian reasoning, this is *not* the right choice to make because it would ignore the fact that the other person, who knows where the prize can be found, has deliberately not chosen the other cup; thus, there is now more information available about that cup. The logical thing now to do is to switch: *always!* The notion is that when you made your first choice, you had a 1/3 chance of being correct; with only two cups remaining, the fundamental probability has not changed; therefore, if you stick with your choice, you now have, as it were, a 2/3 chance of being wrong – or less than a 50% chance of being right with two cups remaining. (It may not feel the right thing to do and if you do not accept this conclusion – and we agree it does not *seem* correct – you are not alone. This is also known as the Monty Hall problem, a popular probability puzzle for economics students.)

Second, as any real-world gambler knows, often to their cost, a probability of a 1 in 80 outcome occurring (e.g., a horse winning a race) may not come about any time soon, and the gambler may go bankrupt long before they realize the wisdom of relying on expected utility theory. Here, we have the problem of short- and long-term outcomes. Let us test this assumption now: take a coin and toss it 10 times. We did this and got the following run: TTHTTHTTHT (7 tails). We would be more confident to get something close to 50/50 heads and tails if we tossed the same (unbiased) coin millions of times (we will leave this to someone else!). In any event, as any real-world gambler knows, the short-term can destroy wealth, even if in the long-term everything turns out as predicted by expected utility theory – assuming, of course, we got our subjective probabilities right in the first place! (Perhaps surprisingly, horse racing markets are some of the most efficient in this regard, as odds do relate to winning *over the season*, but much less so in any given race – if this were not the case, bookmaking would be a less profitable business than it is.)

A similar point was made by John Maynard Keynes in his 1923 book *A Tract on Monetary Reform*: "But this *long run* is a misleading guide to current affairs. *In the long run* we are all dead". To survive and thrive, apparently (neoclassically defined) 'irrational' decisions may turn out to be very rational! And as many bankrupted stock market investors have learned to their considerable cost, as Keynes noted, "the market can stay irrational longer than you can stay solvent". Keynes wrote these words not as a desk-bound academic but as a trader in foreign currency who after a large win suffered a severe loss. Without the experience of gambling one's own money – having 'skin in the game' – it is appealing for academics to extoll the virtues of expected utility theory. (We may well wonder how many of those who advocate the use of expected utility theory test the theory with their own money?) In his 2008 book, *Predictably Irrational*, Ariely quotes a Harvard University economics professor, Al Roth, as saying, "In theory, there is no difference between theory and practice, but in practice there is a great deal of difference". Wise, if uncomfortable, words.

In defense of expected utility theory, neoclassical economists accept that individuals may struggle with calculating and implementing it, but they still assume that the *aggregate* behavior of people conforms to the predictions of the theory (think of the horse racing markets again). In addition, neoclassical economists contend that a logically viable system is better than none at all, and certainly better than one with considerable nonrational (i.e., biased) processing. They have a point, certainly when it comes to decisions made by large organizations that can tolerate and survive short-to-medium-term losses (as in the case of governments with fiat currency systems that can 'print money' to weather temporary losses/deficits).

When thinking about expected utility theory in terms of utility maximization of the consumer and the firm, we start to see cracks appearing. While it may be preferable for large organizations, it seems much less apt: (a) for smaller firms who do not have the financial capacity to survive significant short-to-medium term setbacks; and (b) individuals who, typically, have limited financial, and other, resources. Yet, neoclassical economics continues to insist that expected utility theory is the rational method for decision making. If nothing else, there seems to be a serious disconnect between what neoclassical economists say we *should* (normatively) do and what, we assume even most economists, suggest to their family and friends they might sensibly (descriptively/positively) do.

The above issues are important for neoclassical economics. This is because they construct a vast theoretical superstructure on the foundations of a small number of tenets, assumptions, and principles. Whatever the case, behavioral economists have not been impressed by them, *their* utility to the application to real-world economic problems, and the success of their predictions.

In closing this section, we may note that the three neoclassical assumptions (i.e., rationality expressed in the form of consistent preferences, utility maximization, and full and relevant information), and how they are combined in expected utility theory, allow the neoclassical economist to build an elegant and mathematically rigorous theoretical system to explain the allocation of scarce resources among alternative ends. Such is the appeal of this approach among its advocates, it has been applied to a wide range of economic activity, sometimes very broadly defined. For example, the University of Chicago-based neoclassical economist Gary Becker extended economic thinking into sociology, including understanding racial discrimination, crime, and drug addiction.

EMPIRICALLY CHALLENGED: PREFERENCE REVERSAL

We now know that consistent preferences are at the heart of neoclassical economic thinking, and we know, too, that such preferences should not be blown around on the winds of context, framing, mood, and so on. Preferences should have integrity. Is this the case, though? Well, as explained by Tversky and Thaler (1990), one especially perplexing, and certainly most troubling, finding is so-called 'preference reversal'. This can be illustrated by different examples, and one of the most compelling is the Allais paradox (see text box).

Let us take another, simpler example. Consider the following two bets. Which one do you prefer?

P bet: 29/36 probability to win $2
$ bet: 7/36 probability to win $9

We need to note that the expected utility of the $ bet is higher and the rational individual should, therefore, always choose the second gamble. (Unlike *homo economicus*, you are probably not able to easily calculate $(29 \div 36) \times \$2 = \$1.61$ and $(7 \div 36) \times \$9 = \$1.75$ in your head and conclude that the second gamble provides the higher expected utility of $1.75 – however, note that the denominators are the same in both calculations so we can simply compare 29×2 to 7×9 and conclude that 58 is smaller than 63. We wonder, though, how many people could do even this simpler calculation in their head.)

Lichtenstein and Slovic (1971, 1973) and Tversky et al. (1988) found people *choose* the *P* bet but are willing to *pay* more to obtain the *$* bet. This choice is not rational because whether to choose a bet or pay for it is just a matter of framing the same question differently. What is typically found is that people seem to prefer the *P* bet because the *probability* of winning is higher but prefer the higher *value* of the *$* bet. Slovic (1972) called this outcome the 'compatibility effect', according to which people who evaluate a gamble tend to rely on the monetary aspect of it when a value is expressed in terms of money, even when they have no particular reason to set the value of the gamble based on this monetary aspect. This compatibility effect can turn people into 'money pumps': people purchase and trade gambles in such a way that they are bound to lose money. Companies can frame choices to exploit this effect (see Chapter 7).

As the above example illustrate, preferences are influenced by the *procedure* used to elicit them. According to the neoclassical concept of rationality, this simply should not happen as it violates the assumption of 'procedural invariance': preferences should be stable irrespective of how they are elicited. This observation is yet another example of Richard Thaler's Supposedly Irrelevant Factors (SIFs; see Chapter 1). In Chapter 4, we will see further examples of how easily this assumption is violated.

One interesting way more mainstream economists have attempted to come to terms with the demonstration of preference reversal is to assume *multiple selves*. One is dominant when we are in the state of the far-sighted *planner*, and another when we are in the state of the impulsive myopic *doer*. This makes sense in behavioral terms. We can have all the rational intentions in the world, but are then heavily influenced in the moment by the situation, context, how we are feeling, hunger, and a range of other physiological, psychological, and social states,

THE 'ALLAIS PARADOX'

This is the best-known example of preference reversal – it is named after Maurice Allais (1953). Try for yourself the following set of choices. You are asked to choose between two sets of gambles:

Gamble 1:

Choice 1A:	100% chance of receiving 100 million
Choice 1B:	10% chance of receiving 500 million, 89% chance of receiving 100 million, and 1% chance of receiving nothing

Most people prefer 1A although this safer choice does not yield the higher expected utility (see above).

Gamble 2:

Choice 2A:	11% chance of receiving 100 million, and 89% chance of receiving nothing
Choice 2B:	10% chance of receiving 500 million, and 90% chance of receiving nothing

Most people prefer 2B, reflecting higher expected utility even though it is a riskier choice. If expected utility theory is true, then the preference 1A > 1B should imply a preference for 2A > 2B. However, this is not the case: individuals prefer 1A > 1B, *but* 2A < 2B. We seem to place more weight on the difference between 100 and 500 million, and much less on the difference between 89% and 90%. However, this might not be a great example – although it is one very widely cited in behavioral economics – because who among us can *easily* calculate the expected utility of these choices? Again, we have the practical problem of calculative (in)ability.

many of which we are unaware of. As we see elsewhere in this book, one way to constrain our more in-the-moment, impulsive self is to use a commitment device – in this way, we tie the hands of our future *doer* self who cannot be trusted to follow through with intentions of the farsighted *planner*.

The theory of multiple selves may get us closer to the psychological reality of economic decisions, especially as they are influenced by apparently irrelevant factors, but at the same time, they seem to undermine basic tenets of neoclassical economic notions of rationality – and, if they do not, they most certainly complicate economic modeling which aims to predict behavior. What we might be seeing with this theory is how mainstream economic theorizing starts to segue into *behavioral* economics; it is certainly more complex, but also more realistic, and in this way more predictive of actual economic behavior.

INTERTEMPORAL CHOICE

Another example of *preference reversal* is seen when we make choices distributed over time – this is the field of *intertemporal choice* (a good overview can be found in Berns et al., 2007). It is about how we place value on 'now' and the 'future'. To give an example, if we offer individuals the choice to receive $100 either today or in one week, most will quite sensibly choose the immediate reward because they attach more value to it – in other words, they *discount* the future reward and value it less than $100 received now (it is for this reason that banks pay interest on deposits – inflation and uncertainty play a large part). This choice may be obvious; however, it is less obvious when individuals are asked to choose between $100 today and $110 in one week. Depending on how much people discount the future sum, they will either pick the smaller-sooner-reward or the larger-later-reward. In experiments, many individuals prefer the smaller, immediate reward, which is an expression of 'present bias' – I want it now! Things get a little more interesting when the one-week delay is at some point in the future: most respondents will gladly wait an additional week if the same choice is presented as: $100 in 50 weeks or $110 in 51 weeks? People are more impatient about a one-week delay when immediate gratification is possible, but not when it is some way off in the future. What this shows also is that our 'now' preference reverses as a function of time. All very irrational in neoclassical economic terms! We could anticipate ourselves as identical in 50 and 51 weeks' time, but we see our self today and tomorrow as different. The neoclassical economic view is that the trade-off between consumption now versus one week from now should be the same as the trade-off between consumption in 50 weeks and in 51 weeks – it is the same delay in both cases – but this is not how most of us see things and we treat these same periods of time differently. (Once again, we have to assume that all else is equal, for example, expected inflation or changes in interest rates are not confounding factors.)

What such studies reveal is that we do not discount the future at a constant rate. *Exponential* discounting makes the most sense to neo-classical economists because it assumes a constant rate of discounting where periods of time are treated equally. But people do not conform to exponential discounting; instead, they engage in *hyperbolic* discounting which is characterized by much steeper initial discounting which flattens as time moves into the future. The preference reversal we described above – where the choice between two outcomes ($100 now or $110 one week later) changes when the choice is moved to the future – can be explained by hyperbolic discounting.

BOUNDED RATIONALITY

It has long been recognized that the ideal image of *homo economicus* (ECON) is not reflected in typical economic behavior. This obser-vation is not new. This fact led Herbert Simon in the 1950s to sug-gest that we have, what he called, 'bounded rationality' (Simon, 1955, 1957). This refers to the limitations to our ability to process informa-tion in an optimal (fully rational) manner. However, although we may not reach the heights of perfect rationality (as defined above), we may still be 'procedurally rational' (Barros, 2010): we are doing the best job possible under (cognitively and emotionally) difficult conditions. Simon also argued that we are content to arrive at lower-than-optimal utility which he called *satisficing* – this is a portmanteau of 'suffice' and 'satisfying'. But, again, this might be quite (in a looser sense) rational because it means we avoid the disutility associated with further effort expended, self-control, information search, and so on. Something which later commentators focused on, Simon was influenced by a dis-tinction made by population biologists: between survival and maxi-mization. This might be the most rational objective if the intention is to 'stay in the game' (of life), even if this means not maximizing *in some sense* – that is, not taking the option with the largest expected utility, which could entail a small chance of absolute ruin. Better to survive, to 'fight another day'.

It is interesting to learn that Simon's ideas on *bounded rationality* and *satisficing* came out of the marginalist debate of the 1930s, which showed that it is not the case that entrepreneurs follow the marginalist principles of profit-maximization/cost-minimization – they can get by on a less-than-perfect solution. Given the complexity of information and uncertainty, and the demands of complex computations, most of us are perfectly content to make decisions that are not optimal as defined in mathematical terms but that are good enough to provide a sufficient degree of happiness, pleasure, and well-being – as well as relief from all the hard work needed to strive for perfection. With only a few exceptions (e.g., Reinhard Selten, a Nobel Prize winner in Economics), at the time and until quite recently, Simon's work had less of an influence on mainstream economics than it deserved. The accusation was that it was too vague to be of help in 'proper' economic theorizing and analysis – of course, it only remains 'vague' when we do not have a proper theory. The principal ambition of behavioral economics is to provide *coherent* theoretical accounts of such apparent vagaries of economic behavior.

JUSTIFYING NEOCLASSICAL ASSUMPTIONS AND PRINCIPLES

Given the limitations of HUMAN decision making, as revealed by the examples above and further detailed in Chapter 4, where does all of this leave us with regards to justifying neoclassical assumptions and principles?

Along with Leonard Savage, the famous free market economist Milton Friedman put forward an argument in 1948 to defend neoclassical economic assumptions, and this has been repeatedly used since (we have already seen Freidman's justification of Marshall's theory of the firm above, and here, we examine his justification of the rational individual consumer). The argument goes that, *of course*, individuals are not perfectly rational and not all can make lightning-fast calculations – and some of us are plain dumb. But it is argued, when the 'chips are down' and we are sufficiently incentivized and motivated, to the best of our ability, we behave 'as if' we were using the rational principles as contained in neoclassical economics. Furthermore, Friedman claimed in 1953 that economic theories should neither be assessed by their descriptive realism nor by their ability to account for psychological processes, but by the criteria of whether they are "sufficiently good approximations" of the world and "whether the theory works" in terms of leading to "sufficiently accurate predictions".

Friedman and Savage defended their 'as if' argument with the example of an expert billiard player. They say that it is not unreasonable to accept the hypothesis that the billiard player makes shots 'as if' they knew the complicated mathematical formulas governing the direction of travel, angles, speed, and so on – the fact that this is not done consciously is irrelevant. (We will turn to the issue of conscious processing and free will in Chapter 4.)

Whatever the truth, what distinguishes behavioral (and more generally experimental) economics from neoclassical economics is the lesson from psychology which stresses the value of testing hypotheses rather than just assuming that 'axiomatic' assumptions are inherently true, or useful (even if not entirely true) – this is now routine research practice (Vernon Smith shared the Nobel Prize with Daniel Kahneman for his pioneering work in *experimental* economics). In any case, in deciding between alternative theoretical positions, Friedman is surely right when he declared: "theory is to be judged by its predictive power for the class of phenomena which it is intended to 'explain'". In this way, the predictive power of neoclassical economics (and, of course, behavioral economics) needs to be judged by experimental or other forms of empirical observation. *Prediction* of the future is the gold standard of a scientific theory; *postdiction* of the past is the lead standard.

HETERODOXY

As we have seen in this and previous chapters, much is made in neoclassical economics of the free market, the nature of the firm and that of the consumer – although these are clearly idealized notions, they *are* intended to explain important economic phenomena. As discussed in Chapter 2, there is much dissent over these issues. J. K. Galbraith (1958, 1967) noted that 'the market' of modern society is no longer made up of numerous small firms, competing with each other and complying with the laws of supply and demand. Instead, there are multibillion dollar global conglomerates who can, and do, influence the demands of the consumer via advertising, brand management, and indeed by self-perpetuating fashion and resulting peer pressure (these highly expensive ploys also prevent entry into the market by potentially more innovative and competitive firms). Of course, companies have to provide goods and services that are within the consumer's 'zone of tolerance', but we may assume this to be fairly wide.

Galbraith further noted that many commercial firms are funded by government and military sources, especially in the United States, something which he termed the 'military-industrial complex' – adopting the phrase from US President Dwight D. Eisenhower's farewell address in 1961. Galbraith also observed that while CEOs may be praising the wonders of the 'invisible hand' of the free market they may, at the same time, be lobbying governments for subsidies and trade tariffs to protect their companies from 'unfair' global competition.

Galbraith lampooned the notion that the modern firm is merely seeking to maximize profits (or some other shareholder related value); instead, it may be seeking to maximize the utility of the management in the form of high salaries, generous bonuses, tax-free luxury cars, and the like, which comes, of course, from having great products and services. Is it *really* the case that nonshareholding managers work, plan, innovate, and invest merely to maximize the profit of people they do not know? This would *truly* be altruistic – and not entirely consistent with neoclassical economics' own tenets. Galbraith presented us with an amusing metaphor, "… of a man obsessed by sex who devotes his life to enhancing the sexual opportunities of other people whom he has not met". If we prefer to take our economic lesson not from a staunch liberal economist but a titan of the business world, we hear much the same: in 2009, Jack Welch, former CEO of General Electric, asserted that this is "the dumbest idea in the world", adding "shareholder value is a result, not a strategy" (Quoted in Guerrera, 2009). As we saw also in Chapter 2, notable intellectuals (e.g., Veblen and Chomsky) have challenged the market-driven definition of 'value' – who really decides what has value? Much earlier, Adam Smith expressed a similar sentiment.

THE DAWN OF BEHAVIORAL ECONOMICS

We do not only have the dissenting voices of economists and other intellectual observers; we now have too many behavioral anomalies accumulated to suggest anything other than that, at the very least, core neoclassical economic assumptions need reconsideration and some refinement, and perhaps even wholescale renewal. This pressure came about at around the same time in the 1960s when psychology was experiencing its own revolution with the advent of cognitive psychology. This placed emphasis upon 'mental' processes and argued that focus exclusively on overt ('revealed') behavior and how it is affected by reinforcement (e.g., incentives) is a major shortcoming – of note, Chomsky was a major figure in this revolution with his theory of universal grammar. In particular, the mind came increasingly to be seen as an information processing machine – the development of computers was a major technological impetus to this view. Now, once we start to think about mental processes such as memory, language, and decision making, a whole landscape of intriguing possibilities opens up. These only increase when we add social psychology, which views individual thought, feeling, and behavior as socially influenced and shaped, if not entirely constructed. The intellectual flood gates started to open, slowly at first, but then a fully flowing tide washed away many of the old assumptions that seemed so water-tight not too many years before.

Despite strong resistance, which continues to this day, standard neoclassical economic models would never be quite the same again. Amos Tversky and Daniel Kahneman, in particular, proposed radical new ideas and provided compelling empirical evidence to show some remarkable findings. In 1974, their *Science* article proposed that we use mental shortcuts – 'heuristics' – when making judgments (these are detailed in Chapter 4).

Tversky and Kahneman noted that typical human judgments deviate markedly from supposedly rational decisions and, crucially, are systematically biased – they are not merely random error ('noise'). The influence of their 1974 article was added to in 1979 when they proposed 'Prospect Theory' to account for decision making under risk. This work demonstrated significant violations of standard economic models (e.g., expected utility theory). Importantly, Tversky and Kahneman provided a theory that could be *tested* and, if shown to be wrong, disregarded – the fact that we are still talking about it today attests to its success. Their paper was published in a highly influential journal, *Econometrica*, written in the style favored by economics, and contained enough mathematics to give it a respectable academic gloss: it could not easily be ignored – although many dyed-in-the-wool neoclassical economists gave the impression that they had achieved this feat of self-denial. By 1997, some kind of acceptance was seen with the publication of a special issue of the journal, *Quarterly Journal of Economics*, devoted to behavioral economics.

As noted by Camerer and Loewenstein in 2003, these early papers set the tone for those that followed. The first task was to identify normative assumptions or models widely used by economists (e.g., rationality). The second task was to identify deviations from predictions by clear and unambiguous empirical findings – of course, to win acceptance, this means ruling out alternative explanations that are consistent with neoclassical assumptions (e.g., participants in the studies were confused or they were insufficiently incentivized). Once these two tasks had been achieved, the next step was to formulate alternative theories to replace the flawed neoclassical ones and, finally, to construct new economic models and propose how they should be tested. The idea is not only to account for the failure of neoclassical economics, but to generate new knowledge by applying novel concepts from behavioral science.

Some of the leading figures in early economics anticipated as much. It is appropriate that Richard Thaler opens his 2015 book, *Misbehaving*, with a quote from Vilfredo Pareto (1906):

> The foundation of political economy and, in general, of every social science, is evidently psychology. A day may come when we shall be able to deduce the laws of social science from the principles of psychology.

That day has arrived.

CONCLUSIONS

Neoclassical assumptions, principles, and applications have enjoyed remarkable success over the past one hundred years. Economists trained in this tradition are much sought after by government and businesses alike. Students of economics are highly employable because they have been taught to think in systematic and logical (i.e., mathematical) ways, and this analytical rigor can be applied to all types of problems – these are skills with a high utility even when knowledge of neoclassical economics may have become something of a distant memory.

In the discussion of the virtues and vices of neoclassical economics, the important issue, as Milton Friedman pointed out, is the extent to which people conform to a good enough approximation of rational *homo economicus*. But, as behavioral research shows, in too many specific respects, neoclassical economics seems in dire need of revision to incorporate newer empirical findings that provide a much more psychologically realistic understanding of how people make decisions in real life. To this topic, we turn in the next chapter.

FURTHER READING

Angner, R. (2012). *A course in behavioural economics*. Palgrave.

Frank, R. H. & Cartwright, E. (2016). *Microeconomics and behaviour* (2nd European Edition). McGraw-Hill Education.

Harford, T. (2007). *The undercover economist*. Abacus.

Mell, A. & Walker, O. (2014). *Rough guide to economics*. Rough Guides.

REFERENCES

Allais, M. (1953). Le comportement de l'homme rationnel devant le risque: Critique des postulats et axiomes de l'école americaine. *Econometrica*, *21*, 503–546. https://doi.org/10.2307/1907921

Ariely, D. (2008). *Predictably irrational: The hidden forces that shape our decisions*. Harper Collins.

Barros, G. (2010). Herbert A. Simon and the concept of rationality: Boundaries and procedures. *Brazilian Journal of Political Economy*, *30*, 455–472.

Berns, G. S., Laibson, D., & Loewenstein, G. (2007). Intertemporal choice – Toward an integrative framework. *Trends in Cognitive Sciences*, *11*, 482–488. https://doi.org/10.1016/j.tics.2007.08.011

Camerer, C. F., & Loewenstein, G. (2003). Behavioral economics: Past, present, future. In C. F. Camerer, G. Loewenstein, & M. Rabin (Eds.), *Advances in behavioral economics*. Princeton University Press.

Friedman, M. (1953). *Essays in positive economics*. The University of Chicago Press.

Friedman, M., & Savage, L. J. (1948). The utility analysis of choices involving risk. *Journal of Political Economy*, *56*, 279–304. https://doi.org/10.1086/256692

Galbraith, J. K. (1958). *The affluent society*. Houghton Mifflin Harcourt.

Galbraith, J. K. (1967). *The new industrial state*. Houghton Mifflin.

Guerrera, F. (2009, March 12). Welch condemns share price focus. *Financial Times*. https://www.ft.com/content/294ff1f2-0f27-11de-ba10-0000779fd2ac

Kahneman, D., & Tversky, A. (1979). Prospect theory: An analysis of decision under risk. *Econometrica*, *47*, 263–291. https://doi.org/10.2307/1914185

Keynes, J. M. (1923). *A tract on monetary reform*. Macmillan.

Keynes, J. M. (1936). *The general theory of employment, interest and money*. Palgrave Macmillan.

King, M. (2016). *The end of alchemy: Money, banking, and the future of the global economy*. Hachette.

Lichtenstein, S., & Slovic, P. (1971). Reversals of preference between bids and choices in gambling decisions. *Journal of Experimental Psychology, 89*, 46–55. https://doi.org/10.1037/h0031207

Lichtenstein, S., & Slovic, P. (1973). Response-induced reversals of preference in gambling: An extended replication in Las Vegas. *Journal of Experimental Psychology, 101*, 16–20. https://doi.org/10.1037/h0035472

Marshall, A. (1890). *Principles of economics*. Macmillan.

Pareto, V. (1906). *Manual of a political economy (published in French; edited with notes, in 2014, by A. Montesano, A. Zanni, L. Bruni, J. S. Chipman, M. McLure)*. Oxford University Press.

Savage, L. J. (1954). *The foundations of statistics*. Wiley.

Sills, D. L., & Merton, R. K. (Eds.). (2000). *Social science quotations: Who said what, when, and where*. Transaction Publishers.

Simon, H. A. (1955). A behavioral model of rational choice. *The Quarterly Journal of Economics, 69*, 99–118. https://doi.org/10.2307/1884852

Simon, H. A. (1957). *Models of man, social and rational: Mathematical essays on rational human behavior in a social setting*. John Wiley and Sons.

Slovic, P. (1972). From Shakespeare to Simon: speculations – and some evidence – about man's ability to process information. *Oregon Research Institute. Research Bulletin, 12*, No 2.

Tversky, A., & Kahneman, D. (1974). Judgment under uncertainty: Heuristics and biases. *Science, 185*, 1124–1131. https://doi.org/10.1126/science.185.4157.1124

Tversky, A., Sattath, S., & Slovic, P. (1988). Contingent weighting in judgment and choice. *Psychological Review, 95*, 371–384. https://doi.org/10.1037/0033-295X.95.3.371

Tversky, A., & Thaler, R. H. (1990). Anomalies: Preference reversals. *Journal of Economic Perspectives, 4*, 201–211. https://doi.org/10.1257/jep.4.2.201

von Neumann, J., & Morgenstern, O. (1944). *Theory of games and economic behavior*. Princeton University Press.

HUMAN
HOMO PSYCHOLOGICUS

People systematically deviate from how they *should* behave according to neoclassical economics. For example, the context in which decisions are made is often more important than the informational content. The focus of this chapter is how people *actually* form judgments and make decisions according to psychological research. Heuristics and biases are central to this discussion – heuristics can be thought of as mental shortcuts that are automatic, intuitive, and do not require conscious thought. Tversky and Kahneman initially outlined three heuristics in 1974: availability, representativeness, and anchoring and adjustment, and others have been identified since. The formulation of Prospect Theory by Kahneman and Tversky in 1979 proved especially influential by combining psychological insights with economic phenomena. It provides an elegant explanation of why people dislike losses more than gains of an equivalent value. In particular, Prospect Theory calls attention to the importance of *reference points*: we do not look at things in *absolute* terms but, rather, we focus on *relative* changes around a starting point, and these can be influenced in various, sometimes arbitrary, ways. The chapter also explores how behavioral economic phenomena are the result of specific brain–mind cognitive and affective systems that are specialized for different psychological functions.

DOI: 10.4324/9781003166900-4

INTRODUCTION

By now we know that behavioral economics is rooted in the history of classical economic thought. We also know that dissenting voices (e.g., J. K. Galbraith) anticipated some of the themes that occupy behavioral economics today (e.g., the degree of rationality of the consumer and the power of consumerism). To these views from economics are added insights from psychology: much is now known about how people *actually* form judgments and make decisions, and how these impact economic choice and behavior. These psychological insights have heavily influenced the whole field of behavioral economics. To a large extent, they define it – especially as they provide coherent theoretical models that supplement, sometimes replace, mainstream economic models. These insights are the focus of this chapter. We see how the *homo economicus* (ECON) depiction described in Chapter 3 needs to be modified by the far more typical *homo psychologicus* (HUMAN). Among other things, we see the importance of (psychological) *context* over (informational) *content*.

To gain a good understanding of what can be a complex literature, we start with a survey of what many consider to be one of the most important findings in the whole of behavioral economics: loss aversion. It is a useful starting point because it helps us appreciate the truly psychological nature of economic phenomena. In addition, its influence is seen across many different domains, and it plays a pivotal role in the major alternative perspective to neoclassical economics: prospect theory.

LOSS AVERSION

Loss aversion is one of the best-known phenomena in behavioral economics (an overview of it can be seen in Kahneman et al., 1991). It states that losses loom larger than equivalent gains (Kahneman & Tversky, 1984). In other words, the pleasure of gaining $10 is less than the displeasure of losing $10 – depending on how it is measured, the effect is estimated around twice as much.

It is remarkable to think that well over 200 years before Kahneman and Tversky's (1979) seminal work on Prospect Theory (described below), Adam Smith already identified loss aversion, as well as much else current in behavioral economics (e.g., the influence of social factors and emotions). Smith elegantly articulated loss aversion in his 1759 book, *The Theory of Moral Sentiments*:

> Pain [...] is, in almost all cases, a more pungent sensation than the opposite and corresponding pleasure. The one almost always depresses us much more below the ordinary, or what may be called the natural state of our happiness, than the other ever raises us above it.

(Smith, 1759)

Some one hundred years later, Charles Darwin said something similar to Smith: we place a higher value on blame than we do on praise – more generally, the negative dominates the positive. (How many "I love you" are necessary to compensate for one hurtful comment to your romantic partner?)

More formally in current-day behavioral economics, when the potential of loss is salient (an important caveat), loss aversion refers to the stronger tendency to prefer avoiding losses to achieving gains of the *same magnitude*. However, perhaps somewhat surprisingly, given the prominent role it plays in behavioral economics, the appearance and strength of loss aversion very much depend on how the feelings of loss are made salient and elicited – this is yet another manifestation of the lack of *method invariance* (mainstream economics assumes that such phenomena should not be strongly influenced by the method of their elicitation; that is, they should be 'method invariant'). Empirical studies have demonstrated that under certain circumstances (e.g., when the loss is not made salient), loss aversion can be lower or, even, nonexistent – in fact, there is now much debate over the robustness and implications of the phenomenon (Gal & Rucker, 2018).

Loss aversion is, nonetheless, a good way to start taking a psychological perspective on economic choice and behavior; it is also a good way to start to appreciate the importance of context, framing, and such like. We will see how the conceptualization and measurement of core principles in behavioral economics are affected by such factors, especially the influence of how information is presented. The common caveat in neoclassical economics, *all else being equal*, rings hollow in the face of the pervasive influence of such psychological factors.

ENDOWMENT EFFECT

The influence of loss aversion is evident across a range of behavioral economic phenomena.

THE ENDOWMENT EFFECT – COFFEE MUGS

Imagine yourself in the coffee mug study (Kahneman et al., 1990). The 'sellers' in this study were given a Cornell University coffee mug. They were asked at what price they would be willing to sell it. The 'buyers' in this study were asked what price they would be willing to pay for it. The surprising outcome is that these prices were very different. The median price for sellers was $7.12, nearly 2.5 times the median price for buyers, at $2.87. In another study, of those given a choice to sell, 75% decided to keep the mug if the price was $3.12 on average. Merely owning a product seems to enhance its value: the explanation being that we are averse to the potential loss and we would prefer to keep possession of the coffee mug – there may also be a status quo bias in play, discussed below.

One good example is the *endowment effect*, a term first coined by Richard Thaler (1980). This effect relates to the finding that we value the things we own much higher than the things we do not. For example, our house will always be worth more to us than to a potential buyer. The endowment effect is seen in people wanting to *sell* consumption goods at higher prices than they would be willing to *pay* for them. This was shown in a simple and elegant experiment by Kahneman and colleagues in 1990 using coffee mugs (see text box).

Another interesting form of loss aversion is seen in the 'money illusion'. As noted in Chapter 2, even high-profile neoclassical economists sometimes find cause to scratch their professional heads in disbelief at the notions lay people hold about money. Irving Fisher (1867–1947) – once called 'the greatest economist the United States has ever produced' – wrote about the *money illusion* (indeed, he devoted an entire book to the subject, published in 1928). The money illusion is the tendency to think of currency in terms of the numerical/face value (the nominal value; e.g., $1) rather than in terms of its purchasing power (the real value).

The real value of money reflects how much of a good and/or service can be acquired with the money (consider the eroding purchasing power effect of hyperinflation). Think about what you can buy for $100 today compared to what your grandparents could buy for $100 when they were your age – you have now got the point! However, the money illusion remains tenacious. The argument from behavioral economics is that it reflects the use of a heuristic: nominal prices provide a rule of thumb for deciding the value of a good or service. Real prices, on the other hand, are not taken into consideration unless they are made highly salient – we tend to ignore, or not understand, or at least downplay, the purchasing power erosion of inflation.

The money illusion can be seen in perceptions of outcomes. For example, generally, we see a 2% cut in nominal income (e.g., wages) with no change in purchasing power (the real value of income, i.e., what can be purchased with that income) as unfair – we would be taking home 2% less purchasing power. In contrast, we have far less difficulty in viewing a 2% rise in nominal income as fair even when there is 4% inflation (which decreases real income) – again, we would be taking home roughly 2% less purchasing power. What might be going on here? Well, usually, the immediate increase in income is much more salient than the larger, seemingly more remote, increase in inflation, which appears an altogether more abstract concept (and possibly one we could mitigate by changing our purchasing behavior). Despite the fact that these outcomes are, in rational terms, almost equivalent, they simply do not *seem* that way to us and we have very different feelings and thoughts about them. Such outcomes are consistent with a related phenomenon, 'myopic loss aversion', described by Benartzi and Thaler in 1995. As the name implies, this phenomenon refers to a short-sighted greater sensitivity to apparent losses, compared to gains of an equal amount – objective value, as opposed to subjective value. In addition, as people are accustomed to getting (albeit in nominal terms) a pay rise and not a cut, the prospect of a cut is much more unusual and, therefore, psychologically attention-grabbing, leading to discontentment and a sense of apparent unfairness.

MONEY: MENTAL ACCOUNTING

Recall the discussion of money in Chapter 1 – as ABBA sang, it can be a funny thing. We now need to know something important about money: it is *fungible* – it buys food and Fords, meaning that one coin/note can be exchanged for another of equal value, and they have the same purchasing power. Also, recall from Chapter 1 the working patterns of New York City taxi drivers who work 'one day at a time'. One interpretation of the taxi drivers' behavior is that they have mental bundles of preferences: work, leisure, family, and so on, which are not *easily* interchangeable (i.e., fungible). There is something especially peculiar about the psychology of money: *mental accounting* (see Thaler, 2008). Think of the money in your pocket, in your bank account, in your investments, and even maybe money in the tin on the kitchen sink. Do you treat these bundles of money equally? Probably not. Given the importance assigned to money, and especially its fungible nature, this is something that baffles the neo-classically inclined economist – although surely, in their personal life, they treat money in much the same nonfungible manner.

Most of us – however, apparently nonrationally – bundle our financial resources according to their intended purpose. For example, we may have a holiday fund, shopping fund, leisure fund, and so on – these are not so easily interchangeable in psychological terms. The interesting thing is that we spend these funds in what appears to be inconsistent ways. For example, we may search the supermarket shelves to find value-for-money products, while on the same day, we may not be the least concerned about spending another bundle of money on something of extravagance (e.g., an expensive restaurant meal). Are we behaving inconsistently?

Example: Mental Accounting

Imagine the following situation. You have decided to see a band that happens to be playing close to where you live. The admission charge is $10 per ticket. As you enter the venue, you discover that you have lost a $10 note (you have other money with you). The question is, would you still pay $10 for a ticket to see the concert? Something like 88% of people who are asked this question say they would – 12% would not (Tversky & Kahneman, 1981).

Now consider this situation. You have decided to see the same band and have already bought a ticket for the admission price of $10. As you enter the concert hall, you discover that you have lost the ticket – without the ticket, you will not be allowed into the venue. The question now is, would you now pay $10 for another ticket? Surprisingly, only 46% of people say they would, and most are willing to go away disappointed.

But as you can see, from a money point of view, both situations are identical – either way, if you see the band you would have forgone $20. As this example shows, even when making decisions about money, it is not always about the money! (Other examples of mental accounting can be found in Thaler, 2008.)

Of course, mental accounting helps people to budget and regulate consumption to maximize overall well-being (utility) – seen from this perspective, this is a very rational thing to be doing. It certainly makes the cognitive task of managing money much easier. For example, knowing how much is 'put aside' for household expenditure and how much is available to be spent on nonessential items makes life more convenient and, this alone, contributes to overall utility. But none of this sits well with neoclassical economics: if we want to save money in the supermarket (i.e., we have a preference for this), then why would we then want to splash out on an expensive meal? You can probably think of perfectly good reasons for these, apparently inconsistent, forms of financial behavior.

HEURISTICS AND BIASES

The mental accounting example above shows that some economic exercises require substantial cognitive effort – and compared to others, *these* examples are relatively easy. To deal with them, the human mind has developed strategies to make them more manageable – among these strategies are heuristics, with resulting biases. Heuristics, or rules of thumb, describe the systematic ways we think about problems of judgment and decision making. These mental shortcuts allow us to make decisions quickly and without the expenditure of too much cognitive effort, time, emotions, and inconvenience.

In many people's minds, behavioral economics is all about heuristics and biases. For sure, they are important, but they are far from being the whole story. They serve one valuable function, which is why they have assumed such prominence in behavioral economics: namely, they provide some of the best evidence that we do not always – indeed, very often – conform to the depiction of rational *homo economicus* (ECON). It is now clear that processing heuristics of various types play a large role in economic choice and behavior. Accordingly, any viable economic theory needs to take them into proper consideration.

Recognition of the roles played by processing heuristics has shifted attention away from formal and mathematical rules (e.g., expected utility theory; see Chapter 3) to rules-of-thumb: simple and (reasonably) efficient procedures for forming judgments and making decisions. Heuristics can be thought of as mental shortcuts that are automatic, intuitive, and do not require conscious thought – they just 'feel right' and, often in terms of outcomes, they are right. Sometimes they are fallible, however.

Building on the work of Herbert Simon (see Chapter 3), who first talked about heuristics, the early 1970s saw the emergence of a highly productive collaboration between Daniel Kahneman and Amos Tversky, who went on to list and define a large number of heuristics and associated biases that affect everyday life (for a lively story of their collaboration, see Lewis, 2016). In particular, Tversky and Kahneman's 1974 seminal paper on some of the major heuristics and biases attracted worldwide attention and set the behavioral economics research agenda to this very day. (Later, in 2002, Kahneman won the Nobel Memorial Prize in Economic Sciences – by this date, Tversky had died and Nobel prizes are not awarded posthumously, but had he lived, he most certainly would have been honored alongside Kahneman.)

Although not consistent with the expected utility theory of rationality (see Chapter 3), heuristics – even despite the biases and errors that result – can be seen as rational in a world full of complex problems, incomplete information, and limited psychological resources (e.g., cognitive processing and self-control). Given these limitations, heuristics are good enough in most circumstances and enable judgments and decisions to be made in a timely and usually fairly accurate manner. However, they can lead to errors, sometimes major – and typically less than optimal ones from a neoclassical viewpoint. The major limitation is their focus on only some aspects of the problem – that are salient and seem relevant – to the neglect of other (sometimes more crucial) aspects. Kahneman and colleagues (2021) have elaborated on the implications of *noise* in human decision making. Whereas *systematic* error in judgments is *bias*, noise is variation in either judgments made by different people (e.g., judges in court trying similar cases) or variation in judgments within a given individual. As with all forms of psychological (behavioral) measurement, there will be statistical variation, which is noise, and this needs to be considered when thinking about systematic biases.

Heuristics and biases research is important because mainstream, neoclassical economists contend, reasonably enough, that if people are sufficiently incentivized and motivated, and have full (or good enough) information – *especially when it is about important life decisions* – why would they not show rational and consistent decision making? Mainstream economists say also that, although some people are plain dumb (or choose to behave that way), 'the market' is efficient; therefore, *aggregate* level behavior conforms reasonably well to the principle of optimization and neoclassical assumptions. To assume otherwise, we have to envision human beings going about their daily business, even in important matters, in a bumbling, inconsistent, and inefficient fashion. But as we have already seen in previous chapters, individuals and markets do sometimes behave in astonishingly nonoptimal ways – on a large global scale, the financial crash of 2007–2008 serves as testimony (see Chapter 1). We could surely find plenty of examples of nonoptimal behavior during the Covid-19 pandemic when expert advice was at times ignored by politicians and some members of the public, sometimes with dire consequences.

Tversky and Kahneman (1974) initially outlined three heuristics: *availability, representativeness*, and *anchoring and adjustment*. Others have been subsequently added, for example, those involving making judgments (*judgment heuristics*) and choices (*evaluation heuristics*) easier. Let us consider each in turn.

AVAILABILITY HEURISTIC

The *availability* heuristic relates to the ease with which an idea comes to mind (see text box). It is used to estimate the likelihood or frequency of an event. The basic idea is that when an unlikely or infrequent event springs to mind, we tend to overestimate its occurrence. For example, the likelihood of being caught up in a terrorist incident is tiny, but we do not judge it this way. On the other hand, common and mundane events are not perceived to be as dangerous as, in fact, they are (e.g., a child's death in a home swimming pool is judged less likely than abduction, but the first is much more frequent than the second, and the same is true for suicide and gun deaths in the United States, where gun deaths by suicide are more frequent than ones by murder).

The availability heuristic is used to explain why we are more influenced by a single story that leaves a greater impression than a wealth of statistical data – it is no wonder the UK National Lottery likes to publicize winners with a big public relations splash: "It could be *you*!" (Alas, you have more chance of being struck down by a bolt of

---

LETTER K IN WORDS

Are there more English words with *K* in the first position or with *K* in the third position? It is easy to think of *kangaroo, kitchen, kept*, and so on, but more difficult to think of words with *K* as the third letter (e.g., *lake* or *acknowledge*), but the third-letter position K words are more common. This is an example of the faulty reasoning of the availability heuristic (Tversky & Kahneman, 1973).

---

lightning.) In the world of macabre politics, we see something similar: Joseph Stalin is reputed to have said, "The death of one man is a tragedy, the death of millions is a statistic".

The availability heuristic has also been used to account for *illusory correlation*, which comes from recalling two events to mind at the same time. We tend to perceive a relationship between two variables when, in fact, none exists. Illusory correlations are produced when two separate variables are paired together in such a way that overestimates their frequency (e.g., Chapman, 1967). For example, we may visit a country for the first time, and the first couple of people we meet are very friendly and, then, we infer that all people in this country are friendly, whether they are or not. If we think they are especially friendly and we act in an especially friendly way toward them, then they may well reciprocate in kind, reinforcing our illusory correlation – something of a self-fulfilling prophecy. Also, we may engage in *confirmation bias*: for example, accepting all friendly behavior as typical of the people and less friendly encounters as less typical. We thus unconsciously interpret their behavior in a way that confirms our prior beliefs.

REPRESENTATIVENESS HEURISTIC

The *representativeness* heuristic has an influence when people think in terms of categories (e.g., what seems to characterize nurses and police officers?). The idea is that a stimulus (e.g., a description of a specific person) with high *representativeness* comes about because it is close to the prototype of that category (i.e., this particular person seems to embody what characterizes the typical nurse or police officer). The problem comes when we confuse the stimulus (e.g., a specific person)

STEREOTYPES AND THE DILUTION EFFECT

The representativeness heuristic may explain stereotypes and how they can be reduced: the *dilution effect*. Imagine you are asked whether Paul or Susan are more likely to be assertive – all you know is their name. What's *your* answer? Typically, Paul (as a man) is rated as more assertive. But now, if you are told that Paul's and Susan's mothers each commute to work in a bank, you are less likely to show this stereotype effect – Paul and Susan are typically rated as equally assertive. This effect is explained in terms of the extra information about Paul and Susan, which makes them *less* representative of men or women in general (described in Kunda, 1999).

with the category prototype – although this may seem a little abstract, the example (see text box) helps illustrate it.

The *representativeness* heuristic can be very effective, but it can lead to errors and even prejudice. People can err in one of two ways. They can overestimate the probability that something has a very rare property or underestimate the probability of a very common property. This is known as the *base rate fallacy*. These mistakes violate the rational use of probability information (see text box).

THE CONJUNCTION FALLACY

The representativeness heuristic (and, to some extent, the persistent power of stereotypes) is also reflected in the *conjunction fallacy*, a formal fallacy that once again demonstrates that most of us are far from being star statisticians. Consider the following situation, which is very well known in behavioral economics. Tversky and Kahneman (1983) presented subjects with a brief description of a woman named Linda. She is described as "31 years old, single, outspoken, and very bright. She majored in philosophy. As a student, she was deeply concerned with issues of discrimination and social justice, and also participated in anti-nuclear demonstrations". Subjects in this study were then asked to rank the likelihood of different statements about Linda. These included "Linda is a bank teller", and "Linda is a bank teller and is active in the feminist movement". The results showed that subjects tended to rate the second more specific statement as more likely.

BASE RATE FALLACY

Consider this problem (it is an example of Bayesian reasoning; see Chapter 3) which was published by Tversky and Kahneman in 1982. It involves an eyewitness account of a hit-and-run incident by a taxi. Participants in this study were asked to estimate the probability of a witness identifying the correct color of the taxi *given certain information*. Two taxi companies operate in the city, one with green and the other with blue cabs. The prevalence (base rate) is known: Green = 85%, blue = 15%. The witness to the crime reports that they saw a blue taxi.

When in court, the eyewitness is tested for accuracy of identification under the same lighting conditions as at the time of the commission of the crime. They correctly identified the color presented 80% of the time and failed 20% of the time. The study participants were then asked: What is the probability that the cab involved in the accident was, in fact, blue, as claimed by the eyewitness? Well, what would be your answer? The results revealed that most participants gave a probability greater than 50%; many estimated that it would be 80% or higher. Now, if we did not know the actual color of the taxi, then a reasonable guess would be that there is an 85% chance it was green, but we have additional information on the accuracy of the eyewitness identification to take into account. Given all of this information, the true probability that the taxi involved in the hit-and-run was, in fact, blue is only 41%. These results, which have been replicated in many different contexts, show that participants placed more evidential weight on the testimony of the witness than on the more statistically reliable base rate information.

However, a conjunction of the form "Linda is both a bank teller and in the feminist movement" can never be more likely than the more general statement "Linda is a bank teller".

Put more formally, the probability of a conjunction can never be greater than the probability of its (separate) conjuncts. That is, the probability that two things are true at the same time can never be greater than the probability that only one of them is true. But, in some cases, people judge that a conjunction is more likely than one of its conjuncts on its own. What is happening? It may be that the conjunction suggests a scenario that people can picture more easily than just one of its components: Linda being a bank teller and in the feminist movement – they may also assume that people tend to stay consistent over time. The capacity to imagine seems the vital ingredient to this fallacy. In this example, Linda appears to fit the stereotype of a feminist and not one of a bank teller, so we find it easier to think of Linda as a bank teller who is also a feminist. Lots of other examples show much the same thing. Of interest, Tversky and Kahneman reported they found subjects were very unwilling to give up these judgments, even when they were shown to be illogical.

Another consequence of the representativeness heuristic relates to biased judgments concerning randomness – the *misperception of randomness*. Do you think the sequence 1, 2 3, 4, 5, 6 is more or less likely than any other sequence (e.g., 5, 3, 2, 6, 4, 1)? What about the sequence of heads (H) and tails (T) in coin flips? Which one is more likely TTTTTHHHHH or HHTHTTTHTH? Of course, all of these sequences are equally probable, but we often believe the pattern that appears to be more random is more likely. Casinos exploit this misperception. For example, on the roulette table, they show the sequence of the last black/red numbers that have come up. Some players will see a *run* of red and assume that 'it is now time' for black and bet accordingly (it makes no difference because the ball does not have any memory of where it last landed, even if it cared).

Much has been talked about the *gambler's fallacy*: the tendency to expect outcomes to even out over the short run (e.g., Tversky & Kahneman, 1971). We tend to believe that, for example, a long series of tails in a coin flip game must surely be followed by heads because we intuitively know that with a fair coin, we would roughly see the same number of heads and tails after many coin flips. However, assuming that the coin is, indeed, fair, each individual coin flip is equally likely to result in either heads or tails, regardless of what came before. Gamblers sometimes go bust long before the run has the common decency to correct itself.

Still another consequence of the representativeness heuristic relates to the effects of people's *insensitivity to sample size* (see text box).

ANCHORING AND ADJUSTMENT HEURISTIC

The third major heuristic is *anchoring and adjustment*. It is used when people have to estimate a number. The idea is we start from a readily available number – this is the 'anchor' – and, then, we shift up or down *from that point*. This can be in the form of minimum monthly payments on a credit card or something irrelevant, such as reading your national insurance number before making an estimate. In one such experiment, subjects watched a number being selected from a 'Wheel of Fortune', which they surely knew was random and, therefore, had nothing to do with the task they were then asked to do (Tversky & Kahneman, 1974). After seeing this number, they were asked: "Is the percentage of African countries which are members of the United Nations larger or smaller than x%?" (The percentage number was taken from where the wheel of fortune happened to land.) They were then asked to guess the actual percentage. Even though they must have known that the wheel of fortune number was pure chance, their estimates were closely tied (i.e., anchored) to this entirely irrelevant number.

The upshot of numerous experiments is that people get tied to the anchor, and this contaminates their estimate. Whatever the process that leads to this effect, it would seem to have a wide range of implications for how we estimate numbers. Again, it is interesting to note,

---

INSENSITIVITY TO SAMPLE SIZE

Tversky and Kahneman (1974) presented subjects with the following problem designed to measure their understanding of random variation and its relation to sample size. Start by imagining that over a long period of time, the ratio of male and female babies born in a hospital is 50/50. You are told, if you need to be, this will not be true for all periods of time as we should expect some variation. Tversky and Kahneman asked the question: does the likelihood of deviating from exactly half depend on the number of births for a particular day? What do you think?

Sampling theory tells us that, on average, there will be more variation (i.e., deviation from a 50/50 split) the smaller the sample size. But people's answer to the question does not reflect this fact. Typically, they say that the *number* of births will not affect the sex ratio on any one day – in this specific study, the range was set at a 40–60% sex ratio, and people thought the actual ratio would not fall outside this range. (Of course, on some days, all births would be males or females.) Again, most of us do not possess perfect (even good) statistics skills, unlike neoclassical economics would have us believe.

ANCHORING EFFECT – SEQUENCE OF NUMBERS

The anchoring effect is found also when numbers are combined to form a composite judgment. Estimate in your mind the sum of the following numbers: $8 \times 7 \times 6 \times 5 \times 4 \times 3 \times 2 \times 1$. What is your answer? It is highly likely that whatever it is, it would be higher than if you had estimated the sequence: $1 \times 2 \times 3 \times 4 \times 5 \times 6 \times 7 \times 8$ (Tversky & Kahneman, 1973). As you no doubt calculated in your head(!), the right answer is 40,320.

---

that people find it hard to avoid doing this, even when incentivized, and when challenged to explain their decision, they deny that their estimates were anchored. Perhaps unsurprisingly, the effect is stronger when the decision needs to be made fast. Moreover, the anchors do not even have to appear sensible. For example, when people were asked to estimate the year of Albert Einstein's first visit to the United States, the absurd anchors of 1215 and 1992 were included among more sensible years and influenced the answers just as much (Strack & Mussweiler, 1997). There are many examples of anchoring (see text box).

COHERENT ARBITRARINESS

Examples of the heuristic of anchoring and adjustment are given by Ariely et al. (2003) across six different experiments in which they showed that apparently irrelevant features have influential consequences. Their results demonstrate that arbitrary anchors can affect the initial valuations of products and hedonic experiences. However, the valuations in these experiments appeared to be coherent and thus give the 'illusion' of order – that is, generated by stable underlying preferences. This conclusion is reflected in the sub-title of their paper, 'stable demand curves without stable preference'. Most worrying for neoclassical economics, they conclude that their results show behavior:

(1) cannot be interpreted as a rational response to information; (2) does not decrease as a result of experience with a good; (3) is not necessarily reduced by market forces; and (4) is not unique to cash prices.

Another nice example of this process was given by the same authors. They showed a new class of MBA students a range of consumer products (e.g., computer accessories, wine bottles, and luxury chocolates). Then, after describing these products, the students were asked whether they would buy each good for a certain amount in dollars, which was equivalent to the last two digits of their social security number (which, of course, is an arbitrary number). Then, after their accept/reject response, the students were asked their dollar maximum *willingness-to-pay* (WTP) for the product. Students were incentivized appropriately and, therefore, properly motivated to play the game seriously: both their accept/reject response and their WTP response could influence the purchase. The results were both surprising and remarkable. Students with above-median social security numbers stated values that were considerably higher than those reported by students with below-median numbers – about 57% to 107%. This is despite the fact that the students were not misled about the products and they must have had a good idea of what they were worth. Remember that these MBA students were 'smart cookies' and not easy-to-mislead; but, even they seem not to have the capacity to think straight when anchored to an arbitrary number.

As the authors of this important study concluded, the sensitivity of WTP to anchors indicates we do not make a choice or price a task in the context of an inventory of pre-existing preferences. Instead, we probably have a range of what they consider to be acceptable values, and we base our 'buy' or 'don't buy' on this range. Within the range, anchors exert their toll.

These authors show in five other examples the robustness of anchoring, even when market forces are at play. Such results raise a number of fundamental concerns for neoclassical economic assumptions and principles. Perhaps of most significance – remember the sole assumption underlying utility theory is that people will behave consistently (see Chapter 3) – is the finding that what can appear to reflect preference consistency may not, in reality, be anything of the kind.

AFFECT HEURISTIC

We have now reviewed a number of heuristics that facilitate everyday decision making, but there are still more. For example, the way we *feel* about something influences our judgment and decision making. This is the *affect* heuristic (see text box). We might be excited or fearful about buying shares in a particular company. We can even be influenced by ambient stimuli (e.g., uplifting music in the background)

AFFECT HEURISTIC – DISEASE AND DEATH

Think about this problem. There are two diseases. One kills 1,286 people out of every 10,000 infected. The other disease has a fatality rate of 24.14% (let us assume that 10,000 have also been infected). Which of the two diseases seems most dangerous? Although clearly the second disease is twice as dangerous, when Yamagishi (1997) asked this question, most people said that it was the first disease presumably because they can imagine 1,286 dead people and this affects them more than a percentage figure showing the chances of a single person who is *not* likely to die from the disease (although there will be many more fatalities in total).

which have nothing to do with our decisions but can still affect them. Somehow, we confuse how we are feeling with the hedonic quality of the decision itself, even though there may be no relationship at all.

SYSTEMATIC DEVIATIONS FROM RATIONALITY

As we have seen, everyday behavior is governed by heuristics and biases, which lessens the need for cognitive effort when making judgments and decisions. As a result, humans systematically deviate from rational behavior: we behave more like *homo psychologicus* (HUMAN) than the neoclassical *homo economicus* (ECON). Research has further shown a number of systematic deviations from expected utility theory, discussed in Chapter 3. Some of these deviations are related to systematic, significant, and meaningful differences between people in their aversion or tolerance of risk.

RISK AVERSION

We saw in Chapter 3, the diligent rational person (i.e., economic 'agent' in the lingo of economics) who bases their decision on expected utility theory, in reality, could lose all their money very quickly – especially if the choice with the higher expected utility involves a low probability of winning a large amount of money. It is often far more sensible (rational?) to accept a lower expected utility value with a higher probability of success – thus avoiding the risk of leaving the economic game (whatever it might be) empty-handed – unless, of course, one is playing many iterations of the game and the financial (or other) resources are available to bear the temporary (although it could be relatively long-lasting) financial (and also psychological) pain.

Now, long-term well-being may well be higher if we take the risky gamble many times because the expected value represents the long-run average outcome of repeated gambles; but for one-time choices, it might be wiser to follow the advice of the proverb: "a bird in the hand is worth two in the bush". Also, the typically numerous short-term losses would impose their own *dis*utility, which may need to be subtracted from the longer-term value/utility achieved. In the literature, when we are willing to accept a 'sure-thing' sum that is less than the expected utility theory value, this is interpreted as implying an aversion to risk – that it may well be, but considering the points made above, it might also be the sensible choice.

Risk aversion is especially important in behavioral finance, where it can lead to sub-optimal decisions. It is reflected in the fact that when we are presented with uncertainty, we attempt to reduce this negative state, and this makes us 'risk averse'. Consider this choice. Would you prefer option 1 or 2? Option 1 is a 'sure thing' guaranteed scenario: you get $50. Option 2 involves flipping a (fair) coin to get $100 or nothing. Which option would you go for? Keep in mind that a fair coin is equally likely to land on either heads or tails. The expected value of the coin toss can be calculated as $(0.5 \times \$100) + (0.5 \times \$0) = \$50$, which is exactly the same as in the first scenario. If you go for Option 1, then you are said to be risk averse because you rejected a gamble of the same expected value. However, your decision is surely dependent on your current wealth, or perhaps what you consider to be your long-term *permanent* wealth. Image the sum of money involved is 5 pence, $5, $50, $500, $5,000, $50,000. Are your decisions over these options equally dependent on expected utility theory? It may well be for Elon Musk, but how about you? You probably could not care less about the 5 pence gamble, and you probably could not care more about the $50,000 one. Wealth is important, whether it is actual or perceived.

Under certain circumstances, risk aversion can lead to a willingness to accept a sure payoff which is lower than the expected value of an alternative, but risky choice. For example, we may be willing to put our money in a bank that is paying negative interest; that is, in fact, charging us to store our money – after the 2007–2008 financial crisis, companies bought government bonds with negative yields (i.e., they were willing to pay, quite literally, for the reduction in an uncertain future). Buying government bonds or stashing away money in the bank ensures that it is safe as opposed to investing in an uncertain stock market. All very risk averse but, at the same time, all very sensible perhaps? (Certainly, at the time, the large financial institutions thought so.)

THE EQUITY PREMIUM PUZZLE

Our aversion to risk, and even more so to uncertainty, manifests itself in what is called the 'equity premium puzzle' (Mehra & Prescott, 1985). This puzzle describes the phenomenon that the observed returns on stocks over the past century have been much higher than returns on government bonds (about 6% per year; this has been found over long time periods in many countries; Siegel & Thaler, 1997), implying the stock market has been required to pay over-the-odds to attract investors. The explanation that stocks are much riskier than bonds does not seem a wholly adequate explanation because of the magnitude of the disparity between the two asset classes and the historical record (i.e., information) which show that buying stocks is a sensible, reasonable safe, form of investment. One favored explanation of this puzzle in behavioral finance is that the disparity reflects investor risk aversion for which they must be paid compensation in the form of higher percentage returns. This is another good example of how 'information' is not processed in an unbiased fashion, even when it is available in a clear form and is processed by financial professionals. Sometimes, it just seems "better safe than sorry" – especially if one's reputation and even career might be on the line.

AMBIGUITY AVERSION

Not only do we tend to be risk averse, we tend to be averse to ambiguity, which is sometimes called, 'uncertainty aversion'. Ambiguity aversion is a preference for risks that are known over ones that are not known – in common parlance, "better the devil you know". This form of aversion is illustrated by the Ellsberg paradox (see text box). Despite their apparent similarity, ambiguity aversion is somewhat different from risk aversion. As we saw above, in the case of risk aversion,

THE ELLSBERG PARADOX

People have a tendency to prefer to bet on a known probability. For example, would you prefer to bet that a ball drawn from an urn is red if (1) there are 50 red and 50 black balls or (2) you do not know the number of red/black balls in an urn of 100 balls? People tend to much prefer the known 50/50 split (Ellsberg, 1961).

the probability for each outcome is known; in contrast, ambiguity aversion entails a situation where the probabilities of outcomes are unknown.

All of the above is very much out of step with the assumptions and principles of neoclassical economics, as discussed in Chapter 3.

FRAMING EFFECTS

It is important to note that the above effects do not exist independently of context. How a problem is 'framed' is important − that is, the form in which the content and information are presented. Kahneman and Tversky are rightly famous for highlighting the importance of 'framing' on judgment and decision making. To give a concrete example, consider Tversky and Kahneman's classic 'Asian disease problem' (Tversky & Kahneman, 1981; see text box). The first question is asked in such a way as to establish the reference point that everyone will die; in contrast, the reference point for the second question suggests that no one will die. It may also be the case that the ways these questions are posed primes people to think about them in different ways. For example, maybe the second question makes people focus on trying to save everyone. We will see the practical applications of framing in Chapters 6 and 7. For example, during the Covid-19 pandemic, some governments, and the Behavioral Insights Teams advising them, were aware of the power of framing and chose their messages accordingly. Should people be asked to adhere to social distancing measures to protect (save) vulnerable people and healthcare systems, or should they be told that many people will die if they do not follow social distancing guidance? In the United Kingdom,[1] people were urged by government campaigns to

ASIAN DISEASE PROBLEM

Imagine the following scenario described in a seminal paper by Tversky and Kahneman in 1981. The United States is preparing for an outbreak of an unusual Asian disease, which is expected to kill 600 people. Two alternative programs to combat the disease have been proposed. The exact scientific estimates of the consequences of these programs are as follows: Decision 1: If program A is adopted, 200 people will be saved. If program B is adopted, there is a 2/3 probability that no one will be saved, and a 1/3 probability that 600 people will be saved. Decision 2: If program C is adopted, 400 people will die with certainty. If program D is adopted, there is a 2/3 probability that 600 people will die, and a 1/3 probability that no one will die. Tversky and Kahneman found that 72% of subjects chose A over B, while 78% chose D over C. Therefore, when given these choices with these different frames, people tend to prefer A to B but with a different frame D to C. But note that the only difference between A and C (and B and D) is that the same choice problem is framed in different ways!

"Stay Home – Protect the NHS – Save Lives" – a clear example of gain frame ("save") messaging.

PROMINENCE EFFECT

Related to the framing effect is the *prominence effect* (e.g., Tversky et al., 1988). Let us look at this more closely. Do you agree with the statement that we should not quibble over the cost of road safety if it saves just one child's life? You may well be tempted to agree, but would you still agree if you are then told that the same amount of money could save the lives of many more children suffering from cancer? (This is an example of 'opportunity cost'; see Chapter 2.) In other words, would you prefer to save (for sure!) the life of one child with cancer, or would you prefer to improve the chances of all children suffering from cancer by a tiny fraction (e.g., .01%)? The latter option may actually save the lives of more children. These choices illustrate the importance of prominence, and it is the reason why adverts for charities never talk about the larger population but, instead, show one child, usually giving them a name: this makes it *personal* and it influences the way we think, feel, and act.

PROSPECT THEORY

So far in this chapter, we have seen the ways our choices are influenced by how options are presented and how they are processed in specific ways by the mind – the mind does not simply process information in an unbiased manner. We now know people are typically averse to risk, are easily influenced by framing, by random and relevant numbers that act as anchors, and how arbitrary reference points greatly influence decisions, even among people who would otherwise be considered smart. It seems as if few, if any, of us are immune to these influences. As fascinating or infuriating these observations may seem, do they lend themselves to being described, and even explained, by a parsimonious theory of the type much favored by mainstream economists? It would be a great convenience if we could theoretically corral all of these effects, fallacies, heuristics, and biases. Indeed, the existence of such a theoretic model would go a long way to countering one major criticism of behavioral economics: it proliferates a list of behavioral anomalies relating to deviations from rational judgment and decision making, but then does not provide an elegant, unifying framework with which to work. Certainly, this descriptive approach stands in stark contrast to that of neoclassical economics, which aims at parsimony and elegance – albeit with the price of a lack of psychological realism. Prospect theory answered this major criticism of behavioral economics.

The formulation of Prospect Theory by Kahneman and Tversky in 1979 represented a turning point in behavioral economics: it offered a simple model that can accommodate many seemingly separate effects – like all good economic models, it assumes little and explains much. (Apparently, it was called 'prospect' for no better reason than to make it sound distinctive and to differentiate it from other 'value' theories.) According to the Royal Swedish Academy of Sciences, which awards the Nobel Memorial Prize in Economic Sciences, in 2002, Kahneman's work is important "for having integrated insights from psychological research into economic science, especially concerning human judgment and decision-making under uncertainty". Some years later, in 2017, Richard Thaler was awarded the same Prize for something similar. These prizes gave the official stamp of approval on behavioral economics.

Prospect Theory is about how people *actually* behave, not how they *should* behave according to the normative principles of neoclassical economics. It is powerful because it is simple, very elegant, and can account for many of the phenomena already discussed in this chapter. It is focused on four main areas: (1) certain outcomes are preferred over uncertain ones, even when the expected utility of the latter is greater; (2) there is a greater sensitivity to loss than gains of the same value (loss aversion); (3) decisions about loss and gain are made from reference points and not in absolute terms; and (4) the way information is presented (i.e., framed) is critical, with the same, but differently framed, information leading to differences behavioral outcomes.

Prospect theory is especially influential in providing a theoretical account of, for example, the *endowment effect*, which is couched in terms of loss aversion. The theory calls attention to the importance of *relative* changes around a reference point, and these can be influenced in various ways (e.g., framing). As Richard Thaler (2015) says, contrary to neoclassical economic thinking, the *difference* between losing $10 and $20 (i.e., $10) *feels* subjectively bigger than objectively the same difference between losing $1,300 and $1,310 (i.e., $10). You can probably think of why this might be the case (e.g., in the first case, 50% of wealth has been lost, while in the second case, less than 1%; and the effect of purchasing power in the first case is considerably higher than in the second case). Upon reflection, you might not be surprised at these different affective feelings, and you might even wonder if in the first case these elevated feelings are truly a reflection of *misbehavior*. In any event, if you are not surprised, and can easily think of sensible reasons for the differences, then you have probably not been indoctrinated into neoclassical economic thinking.

Prospect theory is described with a deceptively simple-looking figure (see below). This figure shows the shape of the utility curve under gain and loss relative to a reference point (shown as A). The notion of a reference point helps us to understand how framing works: by establishing a point around which gains and losses are evaluated in a relative way ($20 or $1,310). The important point to note is that the gain curve is concave while the loss curve is convex. What does this tell us? This s-shape reflects that people tend to be risk averse concerning gains while they like to avoid losses and thus act as risk-takers (or risk-seekers) in the domain of loss. Moreover, the shape – in

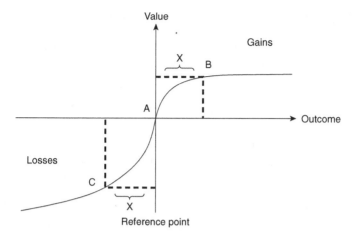

FIGURE 4.1 Prospect theory – the value function

Source: adapted from Kahneman and Tversky (1979), Figure 3

particular, the relative heights of the concave and convex parts of the curve – demonstrates another important point. It means that a one-unit gain (e.g., moving from A to B in Figure 4.1) leads to a smaller change in value (utility) than a one-unit loss (e.g., moving from A to C in Figure 4.1). This gives rise to the somewhat poetic expression, "losses loom larger than gains".

The influence of the reference point has been used to account for many real-life behaviors. For example, people are more willing to back long-shot (e.g., 15 to 1) horses after they have lost money – an example of the 'reflection effect', in this example, risk-taking in the domain of loss. The argument runs that the potential gain is greater when seen with reference to the loss. McGlothlin empirically confirmed in 1956 that people tend to bet more on long-odds horses in the last race, presumably after they have accumulated a loss.

REFERENCE DEPENDENCE

Well, in real life, most judgments and decisions are made in defi-nite contexts and situations. We have seen that this is an important feature in Prospect Theory. A simple example of context can be shown by putting two hands in separate bowls filled, respectively, with hot and cold water, then both hands in one large warm water bowl. Now, the hot hand feels colder and the cold hand feels hotter. This and other easy-to-demonstrate effects show that experience and judgment are not absolute; they are relative as explained by Prospect Theory.

STATUS QUO BIAS

Another important finding in behavioral economics is that we have a preference for the familiar. Prospect theory helps us understand this *status quo bias*: a preference for the current state of affairs (e.g., Samuelson & Zeckhauser, 1988). It is thought to be the result of the combination of loss aversion and the endowment effect (see above). The current baseline (or status quo) is taken as the reference point, and any deviation from this initial point is perceived as a loss. The idea is that we weigh the potential losses of switching from the status quo more heavily than the potential gains from the switch, even when expected utility is greater with the switch. As a consequence, we have a tendency not to switch at all – we wait until the benefits clearly outweigh the costs. It is probably for this reason that we do not readily switch banks and utility companies, or jobs or romantic partners – added to this is the perceived hassle which is a *transaction cost* (see text box).

TRANSACTION COSTS

Transaction costs are entailed when making an economic exchange – it could be as simple as the walk to the local shop (when you would prefer not to be walking anywhere, or somewhere else). Another way of seeing it is the cost of participating in the market. Transaction costs can be of various kinds: (a) search and information costs (finding the good/service and determining its price), (b) bargaining costs (reaching an acceptable agreement with the counterparty to the transaction), and (c) policing and enforcement costs (ensuring that the counterparty adheres to the terms and conditions of the contract). All of this is psychological hassle and entails some degree of risk and uncertainty which people prefer to avoid – none of this seems to be entailed by sticking with the status quo.

Now, even when there is no cost/benefit framing, we still tend to go with the status quo. There may be other factors in play, too, such as the motivation to avoid the possible *regret* resulting from making the wrong decision (see Chapter 7) – especially when opportunity costs are involved. One way to escape from this potential/anticipated regret is to not make a decision at all! But, according to neoclassical economics, this is not rational because we are not seeing the opportunity costs associated with doing nothing – which is understandable because these are much less salient until they are pointed out: that new job might have been much more rewarding; a new romantic partner far more fulfilling, and changing leisure activities could be more enjoyable.

We have now reached a point where we can appreciate the wide-ranging implications of the various heuristics we use, along with the various forms of aversions and biases that contaminate our otherwise neoclassically constrained rational mind. Taken together, they seem to attest to the fact that, indeed, we do not behave in accordance with the strict (or even relaxed) precepts of *homo economicus* (ECON).

The next section examines the cognitive systems underlying the behavioral economic phenomena typified by *homo psychologicus*. They help to explain why we behave the way we do, and why our judgment and decision making fall far short of the standards demanded by neoclassical economics. In Chapter 5, we expand upon these themes by examining the 'social mind' of people, the influence of various affective states (e.g., mood), as well as how personality shapes our behavior.

MIND: SYSTEM 1 AND SYSTEM 2

The cognitive processes that produce economic judgment and decision making are truly fascinating. The thing we call the 'mind' is made up of separate systems, each dedicated to specific psychological functions. There are 'knowledge' structures, called 'cognitive', which are specialized for language, memory, learning, reasoning, decision making, and so on. There are 'affective' systems devoted to emotion, moods, desire, and so on. Sometimes, 'motivation' systems are thought to be separate from the above two systems, but they are probably some combination of the two – they are certainly shaped by them. Sometimes, all three systems are referred to as 'cognitive', as they lend themselves to the typical form of cognitive psychological studies. (In recent years, 'cognitive' has tended to replace 'psychological' in the scientific literature – we now have an all-encompassing 'cognitive science'.) Now, these 'software' structures, systems, and processes are, somehow, instantiated in the 'hardware' of the brain. One of the last frontiers of science is to discover how these seemingly, objective mechanical entities give rise to the subjectively defined experience of consciousness, including the qualia (i.e., conscious, subjective experiences) we experience (color, sound, sight, etc.). Although some might prefer to claim otherwise, the embarrassing scientific truth is that we still have little idea how this happens.

Given the importance of structure, systems, and processes in our understanding of the mind, it is not surprising that they have turned out to be central to our understanding of behavioral economic phenomena. This outcome has largely been the result of the shift in attention away from the view of the mind as a cold, calculating rational machine (a much older version of the rational mind) to one based on the idea that it is often 'hot', heuristics-based and biased.

TWO SYSTEMS OF PROCESSING

Although something of a simplification, two major systems of processing are thought to exist. In behavioral economics, these are referred to as 'System 1' and 'System 2' (e.g., Kahneman, 2011). System 1 is reflexive, fast, automatic, biased, intuitive, emotional, habitual, nonconscious, and prepotent – also called implicit/procedural. System 2 is reflective, slow, controlled, effortful, and can be conscious – also called explicit/declarative. System 2 is said to be 'clean', whereas System 1 is said to be 'dirty' (but in a different sense to the Freudian notion of the unconscious!). There is a vast psychological literature on this dual-processing theory (e.g., Stanovich & West, 2000, Table 3). It is believed that System 2 operates only when there is a definite choice to be made and when System 1 cannot arrive at a solution easily. Behavioral economics lays particular emphasis upon the role played by System 1, especially in terms of the heuristics and biases discussed above.

These two systems need to be put into proper scientific perspective. In psychology and cognitive neuroscience, it is generally accepted that, at the moment of execution, *all* cognition and behavior must be controlled by System 1. This *all* caveat is demanded by the fact that brain processing must come before cognition, feelings, behavior, and so on, and certainly well before complex cognitive processing, and especially anything involving conscious awareness: this takes a considerable amount of time, in the region of 100s of milliseconds, which in brain terms is a very long time (e.g., we recognize faces in as fast as 10–30 milliseconds).

Given what we now know about how the brain works – it generates the mind – it would, indeed, be truly astonishing if brain processing did not come before cognition, feelings, and behavior. Yet, we rarely follow through the implications of this apparent fact – and, as discussed below, they are significant for all forms of judgment, decision making, and behavior, and for economics in general.

System 2 engages when we have a deliberate choice to make and the automatic reactions of System 1 seem neither appropriate nor adequate. But System 2 is limited in capacity, requires attention and deliberative processing – it is prone to fatigue. As such, it cannot be relied upon to deal with the everyday (indeed, every millisecond) business of the mind. We see this readily in everyday life. For example, we do not need to System 2 think about our burning hand if it is placed inadvertently on a hot stove: System 1 reacts in a fast, automatic manner and *only then* is System 2 engaged and we are aware of what just happened. To take another example: we may process the words on this page automatically, but, because this material may be new, it may capture System 2's deliberative processing to grasp the intended meaning. But once we are familiar with stimuli, we quite literally have no 'need to give it a second thought' and System 1 works its magic without bothering System 2.

To the extent that System 1 is in charge of *all* immediate psychological processing, System 2 has been likened to the public relations department of the mind, seemingly in control but, in reality, only the recipient, broadcaster, and 'spin doctor', of decisions and actions already taken by System 1 by fast brain processing.

THE PROBLEM FOR NEOCLASSICAL JUDGMENT AND DECISION MAKING

Well, what does all of this mean for behavioral economics? In terms of neoclassically defined rational decision making, there is a need for considerable computational power and ability, as well as a lot of self-control – just think of what is required when calculating the expected utility of different outcomes (see Chapter 3). From what we know about the brain and cognitive science, it seems we are grossly ill-equipped to process information in such a deliberative, controlled, and unbiased manner. We may want to 'wish away' this problem by invoking Milton Friedman's 'as if' argument (i.e., we behave as if we were doing these complex calculations; see Chapter 3), but the problem remains: some brain/mind mechanisms *must* be doing the computational heavy lifting, and this must rely upon System 1 which, in turn, appears to be unequal to neoclassically defined computational demands.

But there is something even troublesome – something rarely, if ever, discussed in the behavioral economics literature. This important scientific matter, which has been extensively discussed before (e.g., Gray, 2004), is something of a scientific scandal. This is the problem: if all forms of cognition, feelings, and behavior are (System 1) automatic at the *very* moment they occur then how can System 2 ever gain control over these processes? Such scientific problems do not concern neoclassical economics because it is simply assumed that, *somehow*, the necessary processing just happens – a cognitive equivalent of Adam Smith's invisible hand. Here, we start to stray into another contentious, yet important, area of cognitive science: free will.

FREE WILL

Given what we now know about System 1 processing, in what sense can we defend the widely accepted assumption of 'free will'? This assumption seems to be demanded of *homo economicus* (ECON), who is said to process information in a cognitively complex, deliberative, and unbiased fashion where a choice must be made between alternative courses of action with different expected utility values – there needs to be *freedom to choose* between available options. Once again, as commonly conceived, System 1 appears ill-equipped for this task (can it exert free will in any meaningful sense?), and System 2 appears inadequate in terms of speed of processing and limited capacity.

Perhaps not all is lost. There is more support for the power of System 2 to exert 'free won't'; that is, the interruption of System 1 processing. This means that, in terms of behavioral economics, System 2 cognitive processes may be able to inhibit System 1 automatic behavior in situations where heuristics are likely to lead to very sub-optimal judgments and decisions. The evocation of System 2 is likely to happen in complex and ambiguous situations where we know that careful, deliberative processing is required. (It might also be accompanied by the affective warning systems of fear and anxiety in threatening situations – see Chapter 5.)

In any event, it is relevant to consider one of the most comprehensive and dramatic theoretical accounts of the role of affect in decision making as presented by Damasio's somatic marker hypothesis (Bechara & Damasio, 2005; Damasio et al., 1991). In seeking to determine "what in the brain allows humans to behave rationally", Damasio argues that thought is made largely from images, broadly construed to include perceptual and symbolic representations. A lifetime of learning leads to these images becoming 'marked' by positive and negative feelings linked directly or indirectly to somatic or bodily states. When a negative somatic marker is linked to an image of a future outcome, it sounds an alarm. When a positive marker is associated with the outcome image, it becomes a beacon of incentive. Damasio hypothesized that somatic markers increase the accuracy and efficiency of the decision process and the absence of such markers, observed in people with certain types of brain damage, degrades decision performance. The somatic marker hypothesis is yet another instance of a major theoretical account of how the mind works in ways that does not lend itself to neoclassically defined economics. Modern-day cognitive science seems to have little space reserved for the requirements of the rational economic agent, *homo economicus* (ECON).

SYSTEM 1 SOPHISTICATION

This discussion highlights something else of importance. System 2 is usually thought to be more rational than System 1, which is said to be responsible for the biases, errors, and so on that define the phenomena of most interest to behavioral economists. However, the broader perspective on this matter is that System 1 can be very sophisticated, too; indeed, *it must be* if it is in charge of *moment-by-moment* cognition, feelings, and behavior which is often good enough to solve even complex problems. As elaborated by Corr (2010), it seems that once we have learned appropriate cognitive and behavioral routines – and we do this initially by System 2 processing – System 1 cognitive and behavioral routines can be primed and triggered by the situation and context. It is when System 1 processes are *inappropriate* to the situation or context (e.g., when novel, confusing or conflictual stimuli are encountered), or when they have not been developed fully in the first place, that problems occur. More precisely, it is when there is a signal indicating that System 1 processes are not going to plan that System 2 is triggered into action – there can be individual differences in the sensitivity of these triggers (see Chapter 5).

The implication of the cognitive psychology literature is that without a *lot* of training and experience, and the exercise of System 2 processing at appropriate junctures, 'rational' processing just will not happen, at least not as demanded by neoclassical economics. Under these circumstances, we must fall back on usually good enough cognitive shortcuts that in times of stress, ambiguity, or uncertainty, especially, can lead to erroneous judgment and decision making. Sometimes, this is deliberately induced by, for example, high-pressure sales techniques. However, even when things are truly working well, we now know enough from behavioral science to conclude with some confidence that, typically speaking, we are vulnerable to a wide range of influences (e.g., salience) and that good judgment and decision making processes are often hijacked by what Richard Thaler calls 'supposedly irrelevant factors' (SIFs; see Chapter 1). System 2 processes sometimes never get a look-in.

Perhaps, we should not be in the least disturbed by these realizations. After all, the human brain is the product of evolution over millions of years and it has evolved to deal with important matters of life and death, which were the concerns of the human population until comparatively recent times, and still are in some parts of the world. The brain and its cognitive, affective, and motivational systems and processes were not designed to cope with the problems presented by economics and its inventions (e.g., money). In this way, System 1 can be seen as highly rational but not in the contexts and situations of modern economic life where it has not evolved adequate means to deal with its computational problems – instead, it is forced to fall back on 'tried-and-tested' processes that work very well enough in most other contexts and situations, but which can fall short. Here as elsewhere, there is a growing gap between technological advances in society and the capacity of the human brain to comprehend, even control, them. (We see this currently with technologically advanced weapons of mass destruction, and we anticipate the same with the future of artificial intelligence.)

CONCLUSIONS

There are *systematic* deviations from the expectations of neoclassical economics: we *misbehave*. Behavioral economics research provides elegant theoretical frameworks to account for the many forms of misbehavior routinely seen – from a biological perspective, they may not be misbehaviors after all. Kahneman and Tversky's Prospect Theory proved especially influential by combining psychological insights with economic phenomena. Various forms of heuristics explain judgment and decision making much better than standard neoclassical theories – or, at the very least, they explain a wider range of phenomena. Behavioral economic phenomena must be the result of specific brain-mind cognitive, affective, and motivational systems that are specialized for specific functions – they do not *just* happen in some 'as if' and invisible hand manner. Once we take seriously the roles played by these brain and mind processes, we start to touch upon related issues, such as self-controlled processing and free will, which adds considerably to the already heavy burden placed upon neoclassical economic assumptions by empirical behavioral findings. The next chapter explores issues that add further to this burden.

FURTHER READING

Kahneman, D. (2011). *Thinking, fast and slow.* Penguin.
Lewis, M. (2016). *The undoing project: A friendship that changed our minds.* Allen Lane.

REFERENCES

Ariely, D., Loewenstein, G., & Prelec, D. (2003). "Coherent arbitrariness": Stable demand curves without stable preferences. *The Quarterly Journal of Economics, 118*, 73–105. https://doi.org/10.1162/00335530360535153
Bechara, A., & Damasio, A. R. (2005). The somatic marker hypothesis: A neural theory of economic decision. *Games and Economic Behavior, 52*, 336–372. https://doi.org/10.1016/J.GEB.2004.06.010

Benartzi, S., & Thaler, R. H. (1995). Myopic loss aversion and the equity premium puzzle. *The Quarterly Journal of Economics, 110*, 73–92. https://doi.org/10.2307/2118511

Chapman, L. J. (1967). Illusory correlation in observational report. *Journal of Verbal Learning and Verbal Behavior, 6*, 151–155. https://doi.org/10.1016/S0022-5371(67)80066-5

Corr, P. J. (2010). Automatic and controlled processes in behavioural control: Implications for personality psychology. *European Journal of Personality, 24*, 376–403. https://doi.org/10.1002/per.779

Damasio, A. R., Tranel, D., & Damasio, H. (1991). Somatic markers and the guidance of behaviour: Theory and preliminary testing. In H. S. Levin, H. M. Eisenberg, & A. L. Benton (Eds.), *Frontal lobe function and dysfunction* (pp. 217–229). Oxford University Press.

Ellsberg, D. (1961). Risk, ambiguity, and the Savage axioms. *The Quarterly Journal of Economics, 75*, 643–669. https://doi.org/10.2307/1884324

Fisher, I. (1928). *The money illusion.* Adelphi Company.

Gal, D., & Rucker, D. D. (2018). The loss of loss aversion: Will It loom larger than its gain? *Journal of Consumer Psychology, 28*, 497–516. https://doi.org/10.1002/JCPY.1047

Gray, J. A. (2004). *Consciousness: Creeping up on the hard problem.* Oxford University Press.

Kahneman, D. (2011). *Thinking, fast and slow.* Farrar, Straus and Giroux.

Kahneman, D., Knetsch, J. L., & Thaler, R. H. (1990). Experimental tests of the endowment effect and the Coase theorem. *Journal of Political Economy, 98*, 1325–1348. https://doi.org/10.1086/261737

Kahneman, D., Knetsch, J. L., & Thaler, R. H. (1991). Anomalies: The endowment effect, loss aversion, and status quo bias. *The Journal of Economic Perspectives, 5*, 193–206. https://doi.org/10.1257/jep.5.1.193

Kahneman, D., Sibony, O., & Sunstein, C. R. (2021). *Noise: A flaw in human judgment.* Little, Brown Spark.

Kahneman, D., & Tversky, A. (1979). Prospect theory: An analysis of decision under risk. *Econometrica, 47*, 263–291. https://doi.org/10.2307/1914185

Kahneman, D., & Tversky, A. (1984). Choices, values, and frames. *American Psychologist, 39*, 341–350. https://doi.org/10.1037/0003-066X.39.4.341

Kunda, Z. (1999). *Social cognition: Making sense of people.* The MIT Press.

Lewis, M. (2016). *The undoing project: A friendship that changed our minds.* Allen Lane.

McGlothlin, W. H. (1956). Stability of choices among uncertain alternatives. *The American Journal of Psychology, 69*, 604. https://doi.org/10.2307/1419083

Mehra, R., & Prescott, E. C. (1985). The equity premium: A puzzle. *Journal of Monetary Economics*, *15*, 145–161. https://doi.org/10.1016/0304-3932(85)90061-3

Samuelson, W., & Zeckhauser, R. (1988). Status quo bias in decision making. *Journal of Risk and Uncertainty*, *1*, 7–59. https://doi.org/10.1007/BF00055564

Siegel, J. J., & Thaler, R. H. (1997). Anomalies: The equity premium puzzle. *Journal of Economic Perspectives*, *11*, 191–200. https://doi.org/10.1257/jep.11.1.191

Smith, A. (1759). *The theory of moral sentiments.* printed for Andrew Millar, in the Strand; and Alexander Kincaid and J. Bell, in Edinburgh.

Stanovich, K. E., & West, R. F. (2000). Individual differences in reasoning: Implications for the rationality debate? *Behavioral and Brain Sciences*, *23*, 645–665. https://doi.org/10.1017/CBO9780511808098.026

Strack, F., & Mussweiler, T. (1997). Explaining the enigmatic anchoring effect: Mechanisms of selective accessibility. *Journal of Personality and Social Psychology*, *73*, 437–446. https://doi.org/10.1037/0022-3514.73.3.437

Thaler, R. (1980). Toward a positive theory of consumer choice. *Journal of Economic Behavior & Organization*, *1*, 39–60. https://doi.org/https://doi.org/10.1016/0167-2681(80)90051-7

Thaler, R. (2008). Mental accounting and consumer choice. *Marketing Science*, *27*, 15–25. http://www.jstor.org/stable/40057241

Thaler, R. (2015). *Misbehaving: The making of behavioural economics.* Allen Lane.

Tversky, A., & Kahneman, D. (1971). Belief in the law of small numbers. *Psychological Bulletin*, *76*, 105–110. https://doi.org/10.1037/h0031322

Tversky, A., & Kahneman, D. (1973). Availability: A heuristic for judging frequency and probability. *Cognitive Psychology*, *5*, 207–232. https://doi.org/10.1016/0010-0285(73)90033-9

Tversky, A., & Kahneman, D. (1974). Judgment under uncertainty: Heuristics and biases. *Science*, *185*, 1124–1131. https://doi.org/10.1126/science.185.4157.1124

Tversky, A., & Kahneman, D. (1981). The framing of decisions and the psychology of choice. *Science*, *211*, 453–458. http://science.sciencemag.org/content/211/4481/453.abstract

Tversky, A., & Kahneman, D. (1982). Evidential impact of base rates. In D. Kahneman, P. Slovic, & A. Tversky (Eds.), *Judgment under uncertainty: Heuristics and biases* (pp. 153–160). Cambridge University Press.

Tversky, A., & Kahneman, D. (1983). Extensional versus intuitive reasoning: The conjunction fallacy in probability judgment. *Psychological Review*, *90*, 293–315. https://doi.org/10.1037/0033-295X.90.4.293

Tversky, A., Sattath, S., & Slovic, P. (1988). Contingent weighting in judgment and choice. *Psychological Review*, *95*, 371–384. https://doi.org/10.1037/0033-295X.95.3.371

Yamagishi, K. (1997). When a 12.86% mortality is more dangerous than 24.14%: Implications for risk communication. *Applied Cognitive Psychology*, *11*, 495–506. https://doi.org/10.1002/(SICI)1099-0720(199712)11:6<495::AID-ACP481>3.0.CO;2-J

NOTE

1 https://www.gov.uk/government/news/new-tv-advert-urges-public-to-stay-at-home-to-protect-the-nhs-and-save-lives.

THE POWER OF SOCIAL, EMOTIONAL, AND PERSONALITY FACTORS

This chapter further explores the psychological foundations of behavioral economics that help us understand why human behavior often deviates from neoclassical assumptions. The discussion focuses on three related areas. First, we examine social psychological findings about the influence of other people's behavior on our own (e.g., through social norms). Contrary to neoclassical assumptions, we tend to cooperate with others and show altruism in daily life and in economic games played in the labs of behavioral economists. Indeed, we seem to derive personal utility from helping other. Second, we look at judgment and decision making in an evolutionary context by discussing the behavior of monkeys, which is often not that different from our own – fascinating findings suggest that human judgment and decision making are rooted in our evolutionary past. Third, we consider the influence of situation-specific emotions, affect, mood, and physiological states (e.g., hunger) on human behavior. As successful financial traders attest, such 'gut feelings' convey important information about the world. In addition to discussing these transitory *states*, we consider longer-term propensities in the form of personality *traits* (e.g., agreeableness) that shape our preferences and drive our behavior.

DOI: 10.4324/9781003166900-5

INTRODUCTION

We are far from ideal *homo economicus* (ECON): we *misbehave*. In this chapter, we explore the bases of such misbehavior in terms of fundamental principles and findings from psychology. Three related areas are discussed – they are fascinating in their own right and, more importantly, necessary to gain a deeper understanding of the foundations of behavioral economics: (1) social psychological findings, (2) evolutionary pressures, and (3) states (e.g., mood) and traits (e.g., personality).

Before we start, we need to know that rational decision making was typically seen as a *cognitive* process, which is reflected in behavioral economics' initial emphasis on various cognitive heuristics and biases. Only later did noncognitive psychological factors start to play a significant role. For example, the *Irrational Exuberance* in stock market bubbles, which is described in Nobel Prize winner Robert Shiller's book of the same name, is anything but purely cognitive. Another economist, Robert Frank, also highlights the role played by noncognitive factors in his book, *Passions within Reason. The Strategic Role of the Emotions* (1988).

The first area concerns social psychological findings. They reveal that we are influenced by other people and the social waters in which we swim (see text box). Especially, we have a strong tendency to conform to prevailing and fluctuating social norms and expectations. Often, though, we are simply unaware of their influence, even of their existence. None of this is especially newsworthy. Over 200 years ago, Adam Smith famously reminded us of our desire to establish harmonious social relationships, fit in society, and behave in order to please the 'impartial spectator' (see Chapter 2). Again, we see that economics is not all about money; indeed, so often, it is not about money at all.

WHAT'S WATER?

Behavioral economists are fond of telling a joke to illustrate the point that we are influenced by environmental factors of which we are often unaware. Two little fishes are passing the time of day and a big fish swims past and says: "How's the water boys"? The two little fishes look at each other puzzled, and one asks what the other is thinking: "What's water"? The social psychological world is the human equivalent of water to fish.

To maintain harmonious social relations, we do not always, or typically, act to maximize our immediate financial self-interest. What is especially interesting is that our social behavior seems to be heavily influenced by considerations of fairness, cooperation, and the 'warm glow' we feel when we help other people – although getting along and cooperating with others may well be a selfish strategy in the longer-run when the economic games we are playing allow for punishment and reciprocity (see below). (We have seen in previous chapters that utility can come in various guises, such that apparently relatively selfless behavior may be an 'impure' form of altruism.)

The second area concerns the truly fascinating literature on the behavior of monkeys. These findings imply that economic judgment and decision making have deep roots in our evolutionary past. We learn that monkeys' economic behavior is remarkably similar to that of humans and so permits further insights into its biological foundations.

The third area concerns transient psychological (and physiological) 'states' (e.g., hunger) that at any moment affect how we think, feel, judge, decide, and behave. These momentarily fluctuating states can even be induced by irrelevant factors (e.g., background music) unrelated to the economic problem at hand. Susceptibility to these transient states is related to (fairly) stable traits, especially those associated with personality. There is now a growing interest in how the heterogeneity (i.e., diversity) seen in various forms of economic behavior is related to systematic and measurable individual differences in personality (e.g., economically cooperative people tend to be those who score higher on the personality factor of Agreeableness, which describes kind and considerate behavior; see below). As far as we can tell, these associations are not washed away by the tides of incentives and situational influences. The literature highlights the fact that we all differ from one another, and these individual differences have important consequences for economic life.

THE SOCIAL WORLD OF ECONOMICS

Central to social psychology is the notion that, without knowing it, we are subject to influences in the environment that shape our behavior at any given moment, and, in addition, they condition us to behave in certain ways in the future. Sometimes, these are deliberate attempts to influence us: for example, subtle changes to the choice architecture (e.g., in the cafeteria environment, the placing of fruit at the entrance to encourage healthier eating; see Chapter 6) or blatant commercial campaigns (e.g., product advertising; see Chapter 7). Typically, social influences are often not obvious and, more often than not, we are unaware even of their existence – we are oblivious to the social waters in which we swim. More generally, we are subject to tacit influence from other people who, without knowing it, transmit social effects. Such 'social influence' refers to changes in attitudes, beliefs, opinions, values, and behavior *as a result of* exposure to other people's attitudes, beliefs, opinions, values, and behavior. Social influences are central to behavioral economics but alien to the neoclassical economic mind, which places greater focus on information content, not social context – and certainly not other people.

As discussed in Chapter 4, it cannot be assumed that our behavior is autonomous in the sense that we first think and *then* act. It is more the case that we often act for reasons that are not obvious to us. This phenomenon is shown by social priming. Though priming research has been subject to controversy in recent years because some of its classic findings could not be successfully replicated in larger studies (more on this later), it is still worth reviewing this concept as it featured prominently in the early behavioral economics literature.

PRIMING

Priming refers to the scientific theory which states that thoughts, emotions, and acts make further thoughts, emotions, and acts more readily accessible. No conscious or cognitively complex deliberation is required here. The basic idea is that brain networks are activated by an initial 'prime' (e.g., a word, 'Bank'), which then sensitizes the semantic system (i.e., the cognitive system that is concerned with the meaning of words), and this induced state of readiness eases the processing of subsequent stimuli (e.g., speed of recognition of the word 'Money').

As an example of priming, experimental studies have apparently shown that young people who have been exposed to words relating to elderly people start to behave in ways typical of them. In one study of this research program, which is most associated with John Bargh, two groups of participants were exposed to different sets of words: (1) one group (i.e., those in the 'experimental condition') to elderly related words ('Florida', 'Bingo', and 'grey'; the study was conducted in the United States); and (2) another group (i.e., those in the 'control condition') to neutral words that were unrelated to being elderly (Bargh et al., 1996). Even though walking slowly was not included as one of these primed words, those in the experimental condition who had been exposed to the elderly related words tended to walk in the same manner as elderly people when they left the test room. In other words, it was claimed, their behavior was primed (i.e., facilitated) by exposure to elderly related words.

Although this specific set of studies and others in social psychology have been difficult to replicate, and Daniel Kahneman has rightly called for the replication of such classic priming studies, he is in no doubt that priming itself exists (for an incident from his private life, see text box). More broadly, as we have stressed elsewhere in this book, empirical studies need to be replicated so we can be sure that the findings are robust and not statistical chance effects. Such scientific rigor is very much in the experimental spirit of behavioral economics.

PRUDENT SELF-INTEREST AND TRUST

In Chapter 2, we saw how the great classical economist, Adam Smith, conceived of the psychological nature of economic agents. In addition to the *prudence* required to look after our own self-interests, he argued that we are regulated by the desire to be acceptable social beings and to be seen by others in this favorable light. This social perspective makes a lot of sense because we can imagine a society in which there were only selfish people. It would not only be brutal but also inefficient and self-defeating to most individuals – and there would be no room for surviving and thriving for cooperative individuals who would be economically exploited and trampled underfoot. In particular, the economic coordination necessary for a complex society would seem highly unlikely to develop.

Modern-day society is, indeed, built on trust and the expectation that others will reciprocate – in fact, there is good evidence that our expectations closely match how people actually behave. Mervyn King, the former Governor of the Bank of England, noted in his 2016 book, *The End of Alchemy, Money, Banking and the Future of the Global*

DAN ARIELY: HONESTY AT WORK

One of the stars of behavioral economics, the psychologist Dan Ariely, has admitted he "undoubtedly made a mistake" in one of his famous studies, which is now known to be based on falsified data. In a 2012 study in which Ariely was a coauthor, it was reported that if a declaration of honesty appeared at the beginning of a form before crucial information had to be submitted, rather than in its usual position at the end, people were less likely to lie (Shu et al., 2012). If valid, this would be very useful – such was the influence of this study, it was used throughout the world by governments and insurance companies on their declaration forms. Three academics examined the data and wrote that the study was faked "beyond any shadow of a doubt" (Simonsohn et al., 2021). Ariely replied, "If I knew that the data was fraudulent, I would have never posted it" (Lee, 2021). The 2012 article has now been retracted. Ariely was forthcoming about his responsibility for the handling of the data in question and he absolved his coauthors of any scientific misconduct.

Follow-up studies by Ariely and colleagues reported that they failed to replicate the original study (Kristal et al., 2020). Worryingly, however, concerns have been expressed about some of Ariely's other published research, and he was removed from his position at MIT because he conducted an electric shock experiment without ethics approval (Danvers, 2021). These incidents have tarnished the reputation of an important behavioral scientist.

Ariely's case highlights the importance of ensuring the integrity of data, especially when it is collected by other researchers, but this might be difficult in the hectic world of an academic superstar who may not have sufficient time to focus on all research details. It also shows that the scientific literature can be cleaned up by open access to original data and replication studies, which in the case of the declaration forms have failed to support the original findings.

Economy, that economic systems work most effectively when trust can be assumed. Yet, lying and cheating in society are commonplace, as shown by Dan Ariely's 2015 film *(Dis)Honesty: The Truth about Lies* – a somewhat ironic title now given Ariely's own brush with controversy (see text box). We would, of course, be naïve to suppose that people do not use deceptive ploys in pursuit of their self-interests – in this regard,

PRIMING: UNDRESSING THE MAID

Kahneman is fond of recalling in his public talks an example of priming from his private life. He recalls being with his late wife – Anne Triesman, who was an accomplished psychologist – and the host of the occasion was a man that she thought was 'sexy'. Kahneman then heard her say: "He undressed the maid himself", which certainly seemed a distinctly odd thing to say. Upon asking her how she could possibly be in possession of this information, she told him she had, in fact, said: "He rarely underestimates himself". The word 'sexy' had primed Kahneman's brain to try to make sense of what his wife had said about this man that she thought was 'sexy'.

consideration needs to be given to *mis*information in the marketplace designed to deceive other economic players. As we see below, with respect to economic games played in the laboratory, there is something of a Tom and Jerry cat-and-mouse game going on as economic agents struggle to gain an advantage while at the same time trying to maintain social trust and harmonious relations. This tension leads to socioeconomic systems that are vulnerable to being undermined, leading to economic inefficiencies resulting from suspicion and the erosion of social trust. A system of law is important to regulate the economic system by ensuring that economic actors fulfill their obligations (e.g., legally binding contracts).

Despite these potential problems, we now know enough from evolutionary psychology to believe that not only are we altruistic to our biological family – which makes good sense in terms of the 'selfish gene' perspective of protecting and propagating our genes (our own and those of close genetic kin) – but we have a form of cooperation called 'reciprocal altruism' (e.g., Trivers, 1971), which boils down to "you scratch my back, and I will scratch yours" (this is probably better called 'reciprocity' to distinguish it clearly from gene-based 'altruism'). Trust is pivotal to this social process, but as we have already seen, it is fragile and conditional.

The thing to bear in mind is that no one is saying that human beings are truly *selfless* – like rationality, this is bounded and circumscribed (e.g., tit for tat; see text box). But, to get a reputation for being a cheat and not keeping one's word would lead to social exclusion and, likely, retribution in some form. *Successful* long-term, prudent self-interest requires consideration of *other people's* prudent self-interest. This demands some form of mutually acceptable social behavior regulated by social mores and enacted by agreed convention – the nod to the driver who lets you out or the person who holds the door open, oils the wheels of the everyday convivial, and ultimately efficient, social, and economic life.

Despite claims that socially agreeable behavior has gone to rack-and-ruin (Bartholomew, 2004), such is our desire for harmonious social relations, we quite spontaneously coordinate our behavior to ensure this happens (e.g., on the London Underground). George Orwell observed much the same thing many years before in *The English People* (1947), where he noted: "An imaginary foreign observer would certainly be struck by our gentleness; by the orderly behaviour of English crowds, the lack of pushing and quarrelling".

It is easy enough to see the benefits of cooperative behavior in the context of repeated social interactions ('repeated games' or 'iterative

TIT FOR TAT: A SUPERIOR EVOLUTIONARY STRATEGY

Derived from evolutionary theorizing and applied to strategic economic encounters, 'tit for tat' is important in game theory – the analysis of conflict and cooperation in which 'players' anticipate the reactions of others – and is relevant to such games as the repeated prisoner's dilemma (see below). Repeated experimental games confirm that this seemingly simple strategy is remarkably successful in optimizing payoffs (what one receives at the end of the game) and limiting losses. It consists of mirroring the other player's behavior: cooperate with your partner and keep doing this until they 'defect' or cheat, at which point withdraw cooperation. A simple but highly effective strategy to maximize cooperation because if the partner knows your intention, then this will encourage them to continue to cooperate and not to defect or cheat. It works in love and war – knowing the reaction of your partner to your infidelity serves to curb straying, and the enemy is less inclined to 'first strike' if they know the consequences are assured – in the Cold War this was MAD ('Mutually Assured Destruction').

ECONOMIC GAMES (GAME THEORY)

One important way to explore economic strategic behavior is in the form of various economic 'games' (e.g., von Neumann & Morgenstern, 1944). These are highly structured strategic interactive games that allow hypotheses to be tested – for example, do people behave in a selfish or cooperative manner? These strategic games can be 'one shot' (i.e., one interaction) or repeated (also called 'iterative'), when game players have the opportunity to sample the behavior of their opponent – usually, these games are adversarial and zero sum: one player's loss is a win for the other player, although cooperative behavior can lead to nonzero sum outcomes, as seen in the public goods game where contributions to the common pot are multiplied and benefit all players.

strategy games' in the language of the experimental economics laboratory; see text box); but, as discussed below, even in 'one-shot' economic games, where there is no repeated interaction and no opportunity for retaliation, people are surprisingly cooperative and trusting – this seems interwoven into their social fabric

EXPERIMENTAL GAME BEHAVIOR

Well, how do these social psychological processes play out in behavioral economics? We can learn much about these processes from experimental game behavior in the laboratory (for a good introduction to game theory written in simple language, see Dixit & Nalebuff, 2008 – most of the economic games presented below are described in Camerer, 1997). Let us start by considering one standard 'game' used in experimental economics: the Public Goods (PG) game.

PUBLIC GOODS AND NON-SELFISH BEHAVIOR

The Public Goods (PG) game is one of the workhorses of experimental economics with considerable implications for behavioral economics. A public good is defined in economics as nonexcludable (i.e., people cannot be denied use of it, for example, streetlights) and nonrivalrous in consumption (i.e., if one person consumes street lighting, this does not diminish access to other people). Many public goods are provided by the government because it is close to impossible for private companies to avoid free riders (i.e., people who benefit from the public good because they cannot be excluded from its consumption but refuse to pay for it). Other examples include national defense, police protection, and lighthouses.

The basic PG game requires players to decide how much of an initial endowment (e.g., money, points, or tokens) they want to give to the common (public) pot – what they do not give they (selfishly) keep for themselves. One important aspect is that contributions are secret: the players do not see how much others give to the common pot when they make their choice. Whatever is contributed to the public pot is then multiplied by a factor (greater than 1 but less than the total number of players). The resulting public goods pot is then divided among all players. This is seen as an important game that is meant to reflect real-life behavior related to such important matters as taxation, charitable donations, and, more generally, contributing to the public good of society. Quite clearly (because of the multiplication factor), the total payoff of the group is maximized when all players contribute all of their endowments. However, when it comes to the individual player, the best strategy is to make a zero contribution: keep all of one's own endowment and hope that all other players will contribute their entire endowments, which are then multiplied.

Such games may seem abstract and artificial, but we can easily find real-world examples to support them. For example, taxation: it is best for society when every member pays the taxes they owe. All members of society benefit from overall higher tax revenues because these are used to fund schools, the police, and many other government services. However, an individual taxpayer can increase their own wealth by cheating on tax obligations while still benefitting from tax-funded government services. Cheating is, therefore, tempting for the individual – especially the *selfish* type as defined by neoclassical economics. Whether people do cheat in these games partly depends on how it is set up.

In the one-shot version of the PG game, in which there is no chance for other players to retaliate and punish the selfish player, there should be no barrier to expressing maximum self-interest. To be clear, in neoclassical terms, the fully rational agent should be selfish and contribute *nothing* – in this one-shot game, their 'free-riding' behavior maximizes their own (financial) utility, and it is only their own utility

NASH EQUILIBRIUM

John Nash was the subject of the highly popular 2001 film, *A Beautiful Mind*. His mathematical formulation of strategic behavior in noncooperative games won him the Nobel Prize in Economic Sciences in 1994. The Nash equilibrium is the cornerstone of theoretic games: it is defined as the best solution in noncooperative games involving two or more players – that is, changing strategy would not lead to a better pay-off for one player while taking into account the best strategies of other players. In other words, the Nash equilibrium is the solution that maximizes each player's utility given the other player's behavior. To violate the Nash equilibrium is to violate the neoclassical definition of rationality – yet, often we do.

that is seen to count. But, and this is the twist, all of the players know that the best strategy for each individual player is to contribute nothing. The *Nash equilibrium* (see text box) of the one-shot game is, therefore, for everyone to keep all their money and, therefore, lose out on the potentially much bigger shared public pot. So, what actually happens in this game? As a violation of the expectation of selfish rationality of *homo economicus*, people generally do not give a zero amount, even in one-shot games. The amount put into the common pot varies from 0 to 100%, depending on the multiplication factor – however, it declines with repeated trials as players start to learn that others are not fully cooperating.

ULTIMATUM AND DICTATOR GAMES

Two other widely used games in experimental economics have much to say about how we judge fairness and inequality.

In the *ultimatum game*, the first player receives an endowment of money and then decides how they want to share it with a second player. This second player, called the 'responder', chooses to accept or reject the offer. The money is *only* given to each player if the responder accepts it; but, if the responder rejects the division, then the money is lost to both players. (This is usually a one-shot game, so we do not have to worry about reciprocity, retaliation, and the like.) Now, the rational thing might be for the responder to accept *any* offer made to them, as something (however little) is better than nothing, surely? But, this is not

INEQUALITY AVERSION

Inequality aversion (also called inequity aversion) is often invoked to account for less than purely selfish behavior (e.g., Fehr & Schmidt, 1999). It is said to be a preference for fairness: a resistance to inequitable outcomes. Importantly, this is not only perceived inequality due to the action of others but also when one has received a special favor: people may feel guilty or unhappy about their privileged position. Inequality aversion is considered vital for efficient social transactions. Such a process enables an environment in which bilateral bargaining can occur. The argument is that without this rejection of perceived injustice, cooperation would not be sustained.

how things typically work out. If too low an offer is made (in studies, this is usually found to be less than 30%), this is likely to be rejected – in this case, the responder is 'burning' their own money to punish the selfish first player – evidence of spiteful behavior (we see below monkeys behave in much the same way). Of course, the first player knows this may happen – after all, they cannot be assumed to be stupid, and one of the basic assumptions of game theory is that a player considers the other player's reaction – so they tend to make a fair offer of something greater than a third and rarely anything greater than a half (some people opt to give 50% in the interest of absolute fairness). As noted above, what people expect of others is pretty much in line with their actual behavior. All of this seems related to our aversion to inequality (see text box).

But what would happen if there were no chance of retaliation by the responder? To address this question, the *dictator game* was developed. In this game, the first player (the 'Dictator') decides how much of an endowment to share with a second player (who is not really a *player* because their role is passive and they have no say in the game: they get what they are given and cannot respond in any way). Surely, in *this* game, the rational, selfish player should give nothing? Although results vary, the fact remains that most people give away *some* of their money – children even tend to share 50/50. This selfless behavior is open to a number of interpretations:

1   Dictators fail to maximize their utility – they behave in a far from rational manner;

2   The utility function of Dictators may include social factors (e.g., negative effects on reputation and social standing);

3   The utility function of Dictators includes the benefits accruing to the second player, from which they derive some selfish utility in terms of 'warm glow'.

In relation to points 2 and 3, we have seen as much in Adam Smith's notion of the 'impartial spectator', which, as we discussed in Chapter 2, is defined in terms of the idealized person we wish to please in our dealings with other people (it is a form of conscience). If point 3 is invalid, and the first player does not care about the utility of the second player, then they may have negative utility (disutility) related to being seen as a selfish and mean person. Indeed, when interpreting such laboratory experiments, a point that is often overlooked is that people *are* watching the game – if nothing else, the experimenter usually knows the decisions of the first player (or may be assumed to have access to this information). In a similar manner to the impartial spectator, people have a sense they may well be observed, and often they are.

However, the first player's generosity varies between different set-ups of the game. For instance, in some variations, the money that is allocated to the second player is placed in an envelope, which is meant to reduce people's tendency to try to please experimenters and choose a socially desirable action (once again, the power of norms). It is less important for us to know *which* explanation is correct than to appreciate the fact that most people, *for whatever reason*, do not conform to the simplistic notion of selfish ('rational') *homo economicus* (ECON).

THE PRISONER'S DILEMMA

Much the same cooperative behavior is found with the famous Prisoner's dilemma (e.g., Poundstone, 1992), which has widescale implications for economics. The classic situation involves two culprits arrested for some crime. They are taken to the police station, isolated from one another, and interrogated separately – it is assumed that the decision of each suspect will not affect how their partner reacts to them in the future (a dubious assumption in real life!). The police know that they have rather weak evidence to secure a conviction at trial on the more serious charge, and they also know that if neither culprit spills the beans, they will have to charge them with a lesser offense. The police need one of the culprits to crack, confess all, and to 'rat out' their partner in crime. Now, if both culprits refuse to blame each other, then they can expect to serve only one year in prison as they will be convicted of the lesser crime. The police offer them a deal: if they 'defect' and rat out their partner who does not confess, they are set free and their partner serves three years in prison. However, if both confess, they will both receive two years in prison. All possible combinations of actions by each player and corresponding outcomes can be displayed in a 'payoff matrix'.

The payoff below is defined in terms of the length of a prison sentence (shown as a negative sign). The terms 'cooperate' and 'defect' refer to the suspects cooperating with each other (i.e., if neither of them confesses) or defecting (i.e., not cooperating with the other player/confessing). The first value in each cell of the matrix shows the prison sentence that Suspect A might receive, and the second value denotes Suspect B's potential sentence.

		Suspect B	
		Cooperate	Defect
Suspect A	Cooperate	(a)−1,−1	(c)−3, 0
	Defect	(b)0,−3	(d)−2,−2

The strategy that yields the best payoff for a player *regardless* of which strategy the other player chooses is called the 'dominant strategy'. In this example, it is for each player to defect (i.e., confess) as confessing results in the shortest sentence regardless of whether their partner cooperates or defects. Here are the possible outcomes:

- If A and B cooperate and do not confess, both get a 1-year prison sentence (a).
- If A confesses but B does not, A goes free and B receives a 3-year prison sentence (b).
- If A does not confess but B confesses, A will be sentenced to a 3-year prison sentence and B is released (c).
- If A and B both confess, both get a 2-year prison sentence (d).

If both partners could communicate, they would surely decide to both remain silent, which is the socially optimal solution here – however, they would still have the dilemma of whether their partner would keep their word. (This would seem the game theoretic basis for the Omerta code of silence among crime families – and why sometimes it falls short.) In any event, they have been isolated and, therefore, must guess what their partner's decision will be. Each player's best strategy in the Prisoner's dilemma requires little thought: defect. To understand this reasoning, think about what strategy suspect A should follow if they know suspect B will remain silent. In this case, they should confess, which would set them free and result in a 3-year prison sentence for their partner. How about if suspect A knows for sure that suspect B has decided to confess? In that case they should also confess because this would yield 2 years in prison instead of 3. Thus, in both scenarios, the best strategy is to confess (e.g., defect). This is, therefore, player 1's (suspect A) *dominant strategy*, and the same holds for player 2 (suspect B). As both players have the same payoffs, the Nash equilibrium is that both should defect. However, findings from the experimental economics laboratory show that people often decide to cooperate: that is, they do not adhere to the selfish Nash Equilibrium – perhaps more evidence of neoclassical *misbehavior*. When thinking about such issues, what is of most relevance is the extent to which social factors override self-interest when there is a big incentive to behave in accordance with neoclassical assumptions.

We may well cooperate when there is little money 'on the table' (e.g., $10), but what about when there is $100,000 at stake? We cannot really know as, for reasons too obvious to state, no experiments of this type have been conducted. However, there have been some experiments carried out in developing countries where (not very rich) players receive fairly substantial payoffs (cheap for researchers, but a lot of money for them) – this can range from a pay equivalent of a laborer's wages for two days (commonly used) to several times their monthly expenditure. These studies are often cited to show that the amount does not matter (for example, the amount offered by proposers in ultimatum games in Indonesia does not seem to depend on the money at stake; Cameron, 1999).

The game theory examples above show that in social situations, people often do not choose the strategy that would likely maximize their (neoclassically defined) utility. Instead, they remain silent in prisoner dilemma games, share money in dictator games, and contribute to the common pot in one-shot public goods games. What all of these economic games have in common is that the players need to consider the likely behavior of the other player(s). Players who remain silent in prisoner dilemma games seem to *trust* that the other player will do the same. Those who share their money in dictator games seem to care more about fairness than maximizing their monetary payoffs. They all appear to conform to social norms of trust, fairness, and reciprocity.

One criticism of such laboratory-based experimental games, and therefore their implications for understanding economic motivation, is that they do not take adequate account of the social dynamics in the real world, where the human brain-mind has developed over the millennia. In particular, humans have evolved adaptive strategies to get through life in their own and their genetic kin's best interests, and this surely does not include making enemies who could exact revenge – limiting any further utility, economic or otherwise. Maybe these evolved dispositions cannot be overridden by a pure experiment in a socially-sterile laboratory. In any event, what such experimental results show is that, irrespective of the reason, economic agents do not conform to a simple-minded version of *homo economicus*.

SOCIAL NORMS

Perhaps the most pervasive social influence on our behavior comes in the form of social norms – those everyday unwritten rules that guide our behavior, usually without us even knowing. Part of the appeal of the 1719 novel by Daniel Defoe, *Robinson Crusoe*, is the idea of being alone on an island, cut off from the rest of the world and having to rely upon one's own resources. This is very unlike everyday life where we look to others for guidance as to how we *should* behave. There is now a vast literature on 'norms' in social psychology which attests to the fact that we are heavily influenced by what we think *other people expect of us*.

Social norms are the accepted rules of behavior. They lead to *compliance, obedience,* and, once they become internalized, *conversion.* They are usually communicated and received implicitly, that is, without the need for conscious deliberation. Indeed, most of the time, we are not even aware of their existence – at least not until we violate them and, then, in short measure receive corrective feedback (e.g., just try jumping the queue at a train station to experience this social psychological process in action!). A common form of punishment for a rule violation, and a very effective one for most people, is social exclusion – in common English parlance, being "sent to Coventry" (a little unfair on this fine city). Research shows that exclusion and 'social pain' share much in common with physical pain (e.g., MacDonald & Leary, 2005).

Learning social rules does not need an instructor – we learn largely by vicarious means: observing the behavior of others, seeing the results, and emulating. Norms tend to be socially contagious and positive reinforcement (i.e., being rewarded) for norm-following behavior strengthens them. Negative reinforcement (i.e., being punished, or not being rewarded, for not following them) also serves this strengthening function. Norms can establish bad behavior (e.g., littering) as well as good behavior (e.g., recycling). None of this has to be explicit or obvious, and it need not even entail providing people with 'information'. Much more effective are *examples* (i.e., demonstrations) of good norm-following behavior which many people repeat in an automatic manner – "it's the way things are done around here"! After a time, such behavior becomes habitual and automatic, and it is seen as the 'right' way to behave. Such *descriptive* norms are typically more influential than *injunctive* norms, which consist of telling people how they *should* behave.

In all areas of life, social norms serve a number of useful social functions.

- They help to reduce uncertainty about how to behave appropriately – just follow the example set by other people!
- They help to coordinate the behavior of individuals, which reduces 'cooperation losses' for other group members (e.g., the cost of the lack of punctuality).
- They constrain an individual's impulsive responses.
- They reduce cognitive and emotional 'load' (that is, placing a processing burden on the system, which consumes processing resources and requires effort control).
- They facilitate group cohesion.
- They reduce uncertainty in ambiguous situations.

In other words, social norms promote social, and by inference, economic efficiency.

The influence of social norms is especially powerful in the context of ambiguous stimuli. This is shown by the remarkable 'autokinetic

AUTOKINETIC EFFECT

Imagine you are seated in a dark room and there is a spot of light on the wall facing you. Also, imagine you are asked to estimate how much the light is moving about – the 'autokinetic effect' is the *apparent* movement of a stationary light (it seems to move because there are no visual reference points in the environment). If you do this estimation task alone, you form your own 'personal norm' around which there would be some variation. This will differ from other people's personal norms. But, if you were to do this estimation task with other people, then what happens is that a 'social norm' is established: group members converge on an average (e.g., Sherif, 1935). What is now remarkable is that when you, once again, undertake the task alone, you use this social norm and do not develop your own personal norm. This is a simple, elegant, and powerful demonstration of how we come to personalize social norms. If this happens with simple physical stimuli, just imagine what happens with complex social ones!

effect' (see text box); however, we should not assume that they work only in such contrived and artificial situations. They are likely to be influential wherever and whenever the content or the information presented is complex or ambiguous, or, indeed, when the effort to process such information is deemed too much and following the crowd is the much easier route.

MONKEYS: THE EVOLUTION OF SOCIAL BEHAVIOR

The persistence of social norms long after the reasons for why they were established in the first place is shown by a monkey experiment (see text box). This is only one example of many which attest to the fact that monkeys behave in a similar manner to homo sapiens in their economic behavior. This finding suggests that the cognitive, affective, and behavioral phenomena that occupy behavioral economics may not be unique to human beings.

In 2003, Sarah Brosnan and Frans de Waal showed that capuchin monkeys rebel if they see another monkey getting a reward that they consider to be more valuable – the same is found with dogs and birds. (Capuchin monkeys diverged from the homo sapiens line some

FIVE MONKEYS EXPERIMENT: SOCIAL NORMS

This is a well-known account of an experiment, although it seems never to have taken place (Maestripieri, 2012). It is still instructive as an amusing story of how social norms get transmitted. It is also a rather good example of how information in the form of such a story is appealing and people are willing to pass it on – this is an example of a 'meme' which refers to the social transmission of information which is facilitated when it is framed in a certain way (another example is 'rhyme as reason'; see Glossary).

Here is the story. Five monkeys are placed in a large cage. High up at the top of the cage is a bunch of bananas that the monkeys love to eat, but they are beyond their reach. However, help is at hand in the form of a ladder. Being smart, the monkeys work out that they can climb the ladder to get the bananas. But as one monkey climbs the ladder, the experimenter sprays him with a stream of cold water, and then he sprays each of the other monkeys – this they find very unpleasant. All five wet, cold monkeys wait until the temptation is too great. Another monkey tries their luck and is promptly punished with another spray of cold water. The monkeys have now learned that the consequences of trying to reach the bananas are dire and they prevent a third monkey from trying to climb the ladder in order to avoid getting the cold spray. Now here is the twist: one monkey is removed and a new monkey is introduced into the cage who immediately begins to climb the ladder. He is pulled off by the other monkeys. Then, the experimenter replaces another of the original monkeys with a new monkey who does not know about the cold water. The other monkeys pull him off when this new monkey attempts to reach the bananas. Surprisingly, the other new monkey who arrived just before him, *and has never been sprayed,* participates! After a short while, the social norm is not to climb the ladder to the bananas, but none of the newly introduced monkeys has a clue why – if they could talk, they might say: "it's just the way things work around here!".

35 million years ago, and although they share many human cognitive strategies, they were isolated in terms of linguistic, cultural, and technological systems, which are sometimes thought to distort human judgment and decision making.) Monkeys were trained to trade pebbles for slices of cucumber, which they found to be an acceptable

reward. But, when they saw another monkey getting paid with much more desirable grapes, they got agitated, threw the pebbles, and eventually refused to work. *Very* human-like!

What such experiments seem to show is that monkeys and people are less concerned with *absolute* levels of wages, standard of living, and so on, but with their *relative* social standing. We see this clearly in the case of humans. This is elegantly shown by a study on *positional standing* in which Solnick and Hemenway (1998) asked people which of two worlds they preferred.

World A:

Your current yearly income is $50,000; others earn $25,000.

World B:

Your current yearly income is $100,000; others earn $200,000.

(It is assumed that prices and thus the purchasing power of money are the same in the two world states.)

The finding is that approximately 50% of the respondents prefer World A, in which their real, absolute income is lower than in World B, but their *relative* income position is high. Although respondents can only purchase half of the goods and services in World A that they could purchase in World B (prices are the same in both worlds), what appears to be of greater importance is that they can purchase more than their neighbors. Their positional standing seems to matter a lot to them. However, we do not know whether they would make the same choice if this were a real situation; yet, the assumption is that the same outcome would be found. Now, in neoclassical terms, this quite clearly does not make sense: in absolute terms, more of something is always better than less, irrespective of what other people are getting (see Chapter 3), *assuming all else is equal*. But, in social psychological terms, this only rarely is the case.

Something similar was found in related research work by Frans de Waal, who showed that capuchin monkeys refuse to 'work' if they feel they are getting an unequal share of the reward (described in Fisher, 2006). The ingenious experimental set-up involved a heavy tray that needed two monkeys to pull. This tray contained food that was available only to one monkey, called the 'CEO'. The CEO decided how much food to push through a mesh to the 'worker'. Typically, the CEO kept about five times as much food as the worker; but, if they kept any more than that the worker would go on strike and refuse to help, leaving both monkeys hungry. This monkey behavior is very similar to the 'money burning' (spiteful behavior) that is often seen in economic games in the laboratory (see above).

In another study concerned with 'monkeynomics' (you can find an interesting TED talk on the topic by Laurie Santos online, 2010), capuchin monkeys were trained to use shiny metal disks in a similar manner to how we use money. (In passing, it is interesting to note that gold and silver were the shiny metals that long served the function of money in human society – this is well discussed in Adam Smith's 1776 *The Wealth of Nations*.) Similar to human beings, capuchin monkeys responded to price changes by changing their patterns of consumption. They also quickly learned that tokens could be used in exchange for sex – one of the first demonstrations of prostitution in the nonhuman animal world (maybe it is the oldest profession!).

In Chapters 3 and 4, we saw how we tend to be risk averse and often prefer a sure gamble over a riskier outcome with a higher expected utility. Monkeys behave likewise. In addition, studies of horse race gamblers and day traders show that when we are in the 'domain of loss' we tend to prefer greater risk (see text box), and so do monkeys. Like humans, monkeys also display signs of money illusion, loss aversion, and the endowment effect, and they are also reference dependent resulting from the framing of problems as entailing loss or gain, as discussed in Chapter 4.

TRANSIENT STATES AND PERSONALITY TRAITS

Situational factors are well known to influence transient psychological states and behavior. Psychologists have confirmed this in the laboratory and we know this from our own everyday life: some things can delight or disturb us, and these feelings can permeate everything we think, feel, and do. We might even 'get out of the wrong side of the bed' and be in a bad mood for the rest of the day. A rather good example of how physiological states can affect preferences is revealed by hungry office workers (see text box).

EMOTIONS

Emotional associations can powerfully shape our judgments, decisions, and behavior. This fact has long been apparent to economists, for example, John Maynard Keynes who stated in his highly influential

HUNGER AND PREFERENCE: APPLES AND CHOCOLATES

An interesting and informative experiment was conducted by Read and van Leeuwen (1998). Office workers were approached either just after lunch (when they were not hungry) or in the late afternoon (when they were). They were offered a choice of snacks that would be delivered at a fixed time (just after lunch or in the late afternoon) *a week later*. Some of these snacks were 'healthy' (e.g., apples), others 'unhealthy' (e.g., candy bar). We need to note that when the offer is *now*, most people would prefer fruit immediately after lunch but chocolate later in the afternoon. The results showed that irrespective of the *delivery time*, individuals were more likely to choose unhealthy snacks if the choice was made in the late afternoon. The difference in choice has a psychological cause: people are hungrier in the late afternoon and thoughts about the hunger-satisfying properties of food are, therefore, more salient to them, even though they would not be in this state immediately after lunch when their choice would be delivered.

1936 *General Theory* book that financial markets are moved by 'animal spirits'. More recently, one of the world's most successful investors, Warren Buffett, warns us: "If you cannot control your emotions, you cannot control your money".

Emotion (to a specific stimulus) and mood (nonspecific positive–negative feelings) influence decision making – for example, by changing the computation of perceived gains and losses. We are influenced by ambient affect (e.g., financial trading with background music) as well as instrumental affect (perceived feelings of good and bad outcomes of financial trading). Emotions are automatic and difficult to control – often, the real source is not known, but post-hoc inferences are drawn and emotions 'labeled' for social and personal meaning (reference points and frames are influential in this context, too; see Chapter 4).

To appreciate these subjective feelings, consider the 'gut feelings' of financial traders. This is a feeling – more akin to an intuition – that seems to convey information about the market. Famously, George Soros said that he uses a combination of rationality and gut feelings to guide his decisions. In his 1995 book, *Soros on Soros: Staying Ahead of the Curve*, he wrote:

> I rely a great deal on animal instincts. When I was actively running the fund, I suffered from backache. I used the onset of acute pain as a signal that there was something wrong in my portfolio. The backache didn't tell me what was wrong – you know, lower back for short positions, left shoulder for currencies – but it did prompt me to look for something amiss when I might not have done so otherwise.

Soros's strategy stands in contrast to the usual advice given to traders, namely, that they should stick to a proven method and stay disciplined – they are usually advised to ignore gut feeling and base their decisions on the analysis of market information. But their intuition need not be anything magical. Many traders have such a sense. It reflects their years of accumulated knowledge and experience. One way of looking at the brain-mind is to view it as a highly sophisticated pattern recognition machine. With sufficient time and attention, regularities are observed and (apparent) causal relations deduced. All of this occurs at an automatic level – in psychology, this is often called 'procedural learning' and it has been extensively studied. What we are left with is a 'feeling' that something is right or wrong, but it is very hard to put into words: this is the body's way of communicating to the mind that a definite action is required.

What mood, affect, and emotion do is to create widespread activation, which biases thinking and behaviors in the direction of defensive reactions (e.g., fight, flight, freeze) or approach (exploratory curiosity and reward-seeking) – the twin levers of the market: fear and greed. This perspective is very much in accordance with Daniel Kahneman's (2011) view: "… rewards and punishments, promises and threats, are all in our heads. We carefully keep score of them. They shape our preferences and motivate our action …".

'Gut feeling' may have a more literal meaning. Kandasamy and colleagues (2016) found that successful financial traders were better than a sample of the general population at 'reading' their own bodily (interoceptive) sensations – furthermore, the better this ability, the better their trading decisions. The sample comprised 18 male traders who engaged in high-frequency trading (buying and selling futures contracts and holding them only for seconds to hours). Traders were assessed on their ability to detect their own heartbeat – the control group (in this case, the comparison group) were students. The ability to perform this task was also related to the number of years the traders had survived in the profession.

What is going on is difficult to discern. It could be that people who are more sensitive to their own physical processes are also more sensitive to the external world and, thus, they learn more – they are more 'attuned' in some sense or, less abstractly, superior at implicit, procedural learning. Other explanations are possible, too. Successful traders may be more stressed, and thus, their heartbeats are more obvious to them. Or successful traders keep themselves fit (e.g., go to the gym regularly) and this makes them more sensitive to their bodily processes. Irrespective of the reason, sensitivity to bodily states is related to financial trading success – a finding that lends credence to the notion that gut feelings may be important after all.

As already discussed in Chapter 4, Damasio argues that emotions can be viewed as sources of information, especially if they are based on a lifetime of experiences that have been quietly but surely acquired by automatic, procedural means (see Damasio et al., 1991). Other theorists give affect a direct role in motivating behavior, implying that we integrate positive and negative feelings according to some sort of automatic, rapid 'affective algebra', whose operations and rules remain to be discovered. If the activated feelings are pleasant, they motivate actions and thoughts anticipated to reproduce these feelings. If the feelings are unpleasant, they motivate actions and thoughts anticipated to avoid them. In pointing to the limitations of a purely cognitive account of behavior, a long time ago, Guthrie (1952) aptly noted that we must be careful not to leave the organism at the choice point 'lost in thought' – emotions provoke action and, therefore, are functional and often adaptive especially if likened to analytical cognition.

Emotion may also be involved in how effective financial incentives might be – ironically increasing the effectiveness of mainstream incentives. Although we now know that loss aversion is more effective than a gain of the same value, given certain circumstances, financial incentives can be shown to be effective. Consider the study by Berlin et al. (2021), which concluded: "Financial incentives to reward smoking abstinence compared with no financial incentives were associated with an increased abstinence rate in pregnant smokers" (p. 1). Although we should not have too high hopes that such financial incentives would be effective in the general population, among women who are clearly motivated to want the best for their unborn baby, such a mainstream economic approach may work, albeit with psychological enabling factors.

EMPATHY GAP

There is something else about experienced emotional states that bias our thinking about the present and future. We have seen elsewhere in this book that the classical economist, Adam Smith, placed great emphasis on the notion that we regulate our social behavior because we 'sympathize' (i.e., empathize) with other people. There is a literature on empathy and its gaps which tells us something important. The 'hot-cold empathy gap' is a cognitive bias that reflects the fact that people underestimate the influences of visceral experiences on their behaviors and preferences. This idea, made popular by George Loewenstein (e.g., Loewenstein, 2000; Loewenstein & Schkade, 1999), states that when we are in some state (e.g., happy), we find it difficult to appreciate what it is like to be in the opposite state (i.e., miserable). This affects how we behave in relation to other people: we often cannot empathize sufficiently with them (e.g., we may be insensitive to their feelings). It also influences how we see our present and future selves. Being in one state *now* makes it hard for us to appreciate how we could be in another *future* state. Indeed, we tend to underestimate the impact of being in another state to the one we are in now.

For example, in one of many studies that examine the empathy gap, young men in an unaroused 'cold state' could not predict accurately that in a 'hot state' of sexual arousal they would be more prone to risky sexual behavior (Loewenstein et al., 1997). Such findings mean that when we process information about the future, we may be systematically biased by the state in which we *happen* to be in – for example, smoking that cigarette which is giving us pleasure *now* overshadows the displeasure it may bring in the future.

PERSONALITY

Personality represents our characteristic ways of thinking, feeling, and behaving across situations and over time – another way of viewing personality is to say it is the distribution of our psychological states, with the mean representing 'typical' (i.e., trait) values. One very popular descriptive model of personality is the 'Big-5' (McCrae & John, 1992: see text box).

There is an interplay between situational and personality factors. This means that the way we react to a situation depends on our personality. For example, given the *same* situation, people show different behaviors. The reason for this is that genes and physiology are important to how the brain-mind works – and there are individual differences in its workings. We should assume that all social influences go through the brain for them to exert any influence. Differences in brain function, therefore, give rise to individual differences in personality, intelligence, and the like, and determine how we respond to external events (e.g., economic incentives).

Crucial here is the claim that these individual differences in brain (and, therefore, mind) functioning affect the perception and analysis of the 'environment' – more formally, the 'environment' is *constructed* in the brain-mind. As the famous psychologist Hans Eysenck said in 1998: "Our environment is *structured* by ourselves, on the basis of genetic drives". As an example of this fact, some of us see the world, as it were, through rose-tinted glasses, while other peoples' hue is distinctly blue.

In relation to the one-shot prisoner's dilemma, Pothos and colleagues (2011) found that high reward-responsiveness (i.e., a personality factor relating to sensitivity to reward; the goal of the trait is to maximize rewards) individuals are more likely to defect in a prisoner's dilemma game when the optimal strategy is to do so. In contrast, high agreeableness individuals are more likely to cooperate in situations in which the optimal strategy calls for it (high agreeableness is associated with cooperation). In both cases, the behavior is consistent with the goal of each trait.

We see the role played by personality factors in studies of health-related Covid-19 behaviors – along with other behavioral factors, this is summarized in Caki et al. (2021). For example, Bacon et al. (2022) reported the following. Neuroticism (i.e., emotional instability) is associated with poorer mental health. Extraversion is associated with a reluctance to socially isolate. Conscientiousness predicts compliance with safety guidelines. Honesty-humility is associated with prosocial views and abstention from panic buying. (For further Covid-19 personality research, see Bacon & Corr, 2020a, 2020b.)

BIG-5 PERSONALITY

At the most general level of description, there are at least five factors of personality:

Extraversion (E): outgoing/energetic vs. solitary/reserved
Neuroticism (N): sensitive/nervous vs. secure/confident
Openness (O) – sometimes 'intellect': inventive/curious vs. consistent/cautious
Conscientiousness (C): efficient/organized vs. easy-going/careless
Agreeableness (A): friendly/compassionate vs. cold/unkind

These factors are derived from complex statistical analysis of the correlations found between personality-relevant words (e.g., warm, hostile, friendly, diligent, and creative). Although the Big-5 model is not without its criticisms, it is widely used in research across the whole of psychology – more recently, a factor of Honesty-Humility, has been added, which is independent of the above five factors.

More widely, personality can influence even the actions of experts. For example, Sir Professor David Spiegelhalter, none other than the head of the Winton Centre for Risk of Evidence Communication at Cambridge University, admitted that during the early stages of Covid-19, he "didn't take it seriously enough", adding he was "overly optimistic" "and that's why I'm glad I'm not a government adviser" due to his "naturally optimistic personality", as quoted by Sky News, on 7 February 2022 (Mehta, 2022). This is notable because, as the Winton Centre website says of Sir David, "He works to improve the way in which risk and statistical evidence are taught and discussed in society". Given his candid reflections, other features of Sir David's personality are, admirably, self-awareness and honesty.

PERSONALITY AND EMPLOYMENT

On a larger economic scale, there is emerging evidence that personality is important, too. For example, Daly and colleagues (2015) suggested that "the capacity for self-control may underlie successful labor-force entry and job retention, particularly in times of economic uncertainty". Taking into account intelligence, social class, and gender, they found that a low-level capacity for self-control in childhood is related to unemployment across 40 years. (The issue of self-control in economics has fascinated Thaler, who in his 2015 *Misbehaving* book elaborates on this theme – to be a good neoclassical agent, a high level of self-control is most certainly vital.) Similarly, higher levels of conscientiousness (being efficient/organized), as measured at age 16–17, predicted levels of later-life employment in another study (Egan et al., 2017).

Maybe people do, after all, optimize the allocation of their scarce resources to maximize their own utility, as assumed by neoclassical economics. However, their economic preferences (i.e., what supposedly brings them the highest utility) may well depend on personality factors. This means that people may differ markedly in the ordering of their preferences and, therefore, a one-size-fits-all economic model is inadequate. It may also mean that, depending on personality-related preferences, different people may have very different reactions to incentives, information, context, and so on. Therefore, this may work at the micro level of social interactions (e.g., in experimental games), as well as at the macro level, for example, how people react to the incentive structures of employment and state-provisioned social welfare.

Although much more work is needed to explore the extent of personality influences on economic behavior, leading economists are starting to incorporate personality processes in their formal economic models. Many psychologically inclined economists would now agree with Becker and colleagues' (2012) statement (here, heterogeneity refers to diversity/variety):

> What is needed is the development of a comprehensive framework that combines insights from the approaches taken by economists and psychologists to capture sources of heterogeneity in behavior.

We can now see how emotions, personality, and the like influence our judgments and decisions, and they can also cloud our perception of our own behavior. This is shown in one of the earliest examples from the Ancient World. In one version of Aesop's, *The Fable of the Fox and the Grapes*, driven by hunger, a fox tries to reach some grapes, but they are hanging high on the vine and out of his reach. Having failed to reach them, he declares "*Oh, you aren't even ripe yet! I don't need any sour grapes*". This story is used to characterize people who talk

---

COGNITIVE DISSONANCE

Festinger (1957) discovered that people change their attitudes/beliefs to be consistent with behaviors they have performed, even ones they initially disliked (e.g., working on a highly boring task). Performance on such a disliked task induces conflict ('dissonance'), which is an aversive state which people will work to escape – they can do this by coming to believe that the task was, in fact, interesting. Of importance, this change in attitude is not induced when people are highly financially incentivized, showing that such incentives can lead to extrinsic, not intrinsic, motivation. The psychological notion is that people want to maintain consistent attitudes/beliefs and behavior, and they are motivated to eliminate cognitive dissonance, however induced. (There are excellent resources available on the internet.)

---

disparagingly of things they cannot attain themselves, but the main point for us is that the fox engages in face-saving defensive behavior, which has little to do with the fact that he wanted the grapes in the first place. His expressed preference is now the *consequence* of his (failed) action! This is an example of the social psychological literature on cognitive dissonance (see text box).

CONCLUSIONS

Social factors in economic behavior were at the forefront of Adam Smith's seminal thinking at the time he inaugurated what was to become known as classical economics. Subsequent research has done nothing to dampen the relevance of these factors, and much of behavioral economics confirms them. It is especially newsworthy that people have a definite propensity to be cooperative and, typically, they do not behave in an entirely selfish manner, even when it seems to be in their best interests to do so (e.g., in the Dictator game, where the second player is powerless). However, these forms of selfless behavior may be impure in the sense that they serve the longer-term interests of the economic player – especially in situations when there is the opportunity for punishing defectors (as is, indeed, the case in many real-world contexts). Nevertheless, we seem to derive personal utility from helping others: we have a social preference based in *inequality aversion*. Indeed, such is this tendency, we are willing to punish, sometimes by burning our own reward (as seen in the Ultimatum game), those who violate unwritten rules of socially acceptable conduct – we expect others to play fair. We have seen that such behaviors may have evolutionary roots as monkeys display some of the same behavioral economic propensities as humans. In all of this, we need to take into account situation-specific emotions, affect, and mood, as well as longer-term propensities as expressed in personality factors (e.g., agreeableness). Once again, behavior is influenced by many factors other than information and (dis)incentives, as assumed by neoclassical economics.

FURTHER READING

Dixit, A. K. & Nalebuff, B. J. (2008). *The art of strategy: A game theorist's guide to success in business and life.* W.W. Norton & Company.

Frank, R. H. (1985). *Choosing the right pond: Human behavior and the quest for status.* Oxford University Press.

Hewstone, M., Stroebe, W., & Jonas, K. (2015). *An introduction to social psychology.* BPS Blackwell.

REFERENCES

Bacon, A. M., & Corr, P. J. (2020a). Coronavirus (COVID-19) in the United Kingdom: A personality-based perspective on concerns and intention to self-isolate. *British Journal of Health Psychology, 25,* 839–848. https://doi.org/10.1111/BJHP.12423

Bacon, A. M., & Corr, P. J. (2020b). Behavioral Immune System responses to coronavirus: A Reinforcement Sensitivity Theory explanation of conformity, warmth toward others and attitudes toward lockdown. *Frontiers in Psychology, 11,* 566237. https://doi.org/10.3389/FPSYG.2020.566237/BIBTEX

Bacon, A. M., Krupić, D., Caki, N., & Corr, P. J. (2022). Emotional and behavioral responses to COVID-19: Explanations from three key models of personality. *European Psychologist, 26,* 334–347. https://doi.org/10.1027/1016-9040/A000461

Bargh, J. A., Chen, M., & Burrows, L. (1996). Automaticity of social behavior: Direct effects of trait construct and stereotype-activation on action. *Journal of Personality and Social Psychology, 71,* 230–244. https://doi.org/10.1037//0022-3514.71.2.230

Bartholomew, J. (2004). *The welfare state we're in.* Biteback Publishing.

Becker, A., Deckers, T., Dohmen, T., Falk, A., & Kosse, F. (2012). The relationship between economic preferences and psychological personality measures. *Annual Review of Economics, 4,* 453–478. https://doi.org/10.1146/annurev-economics-080511-110922

Berlin, I., Berlin, N., Malecot, M., Breton, M., Jusot, F., & Goldzahl, L. (2021). Financial incentives for smoking cessation in pregnancy: Multicentre randomised controlled trial. *BMJ, 375,* e065217. https://doi.org/10.1136/BMJ-2021-065217

Brosnan, S. F., & de Waal, F. B. M. (2003). Monkeys reject unequal pay. *Nature, 425,* 297–299. https://doi.org/10.1038/nature01963

Caki, N., Krupic, D., & Corr, P. J. (2021). Psychosocial effects of the Covid-19 pandemic. In V. Bozkurt, G. Dawes, H. Gülerce, & P. Westenbroek (Eds.), *The societal impacts of Covid-19: A transnational perspective* (pp. 63–78). Istanbul University Press.

Camerer, C. F. (1997). Progress in behavioral game theory. *The Journal of Economic Perspectives, 11,* 167–188. https://doi.org/10.1257/jep.11.4.167

Cameron, L. A. (1999). Raising the stakes in the ultimatum game: Experimental evidence from Indonesia. *Economic Inquiry, 37,* 47–59. https://doi.org/10.1111/j.1465-7295.1999.tb01415.x

Daly, M., Delaney, L., Egan, M., & Baumeister, R. F. (2015). Childhood self-control and unemployment throughout the life span. *Psychological Science, 26,* 709–723. https://doi.org/10.1177/0956797615569001

Damasio, A. R., Tranel, D., & Damasio, H. (1991). Somatic markers and the guidance of behaviour: Theory and preliminary testing. In H. S. Levin, H. M. Eisenberg, & A. L. Benton (Eds.), *Frontal lobe function and dysfunction* (pp. 217–229). Oxford University Press.

Danvers, A. (2021). *Is this psychology's most ironic research fraud? Did social science best-seller Dan Ariely fake data on honesty?* Psychology Today. https://www.psychologytoday.com/gb/blog/how-do-you-know/202108/is-psychologys-most-ironic-research-fraud

Defoe, D. (1719). *Robinson Crusoe.* W. Taylor.

Dixit, A. K., & Nalebuff, B. J. (2008). *The art of strategy: A game theorist's guide to success in business and life.* W. W. Norton & Company.

Egan, M., Daly, M., Delaney, L., Boyce, C. J., & Wood, A. M. (2017). Adolescent conscientiousness predicts lower lifetime unemployment. *Journal of Applied Psychology, 102,* 700–709. https://doi.org/10.1037/apl0000167

Eysenck, H. J. (1998). *Intelligence: A new look.* Transaction Publishers.

Fehr, E., & Schmidt, K. (1999). A theory of fairness, competition and cooperation. *Quarterly Journal of Economics, 114,* 817–868. https://doi.org/10.1162/003355399556151

Festinger, L. (1957). *A theory of cognitive dissonance.* Stanford University Press.

Fisher, D. (2006). Primate economics. *Forbes.* https://www.forbes.com/2006/02/11/monkey-economics-money_cz_df_money06_0214monkeys.html#636c38313a63

Frank, R. H. (1988). *Passions within reason. The strategic role of the emotions.* W W Norton & Co.

Guthrie, E. R. (1952). *The psychology of learning.* Harper & Row.

Kahneman, D. (2011). *Thinking, fast and slow.* Farrar, Straus and Giroux.

Kandasamy, N., Garfinkel, S. N., Page, L., Hardy, B., Critchley, H. D., Gurnell, M., & Coates, J. M. (2016). Interoceptive ability predicts survival on a London trading floor. *Scientific Reports, 6*, 32986. https://doi.org/10.1038/srep32986

Keynes, J. M. (1936). *The general theory of employment, interest and money.* Palgrave Macmillan.

King, M. (2016). *The end of alchemy: Money, banking, and the future of the global economy.* Hachette.

Kristal, A. S., Whillans, A. V., Bazerman, M. H., Gino, F., Shu, L. L., Mazar, N., & Ariely, D. (2020). Signing at the beginning versus at the end does not decrease dishonesty. *Proceedings of the National Academy of Sciences of the United States of America, 117*, 7103–7107. https://doi.org/https://doi.org/10.1073/pnas.1911695117

Lee, S. M. (2021). *A famous honesty researcher is retracting a study over fake data.* BuzzFeed News. https://www.buzzfeednews.com/article/stephaniemlee/dan-ariely-honesty-study-retraction

Loewenstein, G. (2000). Emotions in economic theory and economic behavior. *The American Economic Review, 90*, 426–432. https://doi.org/10.1257/aer.90.2.426

Loewenstein, G., Nagin, D., & Paternoster, R. (1997). The effect of sexual arousal on expectations of sexual forcefulness. *Journal of Research in Crime and Delinquency, 34*, 443–473. https://doi.org/10.1177/0022427897034004003

Loewenstein, G., & Schkade, D. (1999). Wouldn't it be nice? Predicting future feelings. In D. Kahneman, E. Diener, & N. Schwarz (Eds.), *Well-being: Foundations of hedonic psychology* (pp. 85–106). Russell Sage Foundation.

MacDonald, G., & Leary, M. R. (2005). Why does social exclusion hurt? The relationship between social and physical pain. *Psychological Bulletin, 131*, 202–223. https://doi.org/10.1037/0033-2909.131.2.202

Maestripieri, D. (2012, March 20). What monkeys can teach us about human behavior: From facts to fiction. *Psychology Today.* https://www.psychologytoday.com/blog/games-primates-play/201203/what-monkeys-can-teach-us-about-human-behavior-facts-fiction

McCrae, R. R., & John, O. P. (1992). An introduction to the Five-Factor Model and its applications. *Journal of Personality, 60*, 175–215. https://doi.org/10.1111/j.1467-6494.1992.tb00970.x

Mehta, A. (2022). COVID-19: Cambridge professor admits he was "over-optimistic" at the start of the coronavirus pandemic. *Sky News.*

https://news.sky.com/story/covid-19-cambridge-professor-admits-he-was-over-optimistic-at-the-start-of-the-coronavirus-pandemic-12534429

Orwell, G. (1947). *The English people*. Collins.

Pothos, E. M., Perry, G., Corr, P. J., Matthew, M. R., & Busemeyer, J. R. (2011). Understanding cooperation in the Prisoner's Dilemma game. *Personality and Individual Differences (Special Issue: Personality and Economics)*, *51*, 210–215. https://doi.org/10.1016/j.paid.2010.05.002

Poundstone, W. (1992). *Prisoner's Dilemma: John von Neumann, game theory, and the puzzle of the bomb*. Oxford University Press.

Read, D., & van Leeuwen B. (1998). Predicting hunger: The effects of appetite and delay on choice. *Organizational Behavior and Human Decision Processes*, *76*, 189–205. https://doi-org/10.1006/obhd.1998.2803. PMID: 9831521

Sherif, M. (1935). A study of some social factors in perception. *Archives of Psychology*, *27*, 1–60.

Shu, L. L., Mazar, N., Gino, F., Ariely, D., & Bazerman, M. H. (2012). Signing at the beginning makes ethics salient and decreases dishonest self-reports in comparison to signing at the end. *Proceedings of the National Academy of Sciences of the United States of America*, *109*, 15197–15200. https://doi.org/10.1073/PNAS.1209746109

Simonsohn, U., Simmons, J., & Nelson, L. (2021). *Data Colada blog 98: Evidence of fraud in an influential field experiment about dishonesty*. https://datacolada.org/98

Smith, A. (1776). *An inquiry into the nature and causes of the wealth of nations*. W. Strahan and T. Cadell.

Solnick, S. J., & Hemenway, D. (1998). Is more always better? A survey on positional concerns. *Journal of Economic Behavior & Organization*, *37*, 373–383. https://doi.org/10.1016/S0167-2681(98)00089-4

Soros, G. (1995). *Soros on Soros: Staying ahead of the curve*. John Wiley & Sons, Ltd.

Thaler, R. H. (2015). *Misbehaving: The making of behavioural economics*. Allen Lane.

Trivers, R. L. (1971). The evolution of reciprocal altruism. *The Quarterly Review of Biology*, *46*, 35–57. https://doi.org/10.1086/406755

von Neumann, J., & Morgenstern, O. (1944). *Theory of games and economic behavior*. Princeton University Press.

NUDGE
WHYS, WAYS, AND WEASELS

If citizens make bad decisions, should it be the responsibility of governments to use insights from behavioral economics to nudge behavior in more desirable directions? Such 'nudging' has been applied in countries around the world, for example, to increase pension savings and organ donation rates, and to affect energy consumption in homes. As one goal of governments is to enhance citizens' well-being, nudging may be justified, but it remains a matter of considerable debate (e.g., how can we know people's *true* preferences?). In this chapter, we describe some of the ways 'nudging' is applied, and, also, some of its problems. We discuss why nudges are often more effective than simply using information, incentives, or regulation to change behavior. For example, social incentives and precommitments can help people adhere to their goals and not give in to temptations of immediate gratification. Behavioral insights teams around the world now help governments to design and evaluate behavioral policies. We further discuss how some governments and organizations have highlighted the value of taking into account subjective (i.e., self-reported) well-being – acknowledging that satisfaction, a sense of purpose, and flourishing are important components of the true wealth and health of the nation.

DOI: 10.4324/9781003166900-6

INTRODUCTION

We do not always act in our own best interests, *as judged by ourselves*. We get things wrong, misjudge, and base decisions on irrelevant information. To use Thaler's (2015) felicitous term, such *misbehaviors* perplex mainstream economists who have been brought up on a staple intellectual diet of rationality, self-interest, and the powerful influences of incentives and factual information. In contrast, behavioral economists are inspired by such misbehaviors (see text box). This state of psychological and economic affairs raises an important question: should governments protect us from ourselves by applying scientifically-based strategies to *nudge* us in more desirable directions? Many governments around the Western world have, indeed, concluded they should.

This public policy realization was inspired and guided by the highly influential 2008 book, *Nudge*, by Richard Thaler and Cass Sunstein – the subtitle *Improving Decisions About Health, Wealth and Happiness* captures its purpose aptly. There has been an update in 2021, which the authors called "the final edition" as a commitment strategy for themselves to ensure that they will not agree to work on future editions. This final edition updates dated references (does anyone still use iPods?) and introduces concepts that have gained prominence in the 13 years since the first edition (for example, *sludge* – parts of the choice architecture that hinder good decisions; and *smart disclosure* which can limit sludge). It also provides choice architecture concepts that are more positive for consumers, such as personalized defaults and 'make it fun'.

As discussed below, we have cause to question some of the basic assumptions of nudge theory, but, for now, we assume it is uncontroversial to want to help people make better decisions for themselves, their families, and wider society. The nudge perspective, though, was not an entirely novel approach when it was first published, especially as psychologists, in particular, were never much taken with the idea of the abstract rational economic agent characterized by neoclassical economics. They desired some altogether more psychologically realistic version of the flesh-and-blood economic decision maker. As long ago as 1904, Sigmund Freud devoted a book to *The Psychopathology of Everyday Life*, which had no time for the notion of a rational person – for Freud, the opposite was much more the case. In more academic psychology, whole sub-fields are devoted to less-than-rational everyday behavior.

DIFFERENCES BETWEEN STANDARD ECONOMICS AND BEHAVIORAL SCIENCE

Standard economic practice depends on three main tools to influence behavior: (1) information/education, (2) financial incentives, and (3) regulation. In contrast, psychologically-inspired behavioral approaches depend on: (1) framing, formatting, and timing of messages; (2) social incentives; and (3) nudges. According to nudge philosophy (Thaler & Sunstein, 2008, 2021), nudges retain freedom of choice (they are liberty-preserving); do not involve coercive means such as bans or regulations; and do not alter economic incentives – they can be developed using insights discussed by behavioral economics research, which relies upon the broader field of judgment and decision making, and wider behavioral science more generally.

One example of our less-than-rational behavior is seen in procrastination – we all too readily put off until tomorrow those activities that really should be done today, and then we waste time ruminating on this fact! Of importance, we even behave in this manner when it comes to important life decisions (e.g., saving for retirement), and we seem neither to notice nor care much that, on an everyday level, small things add up to larger ones. Too many of us postpone going to the gym and then wonder why we are not losing weight and getting fitter. Such misbehavior is seen in many other areas of life; for example, we often abandon New Year's resolutions even before we have taken down the Christmas tree. There are countless other examples of how we act in ways that fail to conform to neoclassical notions of rationality (see Chapter 3). In terms of the impulsive here-and-now propensities we so often show, we conform more to Oscar Wilde's witticism (1893): "I can resist anything except temptation". As evidence of this fact, we have a marked impatience for rewards and postpone the costs of decisions until the future; these tendencies are reflected in a need for instant gratification – such motivation is the very basis of the credit card industry. Rather than wait for a larger, later reward, we prefer smaller sooner benefits, *now* – in the lingo of the behavioral economist, we are *present biased*. As many years ago David Hume opined:

> There is no quality in human nature which causes more fatal errors in our conduct than that which leads us to prefer whatever is present to the distant and remote.
>
> (Hume, 1738)

Helping people to correct their bad decisions is especially relevant in financial life where the cost of mistakes is high for both the individual and society. Pension provision is one such area. Too many of us fail to save enough (or anything) for retirement, even though this is a tax-efficient way to put money aside for the future. We seem too prone to agree with the rose-tinted worldview of the character from Charles Dickens's 1850 novel, David Copperfield, Mr. Micawber, "something will turn up" – but for many retired people, the only thing that turns up is relative poverty. (Dickens had personal experience of the consequences of this worldview: Mr. Micawber was modeled on his own father who ended up in debtor's prison.)

This chapter has several aims. First, to describe 'Nudge'; second, to discuss the ways it is applied; and third, to present some of its problems, even dangers. These are the *Whys, Ways*, and *Weasels* of the alliterative subtitle – a 'weasel' is a term used in the advertising world to refer to *suggestio falsi* (Ogilvy, 1963 – see Chapter 7). We also consider the importance of subjective well-being in terms of governmental attempts to enhance human welfare, and how this approach may overcome some of the problems associated with the nudge philosophy and approach.

WHAT IS NUDGE?

The concept of nudge is based on the idea that people do not make good decisions *in terms of their own preferences* and, therefore, fail to maximize their utility. What it means is that our 'revealed preferences' do not reflect our *true* preferences. As we saw in Chapter 3, preferences are identified by such *manifest* behavioral choices. The idea that these choices may not reflect our true preferences is deeply unsettling for neoclassical economics. Notwithstanding, a cursory inspection of everyday life quickly confirms that we go about our business in ways that seem less than fully satisfactory – in the eyes of the mainstream economist, we are being inefficient and wasting scarce resources (in terms of time, effort, emotion, opportunity costs, and so on). All these behavioral imperfections seem ripe for a nudge intervention.

According to Thaler and Sunstein (2008): "A nudge is any aspect of the choice architecture that alters behavior in a predictable way without forbidding any options or significantly changing their economic incentives. A nudge must be easy and cheap to avoid". The emphasis is upon the *availability* of choice, and altering people's judgments, decisions, and behaviors should not impose significant costs on the chooser in terms of time, social sanctions, effort, and such like. Importantly, a nudge should allow people to perform rationally *in terms of their own self-declared interests* – according to Nudge, it is *not* for the choice architect to decide what is best for them.

It remains a matter of debate whether people should be nudged, but if we want to achieve behavior change, how should we go about the task? For a start, to change behavior, it is often not enough simply to provide people with the option – sometimes, they just ignore it. Nor is it enough simply to provide more information about the consequences of following option A over option B. For instance, how many smokers *really* do not know the very serious health consequences of their habit? What more information could be given to change their behavior? There is a psychological barrier to overcome. We know that human beings have a wonderful facility to 'wish away' unpleasant outcomes – indeed, there is a whole social psychological ('cognitive dissonance') literature devoted to this very topic (see Chapter 5). This shows just how easily we change attitudes, beliefs, etc. to maintain consistency with our behavior – contrary to what is commonly believed (i.e., attitude/belief more often leads to behavior, not vice versa).

MR. MICAWBER NUDGED

Returning to the case of pensions, government-inspired attempts to get more people to save for retirement have been hailed as one of the finer achievements of the nudge approach, and with some justification. Since 2012, in the United Kingdom under the 2008 Pensions Act, firms are required to enroll their employees automatically in a pension scheme – this started with larger firms but since 2018 applies to all firms. This is a good example of the power of 'defaults' – going with the flow (see below). If employees want to opt out of the pension scheme, they are free to do so, but this will require the expenditure of effort, cognitive resources, and time, and may even some psychological conflict. The idea is that because we are prone to cognitive laziness, not many people will pursue this opt-out option, and this has proved to be the case. As a result of this recent change in employment law, vastly more people are now in a pension scheme and comparatively few have bothered to go to the trouble of opting out – of course, they may stay in the scheme because they clearly see the benefits, but these benefits were not salient enough to encourage them to opt-in before the nudge intervention. (One fly in the ointment is that employers have an incentive to encourage and enable employees to opt out as this will save them making their own contributions.)

NUDGE AND STANDARD ECONOMIC POLICIES

Nudge policies stand in contrast to the typical toolkit of the policymaker who has traditionally relied upon taxing behavior that is deemed undesirable (e.g., taxes on cigarettes) and subsidizing behavior that is seen to improve well-being (e.g., tax relief on pensions). Taxes and subsidies work well in some domains of life by changing the (dis)incentives in the cost-benefit calculation – this is very much along the lines of the ECON model. However, these incentives are purely economic and do not take much if any account of the impact of the social context. For instance, nudge can capitalize on the fact that behavior change programs may be more successful when networks and peers are involved, who can act as a *commitment device* – this is designed to help HUMANS adhere to their goals and come in many different forms (e.g., Brocas et al., 2004). For example, this may be social: declaring to everyone who is willing to listen that you are going to give up smoking or lose weight. If you fail in this publicly declared goal, there will some psychological egg on your face which might be rubbed in by those who want you to fail – this is a fine example of loss aversion motivated compliance with the self-avowed goal.

To achieve behavior change, governments could well choose 'hard' measures such as regulations, mandates, and bans, which force citizens and corporations to adopt or avoid certain otherwise preferred actions. For instance, in the United Kingdom, it is an offense to smoke in certain designated public places. The prospect of paying a steep fine certainly deters many people from violating such regulations. Hard measures are usually seen to be desirable and necessary when behavior is detrimental to society and needs to be avoided (e.g., Covid-19 lockdowns). Even here, we might prefer to adopt behavioral means to encourage desirable behavior, for example, stressing the importance of social norms or using commitment devices. (Although it can only be speculation, we might wonder whether this alternative strategy might have discouraged those behaviors which led to the then Prime Minister of the United Kingdom, Boris Johnson, along with colleagues and officials, being fined for violations of the laws in the very buildings where they were designed and communicated to the general public.)

In any event, there are whole areas of human behavior where standard policies are particularly ill-suited. For example, getting people to eat more healthily, exercise more, drink less, and so forth. To use coercive means to affect change in these areas would not be politically viable and would be very difficult to implement – it is doubtful they would be effective in any case. In such areas, the other option in the government's toolbox is to rely on 'soft' measures, such as voluntary agreements – a 'psychological contract' designed to ensure consistency with agreed courses of action. This is the way that many governments around the globe have decided to go. For example, the UK government has used subtle tactics to encourage people to get back to work (for an example, see text box). In this example as well as others, it must remain a matter of opinion whether this is a dubious application of psychological science or a harmless trick to help people re-enter employment – the choice architect could retort: "As we are going to send a letter in any case, why not design it for maximum effectiveness"? There are other forms of nudges that are much less problematic, and some are quite amusing. A delightful example is seen at Odenplan metro station in Stockholm, Sweden, where the stairs to the side of the escalator contained touch-sensitive pads designed to represent piano keys. (Search the internet to find it.) As people walked up the stairs, piano notes played. This fun and novel initiative encouraged people to use the stairs – in fact, 66% more people than normal.

CHOICE ARCHITECTURE

If information by itself is not sufficient to alter behavior, then what is? One major factor is a design change in the environments in which people make choices. This entails the concept of what is known as *choice architecture* which describes the careful design of how *choices are presented* (Thaler & Sunstein, 2008, 2021).

There is now ample evidence that making food portions, food packages, and even plates smaller reduces how much people consume – even

PERSONALIZED LETTERS TO THE UNEMPLOYED

As reported by the BBC (Easton, 2015), the UK Behavioural Insights Teams was asked if it could get more unemployed people to come to job interviews. To test the effects of several types of messages, they sent different versions of an invitation to a job interview to unemployment claimants. The first text was simple, telling claimants about an interview:

> "Eight new Customer Assistant jobs are now available at Tesco. Come to Bedford Jobcentre on Monday 10 June between 10am and 4pm and ask for Sarah to find out more."
>
> About 11% turned up. The second message was exactly the same, but they added the claimant's first name, for example: "Hi Sam, eight new Customer Assistant jobs are now available at Tesco ..."

The percentage of people turning up to the interview increased to 15%. The largest increase in the interview attendance rate, rising to 27%, was observed when the Jobcentre adviser signed the message and wished the claimant good luck:

> "Hi Sam, eight new Customer Assistant jobs are now available at Tesco. Come to Bedford Jobcentre on Monday 10 June between 10am and 4pm and ask for Sarah to find out more. I've booked you a place. Good luck, Michael."

This small, but highly effective change, which simply consisted of adding a personal touch to the message, is now used by every job center in the country. Maybe the claimants simply needed to feel that somebody cared about their future.

eating off a red plate reduces consumption (for further examples, see Chapter 7). The point is that nobody is being told, let alone compelled, to make a specific choice. For example, in a nudge-designed cafeteria, no one is stopping anyone from consuming as much unhealthy food as they can shovel down their throats. This is an important point in the philosophy of nudge. We are still *free to choose* – to use the title of one of Milton Friedman's most popular neoclassically-based books

(Friedman, 1980). Instead, *choice architecture* exposes us to subtle cues that guide us in one direction (to healthy fruit) and away from less desirable foods (chocolate bars) – however, if we want to go our own way, we are still at liberty to do so.

In the specific example of a cafeteria designed by a choice architect, and following the social psychological principles discussed in Chapter 5, people can be nudged to assume that the *social norm* is for a plate of food to be of a certain size or to contain a certain variety of items (e.g., vegetables and fruit). People do not need to be told this explicitly; all they need is the opportunity to observe and learn from others, and then to be reinforced for adhering to this social norm. As a result, it is hoped they will adjust their expectation of what constitutes an adequate food portion – their attitudes and beliefs will then follow their changed behavior – and as a pleasing consequence, they will then serve as a model to pass this norm on to other people! Although there are different ways of looking at how best to nudge (see below), one useful way is given by the BASIC model (see text box).

THE BASIC NUDGE MODEL

A way of identifying behavioral problems that may be amenable to a nudge intervention is given by the Danish organization iNudgeyou, which uses the BASIC model to design interventions. The acronym stands for: B = Behavioral mapping: collecting data to define the problem – the *what* phase. A = Analysis: why people are currently behaving as they are – the *why* phase. S = Solution mapping: this is the scientific and systematic process of making suggestions – the *how* phase. I = Interventions – this is the testing of possible nudge solutions before full implementation – this is the *test* phase. Once a nudge intervention has been selected, there is then C = Continuation: solutions may fail due to poor implementation or lack of maintenance, so a process of ongoing monitoring of the target behavior is needed, as well as an evaluation of possible unforeseen side effects – the *results* stage.

An approach such as BASIC is needed whenever nudging is being considered – especially as jumping from general knowledge to specific behavioral problems is fraught with problems. An excellent example of the application of BASIC is seen in the nudge intervention to move smokers away from entrances at Copenhagen airport (Schmidt et al., 2016).

EVIDENCE-BASED POLICIES

With the nudge philosophy of public policy design and implementation, there is a growing consensus on the need for government initiatives to be evidence-based, meaning that they should be informed more by (empirical) data than (political) dogma. The 'gold standard' for such empirical evidence is the randomized controlled trial (RCT). How does it work?

Participants in a typical RCT are *randomly* assigned to two (or more) groups, and these groups are subjected to different conditions (e.g., the 'treatment' group may receive a certain message, whereas the 'control' group does not) – for example, a personalized vs. a generic letter. The random allocation of participants to groups is a crucial design feature because it allows the avoidance of *systematic* bias effects: if we observe differences in the behavior of the groups, then these differences may be ascribed to the treatment and not because the members of the two

NUDGING WARFARIN MEDICATION ADHERENCE

One major health issue is that, too often, people do not adhere to prescribed medicine, even for serious medical conditions. One study used an RCT, employing a lottery technique, to encourage stroke patients to take warfarin (Volpp et al., 2008). The (nudge) treatment group had a 1% chance of winning $100, but this was conditional upon taking their pills correctly. The control group did not receive any incentive – at least, not beyond the increased risk of dying by not taking their warfarin correctly. The result was a marked increase in medication adherence in the experimental group – as assessed by an InforMedix Med-eMonitor System with a daily reminder feature. This was a pilot study with only a small number of patients in each group.

However, a second similar (but much larger) study failed to show a statistically significant difference between the treatment and control groups in warfarin patients, although there was evidence of a positive effect in a group of patients at higher risk *a priori* of poor adherence (Kimmel et al., 2012). The difference in results between these studies raises the general issue that all such experimental studies need to be replicated before they can be said to be robust and generalizable to the wider population, especially when small and perhaps nonrepresentative samples of the target population have been used.

groups were different from each other at the start of the trial. (Without such randomization, it is notoriously difficult to avoid systematic allocation bias, however well intended the researcher.)

A typical RCT might involve sending different (and there could be many) variations of a letter to nudge people to pay their taxes on time – for example, including mention of the percentage of people in the local area who have paid their taxes by a certain date. The letter that achieves the highest level of compliance is then assumed to be the most effective in nudging people – this type of 'market testing' is widely used by commercial companies to hone their appeal to customers and to turn browsers into buyers (see Chapter 7). Nudges have been applied in many areas of life, and, in most cases, consumers and citizens are unaware of their use or influence.

Here, we see again how choice architecture and its clever use of defaults underpin many of the little decisions we make every day – and small everyday decisions can mount up to big changes (e.g., recycling of waste).

LIBERTY PRESERVING

According to Sunstein and Thaler (2003), nudges are *liberty preserving*; that is, they steer people in a direction that does not take away their choices. This is a critical aspect of their oxymoronically sounding phrase: *libertarian paternalism* – this is used to reflect the idea that behavior can be manipulated and changed in a way that maintains freedom of choice (Thaler & Sunstein, 2003). According to this view, people are *at liberty* to make their own choices, and, importantly, they are not restrained from doing so. However, this takes place in a context where a choice architect engineers the environment to influence decisions in ways that make the target groups better off, *as judged by themselves*. According to Sunstein and Thaler (2003), illiberal paternalism is avoided by the fact that "people should be free to opt out of specified arrangements if they choose to do so" and this opt-out is said to "preserve freedom of choice". The claim is made that the choice architect is nudging people merely in the direction of choices that they would have made, if only they were better able or motivated.

Libertarian paternalism is similar to *asymmetric paternalism* (Camerer et al., 2003). This refers to policies designed to assist people who seem to be behaving in ways that appear to be nonrational and who by so doing are not seemingly maximizing their utility, while at the same time interfering only minimally with people who are behaving (neoclassically speaking) rationally. Nudge policies are asymmetric in a related sense: they should be acceptable both to believers in human rationality and to those who believe that people often behave nonrationally.

In nudge theory, retaining the element of choice is all important. For example, people can still choose to purchase the electrical appliance with the worst energy rating – maybe they care more about the color or price, or they have money to burn (some people have a preference for contrariness too – it is *their* choice after all). Nudge theory declares that it does not take away this personal choice.

MINDSPACE

An attempt at summarizing noncoercive principles of behavior change was undertaken by the Institute for Government, along with the Cabinet Office, in the United Kingdom in 2009, which set as its goal to provide a simple checklist for policymakers. The result was MINDSPACE which stands for nine principles that influence human behavior, described below. (We partly borrow the short explanation of each of the nine letters from the original MINDSPACE document (Dolan et al., 2010), and advise the reader to find the document online to see further examples.) For clarity of exposition, we illustrate these principles in relation to nudges to get motorists to slow down close to schools.

ELEMENTS OF MINDSPACE

M – MESSENGER: WE ARE HEAVILY INFLUENCED
BY WHO COMMUNICATES INFORMATION

The messenger of information matters, for example, their perceived authority. There are data to show that people more favorably receive information from experts (e.g., a doctor in a white coat), so long as they are trusted. Similarities between the information giver and receiver are important – for example, the sign: "Kill your speed, not a child" is communicated better by a smiling child than a stern-faced government official. The feelings we have toward the messenger are also important – if we dislike them, their advice is more likely to be discounted or even ignored, or otherwise explained away. We can see that this principle is consistent with the cognitive response model of persuasive messages, discussed in Chapter 6.

I – INCENTIVE: OUR RESPONSES TO INCENTIVES
ARE SHAPED BY PREDICTABLE MENTAL SHORTCUTS
SUCH AS STRONGLY AVOIDING LOSSES

Incentives are widely used by governments, but their influence depends on factors such as timing, type, and magnitude. Incentives can be about money (i.e., the costs and benefits associated with different behaviors); but social aspects of incentives are also important, too. As discussed in Chapter 4, we need to consider a number of psychological factors. For example, our general propensity to loss aversion means we dislike losses more than we like gains of the same amount. Therefore, instead of saying that x number of children die or are injured by speeding cars, we could say that y children would be saved by a 5-miles per hour reduction in speed. Some countries do not add penalty points for speeding but take away points from a predetermined number – people have the sense they are losing something of value, rather than accumulating penalty points as something of a 'boy racer' badge of honor!

We also use reference points: the value of something depends on our frame of reference. As discussed in Chapter 4, we allocate money to mental bundles, so the incentive must be tied to whatever bundle is related to the behavior change in question. Also, we prefer to receive our incentives today, and not at some point in the (uncertain) future

CROWDING OUT IN THE BEDROOM

Recall that one of the major assumptions of neoclassical economics is that more is better than less. George Loewenstein put this hypothesis to the test in the bedroom – perhaps appropriately as Loewenstein is related to Sigmund Freud. Along with colleagues, his 2015 study reported that when couples were required to double the amount of sex they had, this made them less happy, they wanted sex less often and did not enjoy it as much. Their otherwise intrinsic motivation and utility/satisfaction were crowded out by the extrinsic (imposed) motivation – having sex to conform to the requirements of a scientific study must appear high up on the list of passion killers!

(even when this future amount is larger). However, there is a downside to using incentives, even social ones: as an external source of motivation, they can 'crowd out' intrinsic motivation (doing something for its own sake – for an amusing example, see text box), and this can undermine long-term behavior change.

N – NORMS: WE ARE STRONGLY INFLUENCED BY WHAT OTHERS DO

What people *expect* about social behavior influences how they behave. Social norms can be obvious ("No smoking here") or more covert (social conventions when you meet someone for the first time). We tend to take our social norm cues from observing what other people are doing. Simply informing people about the existence of social norms can influence behavior, though (e.g., how many passengers in cars wear seat belts). Telling people that most guests in hotels recycle their unused towels encourages similar behavior. Telling drivers that other motorists slow down outside a school is effective, especially if it comes from a child.

Norms are spread through social networks and policymakers are wise to take these into account (e.g., typical community behavior). Nevertheless, people need to be reminded about norms as they can quickly forget – in other words, norm-following behavior needs to be reinforced (see Chapter 5). But the use of social norms in nudging can sometimes backfire. If we learn that our neighbors are using more water than us, then we may well *increase* our usage, perhaps in an attempt "to keep up with them", or to feel we are "getting our fair share"! Another example of backfiring norms is seen with signs at a national park in the United States (Cialdini et al., 2006). One sign tried to deter people from taking home wood (it showed thieves stealing wood); the second sign showed a single thief. Both signs led to *more* wood being stolen because the signs served to reinforce this harmful social norm, and they covertly conveyed the message: "take wood while stocks last!" Relatedly, there is a highly relevant social psychological literature on 'social proofing', referring to the findings that we look to others for guidance on social behavior – we often see this in adverts where people *like us* (those in our demographic group) are observed participating in and enjoying the product or service on offer. There are obvious ways this could be used outside schools to slow down traffic – try to think of some.

D – DEFAULTS: WE 'GO WITH THE FLOW' OF PRESET OPTIONS

Much of our everyday behavior is just going with the flow, and we usually do not even notice it – it is a form of taking the easy option, the path of least resistance. Defaults are preselected options that do not involve an active choice: we tend to take what is on offer (e.g., automatic enrolment in an organ donation program). Most people stick with the default, and rates of participation in organ donation programs are significantly higher than without it.

In our road safety example, markings on the road which give the impression of speed could help encourage people to slow down outside schools – we see the use of such floor markers in supermarkets to influence the speed of customer travel (see Chapter 7).

S – SALIENCE: OUR ATTENTION IS DRAWN TO WHAT IS NOVEL AND SEEMS RELEVANT TO US

Information to which we are attentive attracts cognitive processing. Although attention is not required for all forms of processing, it is often important for the effectiveness of certain types of messages. We are more likely to process information that is novel, accessible, and simple. This could be in the form of funny messages – to deter littering on Bondi beach in Sydney, Australia, "Don't be a tosser" was written on the bins (described in Tribe, 2016). In the school driving example, pictures drawn by children could be used to convey the message to drivers to "kill their speed, not children".

The concept of salience addresses a problem confronting the brain-mind: it is bombarded with stimuli and it must make a choice what to process – grabbing attention by salience is helpful in this respect. Salience also refers to *peak* moments – a sharp pain at the dentist is remembered more vividly than a longer period of sustained discomfort: we especially remember what was salient to us, and easily forget the rest.

P – PRIMING: OUR ACTS ARE OFTEN INFLUENCED BY SUB-CONSCIOUS CUES

Exposure to stimuli – sights, sounds, and smells – can prime (i.e., make more likely) subsequent behavior (we have already discussed this in Chapter 5). These stimuli can be complex (e.g., words) or simple (freshly baked bread). Priming can happen outside of cognitive awareness and does not need elaborate processes to be effective. For example, regarding exposure to words, when people make a sentence out of scrambled, fitness-related words (e.g., 'fit' and 'lean'), they are then immediately more likely to use the stairs instead of the lift (Wryobeck & Chen, 2003); happy faces lead people to drink more (Winkielman et al., 2005); the smell of cleaning products in a canteen leads to more people clearing their tables (Holland et al., 2005); and the list goes on (these examples are all taken from the MINDSPACE document; Dolan et al., 2010).

However, as mentioned in Chapter 5, it should be noted that many priming studies have been impacted by the replication crisis in social psychology (i.e., researchers often do not manage to find the same results as classic priming experiments; however, Kahneman, who is a severe critic of these studies, is in little doubt that the phenomenon exists; see Chapter 5).

Streets surrounding schools could display pictures of children, and then as drivers approach the school, messages related to slowing down would be primed and, therefore, processed faster.

A – AFFECT: OUR EMOTIONAL ASSOCIATIONS CAN POWERFULLY SHAPE OUR ACTIONS

The experience of affect (mood, emotion, and other subjective states) influences judgment and decision making (see Chapter 5). For example, being in a good mood can lead to being overly optimistic, and being in a bad mood to being inappropriately pessimistic – both can impair concurrent judgment and decision making. Even the mood-inducing effects of background music can do this, and it need not even be task-relevant – for example, seeing an attractive, smiling face on a loan advertisement leads to increased demand, similar in magnitude to the demand created by a 25% reduction in the interest rate (Bertrand et al., 2010). (This study was also described in the MINDSPACE document.) The influence of affect is much more prevalent than commonly thought, especially by neoclassical economists, and much of what we process is imbued with emotion.

Affect needs to be used with caution. Images of happy children may make drivers more risk-tasking and over-confident in their driving ability, so perhaps an image of a less-than-happy child may be needed at critical junctures on the road where speed is especially dangerous. This cannot really be known in advance, so experimental studies are needed to test such interventions (see RCTs, above).

C – COMMITMENT: WE SEEK TO BE CONSISTENT WITH OUR PUBLIC PROMISES, AND RECIPROCATE ACTS

A lack of willpower is a major reason why we do not always act in our own best self-interest. Commitment devices can be used to achieve long-term goals. Such devices tend to become more effective as the costs for failure rise. A good example is smoking. Smokers were offered a savings account (Giné et al., 2010) in which they had to deposit money for six months, after which time they took a nicotine test. If they passed the test (i.e., they were nicotine-free), their money was returned; otherwise, they lost it (clearly, there is a loss aversion aspect here). After 12 months, this commitment device raised the chances of quitting smoking by 30%. Much the same is found with exercise. The mere act of signing a contract that specifies the amount of exercise leads to adherence, despite no monetary consequences of succeeding or failing. As discussed in Chapter 5, we like to remain consistent in our intentions and actions.

Getting drivers to agree to the statement that motorists should be especially careful around schools should help to lock them into this commitment mindset – then reminders, strategically placed along the road, would serve to reinforce their commitment.

E – EGO: WE ACT IN WAYS THAT MAKE US FEEL BETTER ABOUT OURSELVES

We have a desire to be consistent in our behavior, so if our behavior and beliefs are in conflict, our beliefs often change (this is accounted for by cognitive dissonance theory; see Chapter 5). In addition, we tend to attribute good outcomes to ourselves and bad outcomes to other people or situations: we take praise with one hand and give blame out with the other. Attributions to our own behavior and that of others form a central part of social psychology, and they are used widely, especially in the commercial world. For example, males donate more to charity if they are approached by an attractive female, suggesting the giving of money reflects a desire to present a positive self-image. If we place an expectation on someone, this is often sufficient to encourage them to perform better – they have internalized these expectations (i.e., assimilated them with their self-image) and then used them to guide their behavior. This can lead to a self-fulfilling prophecy – of course, this could be a vicious as well as a virtuous circle.

We have also a strong tendency to compare ourselves to other people: this is *social comparison*, which we engage in to be better able to evaluate ourselves. But it can lead to biased judgments; for example, most people think they are above the average in terms of driving ability, which can lead to over-confidence and risk-proneness. Given that drivers do not want to think of themselves as potential child killers, they should feel a warm glow about being good citizens after committing to a statement that extra care is needed outside schools.

Now, in order for the effects of nudge interventions to persist over the longer term, it is important that people 'buy into' them. As discussed in Chapter 5, the process of *conversion* must be working because if only *compliance* is in operation, the behavior will stop once active measures are not in place to maintain them.

OTHER NUDGE FRAMEWORKS

There are other models of behavior change that have been adopted by organizations. For example, the EAST framework, published by the UK Behavioural Insights Team in 2014, postulates four main principles to design effective behavior change policies and is perhaps easier to adopt than Mindspace (The Behavioural Insights Team, 2014). The EAST acronym stands for Easy, Attractive, Social, and Timely – and it is hoped that this simple framework can be easily memorized by busy choice architects, such as policymakers. Similarly, the COM–B model (see text box), which has been used in public health settings in the United Kingdom, can be used to design behavior interventions.

THE COM-B MODEL OF BEHAVIOR CHANGE

The COM-B model, which was developed by Susan Michie and colleagues in the United Kingdom (e.g., Michie et al., 2011; West & Michie, 2020), identifies three important factors for behavior change to occur:

- C = Capability: can the behavior be accomplished? Do people have the psychological and physical ability to engage in the behavior?
- O = Opportunity: do the external factors exist to make the behavior possible?
- M = Motivation: are people sufficiently motivated to change their behavior?

With any choice architecture, there must be an architect who decides on, for example, default options. How should they go about their business? One option would be to select the rule that most people would select if they were well informed. As we have seen before, people are not fully informed and, therefore, do not always make optimal decisions. For instance, most people would select to make additional payments to their pension plans or to sign up for their company's pension plan if they fully appreciated what it is like to live with too little money in old age. This is an important issue. In 2010, 53% of workers in the United States were at risk of not having adequate funds to maintain their lifestyle in retirement. A clever use of default options would eliminate some of the pain that people feel when they put away money for future consumption. There might even be the opportunity to use present bias to help their future, for example, a mobile app that prompts *impulsive* saving.

TESTING TIMES FOR NUDGES

Given the huge promise of nudges to change behavior – often in relatively cheap ways – it is important to point out that the evidence base of their effectiveness has been contested. Mertens and colleagues (2022) helpfully examined 200 studies with 450 effect sizes in over 2 million people. They report that, overall, interventions promote behavior change albeit with small to medium effect sizes, but these are influenced by techniques used and domains targeted. For example, food choices seem particularly amenable to behavior change with effect sizes 2.5 times larger than those found for other behavioral domains. Therefore, it cannot simply be assumed that a nudge intervention will work and to what extent. However, others have claimed that such meta-analyses do not find nudges to be effective once publication bias is taken into statistical account (Maier et al., 2022). A meta-analysis combines results from separate studies to provide a summary of the literature, taking into account such potential moderating factors as sample size.

Publication bias refers to a big problem in academic publishing as studies with significant results are more likely to be published than studies that do not find any effects. Thus, it is possible that many studies that analyzed nudge interventions and did not find any positive results of nudging are still languishing in researchers' file drawers, while successful interventions gain the attention of governments and the media

To assess the overall effectiveness of nudges, it is important to consider both types of results and to replicate small studies with larger samples. The importance of using as many approaches as possible is highlighted by a 'megastudy' by Milkman et al. (2021) focused on physical health – 'megastudy', as used here, denotes a field experiment with a very large sample size that includes a number of interventions. They found that forecasts by impartial judges failed to predict which interventions would work best. This raises the question of how best to decide which interventions should be used, and which ones should be discarded – there are many potentially effective nudges 'out there' that are yet to be recognized or appreciated for their potential. Whatever the case, a debate rages over the true effectiveness of nudge interventions. Good discussions of this debate are given in a number of informative articles (Hallsworth, 2022; Osman, 2022), where further references may be found.

NUDGING: WAYS AND WEASELS

Nudging may seem a rather uncontroversial approach; even highly desirable and, in common parlance, a 'no brainer'. But not everyone agrees. Some see paradoxes and ironies at its very core – indeed, those with a distinctly uncharitable disposition view nudging as something of a *weasel* concept (cunning and deceptive). One major irony seems to be that, although nudge is quoted as an example of the validity of behavioral economics, ironically it seems to have to rely upon a neoclassical bedrock of consistent and integrated preferences (see Chapter 3). In addition, some critics argue that it *downplays* the true importance of psychology, especially with regard to ideas about the nature of the *economic agent* and their preferences.

Before discussing these conceptual problems in detail, dissenting voices include those who draw attention to the limitations of its efficacy and ethics. For example, Raihani (2013) notes that nudge interventions may vary across contexts: what may work well in one situation or with a group of people may not work well in other situations or with a different group of people. Indeed, this raises the crucial issue of the explanations for the *heterogeneity*, as seen in reactions to nudge interventions, in all forms of economic choices, and more generally (see Ferguson et al., 2011).

Also, we have too scant knowledge to know whether nudges work well in the long term, even if they can be shown to have short-term significant effects. There are also the ethical aspects of nudges, including their moral justification, as well as imposing a cost on those who may not benefit from them. Such is the disquiet with nudge theory, there have been accusations that it has been "weaponized", especially during the Covid-19 pandemic (e.g., Dodsworth, 2021). This serves only to highlight a much earlier concern stated by the UK House of Lords Science and Technology Select Committee 2011 report *Behaviour Change* that there are "ethical issues because they involve altering behavior through mechanisms of which people are not obviously aware".

Now, we turn to some of the major conceptual problems underlying the whole nudge approach.

PREFERENCE PURIFICATION

Robert Sugden of the University of East Anglia is one of the UK's pioneers of behavioral economics. He highlights a number of fundamental conceptual problems with the whole nudge approach – whether we think nudge is a good thing for other (more practical) reasons is quite a different matter. Sugden highlights the apparent 'preference purification' required to make Nudge work *on its own terms*, as well as assumptions about the 'inner rational agent' (Infante et al., 2016).

As seen in Chapter 3, the essential idea of neoclassical economics is that individuals have integrated *latent preferences* which cannot be directly accessed – but we can infer them through *revealed preferences* in their choice behavior. Now, we know that the economic agent's psychology sometimes causes errors in decision making – previous chapters documented that revealed preferences are influenced by context, reference, even moods, and they are anything but pure! The task for economics is, therefore, to *recover* an individual's latent preferences by stripping away these psychological imperfections. Sugden's argument is that nudge theory must do this by *purifying* contaminated revealed preferences; and it is then the satisfaction of *these* purified preferences that nudge theory aims to maximize. These issues may seem a little arcane, but they have important implications for the justification and ethics of government behavioral interventions. Let us start to look at these issues in a little more detail.

Sunstein and Thaler are clear on the topic of behavioral interventions: "Libertarian paternalism is not an oxymoron", they claim in

2003, before going on to assert that paternalism is necessary because, as they put it, the antipaternalist position is 'incoherent' and a 'non-starter'. In their opinion, people are simply too swayed by irrelevant factors (e.g., by the position of food items in a cafeteria) and really cannot be left to their own flawed psychological devices to make the right decision. Sunstein and Thaler say that the point of Nudge is to "make choosers better off, *as judged by themselves*". Continuing this spirited defense, Thaler states in 2015:

> ... a point that critics of our book [i.e., *Nudge*] seem incapable of getting. [We] have no interest in telling people what to do. We want to help them achieve their *own* goals.

Pointing to the "*as judged by themselves*" clause in *Nudge*:

> The italics are in the original but perhaps we should also have used bold and a large font, given the number of times we have been accused of thinking that we know what is best for everyone.... We just want to reduce what people would themselves call errors.

The problem with this position is that when choices are context-dependent, how are we to understand them? And how is the planner (e.g., the cafeteria choice architect) to reconstruct them? The nearest Thaler and Sunstein get to answering these questions is in discussing decision making errors:

> In many cases, individuals make pretty bad decisions – decisions that they would not have made if they had paid full attention and possessed complete information, unlimited cognitive abilities, and complete self-control.
>
> (Thaler & Sunstein, 2008)

Now, it seems we are getting somewhere. It is clear that Sunstein and Thaler categorize such decisions as "inferior decisions in terms of their [i.e., the individuals'] own welfare". The implication is that Sunstein and Thaler's welfare criterion is the satisfaction of the *latent preferences* that would equal individuals' *revealed preferences* if it were not for these imperfections. This is *preference purification*: the reconstruction of what the individual would have chosen in the *absence* of such psychological imperfections. It follows that the implicit assumption is that *latent* preferences are context-*in*dependent – this seems to be the case because Sunstein and Thaler are claiming to solve a problem created by the context-dependence of revealed preferences.

Sunstein and Thaler's rhetorical device is to characterize neoclassical economists as assuming that humans are ECONS who are immune to reasoning imperfections and can "think like Albert Einstein, store as much memory as IBM's Big Blue, and exercise the willpower of Mahatma Gandhi". Sunstein and Thaler say, "the folks we know are not like that" – many of whom are exalted intellectuals with no dearth of reasoning power.

Sugden's criticism is that, according to nudge theory, the economic agent is a faulty ECON – but an ECON *all the same*. This imperfect ECON needs a little help to reveal its true (latent) preferences. So, inside the economic agent is a neoclassically rational ECON with coherent preferences that are struggling to escape the binds of psychological restraints to achieve *true* utility maximization.

Sugden contends that the problem with Sunstein and Thaler's approach is that they do not take psychology seriously enough. Of course, they assume that judgments, decisions, and choice behaviors are (at least, often) psychologically flawed, but they seem not to go further in saying that all preferences of the economic agent are psychologically flawed – as defined by neoclassical economics. This is a fundamental point: nudge theory seems to rely upon the notion of an economic agent who is, at their core, rational (ECON), and the main problem is that they struggle to reveal these consistently integrated preferences in the whirlwind of everyday psychological life. Therefore, it may be claimed, Sunstein and Thaler seem to have a flawed argument in that they must rely upon the unjustified notion of the neoclassically rational economic agent.

SUPERREASONER: OBJECTIVE REASONING AND SUBJECTIVE PREFERENCES

Well, what might be going on? Let us look at the issue more closely. Imagine an economic agent called SuperReasoner, who: has access to all relevant information; gives full attention to all relevant information; has no cognitive limitations; and has perfect self-control (You will also encounter SuperReasoner in Infante et al., 2016.) Let us further assume that SuperReasoner's revealed preferences are not blown around on the psychological winds of reference points, context, mood, and the like – they are *much* too smart for that to happen. As we can see, SuperReasoner has all the fine neoclassical features assumed by mainstream economics – a *real* ECON.

Now, contrast SuperReasoner with an everyday HUMAN, Jo/anne who are in Sunstein and Thaler's cafeteria and choose whichever of fresh fruit or cream cake is displayed nearest to the front of the counter: they have been successfully nudged. Now, imagine SuperReasoner enters the cafeteria. Would they be unbiased and not in need of nudging to make the 'right' (as defined by the cafeteria architect) choice to eat only healthy food? Well, what should we expect of SuperReasoner in this situation? Sugden claims that, given a truly free choice, there is no reason to assume that SuperReasoner would pick the fruit over the cake – why should they? Their processing abilities may be *objective*, but their preferences are *subjective*. Importantly, in their preferences at *that* moment, they would be just as swayed as the psychologically flawed Jo/anne. Although there are enormous cognitive, affective, and motivational differences between SuperReasoner and Jo/anne, this does not allow us to say anything about their personal (subjective) preferences. There just seems to be no determinate answer, accessible by applying unlimited cognitive ability to full information ($2 + 2 = 4$, but there is nothing in economics that says fruit = good, cake = bad). As said elsewhere in this book, although you and I may have a definite preference, there is nothing in neoclassical economics that prefers a short fat life over a long thin one. It is a matter of personal preference, and so long as it is consistent, neoclassical economics is just fine with it.

You may well ask, so what? Why do we need to be concerned with SuperReasoner's *subjective* choice behavior, and are we not getting a little too abstract and 'academic' here? Well, the whole point of nudge theory is that such a SuperReasoner should not need a nudge to make the 'right' choice (fruit over cake) because it has all the information needed and the psychological powers not to make the 'wrong' choice. Well, *as seen from their perspective*, SuperReasoner prefers cake over fruit – and why should they not? In other words, we cannot have any confidence that SuperReasoner's personal (subjective) behavior will conform to what the choice architect thinks is 'correct' – that is, their true preferences. Therefore, it seems that basic psychology is involved in all such choice decisions, even SuperReasoner's. To put things another way, nudge theory may not, as claimed, make "choosers better off, *as judged by them-selves*". They may be better off as judged by the choice architect, and the architect may well be right (in some abstract sense), but this is *not* the underlying rationale of nudge. Indeed, if SuperReasoner is successfully nudged, then they would be worse off, as judged by themselves!

Now, it could be decided that for purely practical reasons, nudge is a very fine thing and should be at the heart of government policy-making. However, this decision would place much more emphasis on 'paternal' and much less on 'liberty'. If the conceptual moral rug has been pulled from under the nudge approach, we may want to demand greater justification for any nudge intervention – and certainly more than is conventionally provided. For a start, there would need to be a greater challenge of the notion that nudge makes choosers better off, *as judged by others*. We might agree that government could simply tell us to stop acting stupidly – we should eat healthier food, not drink/smoke, save for our retirement, and so on – but this would not be *liberal pater-nalism* and in accordance with nudge theory. It would be something else entirely and invoking nudge theory to *justify* it would be wrong: a *weasel*. It would be something much closer to 'nanny state' paternalism.

There are other problems with the nudge approach. For one, does it not impede – indeed, it may serve to erode – people's autonomy in decision making? And as we have already seen, concerns, too, have been expressed regarding the democratic legitimacy of nudging people without their knowledge, or even consent. It may be thought that if people are properly informed, then this potential problem is miti-gated. However, if we accept Daniel Kahneman's view that the power of System 1 thinking (heuristics, biases, etc.) is much stronger than System 2 (reflective processes), this may well not be the case at all – after all, although we must know we are being influenced/manipulated by commercial advertisements, they still work (see Chapter 7).

It is important to recognize that, as with all initially benign initia-tives, there is the ever-present risk that a friendly nudge may segue into a less friendly budge, and finally into a definitely unfriendly shove (these distinctions are well discussed by Oliver, 2013, 2015) – and all underwritten by the belief that it is in the best interests of citi-zens, intellectually bolstered by: *as judged by themselves*. Nevertheless, as a society, we may well want to allow governments to act as a Dutch Uncle, offering words of advice, especially in circumstances where behavior is resulting in 'externalities' (i.e., a negative impact on other people; e.g., the health costs associated with smoking and an unhealthy lifestyle). This might be a paternalistic price well worth paying for a healthier and wealthier society. Whatever decision we make, the philosophical basis of nudge seems unable to provide a justification.

Perhaps, a more fundamental question is whether nudging is appropriate at all in many situations as it places the responsibility of actions (and thus the outcome) on individuals rather than the choice architect. If low pension savings rates are seen as a huge societal problem, is it simply the individual's fault if they opt out of additional pension contributions and end up poor in old age? After all, they were given the choice to opt out so can this choice be truly wrong? As the sub-heading of a recent article in the Financial Times intones: "Is behavioral public policy a distraction from finding systemic solutions?" (Harford, 2022). In many cases where nudging now seems to be the preferred option of policymakers – perhaps to maintain the illusion of limited government intervention – it could be argued that systemic solutions to societal problems are more appropriate. Chater and Loewenstein (2022) elaborate on this view by explaining that behavioral scientists often adopt an "i-frame" where policy problems are framed as individual issues, rather than an "s-frame" which refers to systemic problems and solutions. Echoing the title of a recent book that addresses the need for systemic solutions to pervasive gender discrimination, rather than asking women to "lean in" more (fix the system, not the women; Bates, 2022), we might prefer to advocate to "Fix the system, not the (irrational/biased/etc.) individual". Indeed, according to some notable commentators, focusing on personal responsibility can become an excuse for government inaction (Reicher et al., 2022).

Taking a more sinister turn, the use of psychological ploys to influence people's behavior may be used for malign purposes – arguably, in the commercial (and political) sphere, it already sometimes is (see Chapter 7). History provides too many lessons for us to rest content. For example, Nazi Germany used social psychological processes to further its ends, including social comparison, social norms, cognitive-impaired emotional reactions, and the like – it also depended on the complacency of large sections of the population at the time. Although there is no evidence to indicate that Western democracies are using behavioral science in such a malign way, equally it would take a heroic feat of optimism to believe that this could *never* happen. We may as well start thinking seriously about these possible outcomes in order now to build defenses against them.

BENIGN PATERNALISM

We have reached a point now where we can see that the concept of libertarian paternalism is problematic: there is no reason to think that people's true preferences necessarily serve their long-term welfare – short-term utility satisfaction, blown around on the winds of psychological whim, may well to be the order of the day. Where does this leave us?

One option is to pursue some form of, what we call, *benign paternalism*, which we could define as nudging people in the direction of what *we believe* is good for them, *irrespective of their true preferences*. This truly psychological approach – stripped of the need to purify preferences, as defined above – is aimed at nudging people toward a longer, healthier, and wealthier life (anyone for a short, unhealthy, and poor life?). This benign paternalism retains the liberal component of Sunstein and Thaler's approach as people can choose to reject the nudge, and other options are on the table – although they would be framed as less desirable. This benign paternalism approach has another merit: it avoids the weasel aspect that some people suspect underpins Sunstein and Thaler's nudge approach. In addition, the very name – *benign paternalism* – has a sufficient tone of patronization to serve as a constant reminder that government has to come to a consensus as to 'what is right' – and it may not be 'right' from the individual's short-term (subjective) perspective, even though it enhances their longer-term (objective) utility. Governments may also want to combine this approach with standard economic practices to impose a fine on the behaviors that cause externalities, that is, costs to other people (e.g., pollution). But beyond encouraging people to be healthy, happy, and wealthy, what should be the other targets?

SOCIAL COMPARISON AND SUBJECTIVE WELL-BEING

As we now know, paternalism comes in distinct forms which differ primarily in their understanding of preferences and the goals of nudging: should people be nudged toward the behavior they would choose if they were ECON, or should they be nudged toward the behavior that a benign choice architect considers best for them? In other words: what should be the criteria for nudging?

Instead of trying to identify underlying preferences, we may ask: what is actually important for people's well-being? To answer this question, we need to consider the ultimate goal of benevolent governments, which is beautifully illustrated in a quote by Thomas Jefferson (1809):

> The care of human life and happiness and not their destruction is the first and only legitimate object of good government.
>
> (Reprinted in Looney, 2005)

The idea that the central role of governments is the well-being of their citizens is reflected in the US Declaration of Independence, drafted by Jefferson and adopted in 1776, which famously declares the right to "Life, Liberty and the pursuit of *Happiness*". How should this happiness be measured? One option is to ask people how happy they are and then consider their own, *subjective* evaluation of their happiness instead of observing their revealed preferences – this is captured in measures of subjective well-being (SWB). SWB might be a convenient catch-all measure of happiness (or utility, as economists prefer to call it). All of this is in the spirit of one version of behavioral economics which argues that people are well off to the extent that they are happy or satisfied.

If we were to go down the SWB path as the criterion of happiness/utility/welfare, then we have to consider psychological processes that can influence these subjective evaluations. As we know, choices are often dependent on available options (so-called 'reference dependence'; discussed in Chapter 4). One good example of this is *social comparison* (Festinger, 1954), which we have already encountered in Chapter 5. Here, the reference point – or frame of reference – is a peer group, which consists of relevant others (maybe one's colleagues, friends, or family members). A major finding in the subjective well-being literature is that people often care more about their *relative* utility; that is, their comparative standing in society, rather than their *absolute* utility, especially with respect to income and other material goods (e.g., Easterlin, 2003). This directly contradicts the mainstream economist's understanding of utility maximization, which depends solely on the individual's own consumption and not that of other people, regardless of their relationship (what has my pleasure from eating an apple got to do with yours?). However, people *do* compare themselves in everyday life – and, as we saw in Chapter 5, even monkeys engage in work-related social comparison and can get into a 'strop' if they feel they are not getting their fair share of pay.

One example in humans that seems to bear out this social comparison effect is found in unemployment. Those who are unemployed, but live in regions of low unemployment, are considerably less satisfied than unemployed people who live in regions of high unemployment; that is, the employment status of others in their reference group matters for their own well-being (they are also affected by the employment of their partners and others in their household, though this effect is stronger for men; Clark, 2003). What seems to matter here is not just the loss of income that unemployment brings, but the loss of social status which is damaged less if others are in the same socioeconomic boat.

One major reason for thinking that social comparison is important comes from the work of economist Richard Easterlin, who in 1974 identified a paradox in the relationship between happiness and income: cross-sectional studies (data collected at any one time) show richer countries to be happier than poorer countries; but, when assessed over time, happiness does not increase as a country gets richer. One major interpretation is that how happy we feel has much to do with our perceived *relative standing* in society, which does not change as everyone in a country gets richer.

Social comparison – comparing ourselves to others – typically occurs in life domains where judgments of relative standing are easy to make. We notice when a colleague buys an expensive watch or a friend posts pictures of their new house on social media. We may then adopt their example as a new standard (reference point) for ourselves to which we then start to aspire. As an example, a major finding in the social comparison literature is that *relative* income (i.e., how one's income compares to relevant others, e.g., peers) is more important for subjective well-being than the absolute amount – we discussed this in Chapter 5. From a neoclassical economic point of view, this is plain silly: *assuming* equal buying power, who should prefer an annual income of $50,000 to $100,000? (It should not matter what other people are earning; in these two examples, $25,000 or $200,000 respectively.) This effect plays out within local networks, too. As the writer H. L. Mencken once quipped: "A wealthy man is one who earns $100 a year more than his wife's sister's husband" (quoted in Norton, 2012).

AFFECTIVE FORECASTING

There are other studies that seem to attest to the importance of social comparison effects on subjective well-being. One set of studies relates to *affective forecasting* (e.g., Wilson & Gilbert, 2005). To illustrate, consider the following study, which asked respondents across a number of countries to rate their present well-being, their well-being from five years ago, and to guess how happy they expected to be five years from now. On average, people rated past well-being lower than present well-being and anticipated to be more satisfied in five years' time. However, their well-being actually remained fairly constant over time (Easterlin, 2001). Why did these respondents assume fairly large swings in their well-being as time passes, which actually did not occur? One possibility is that they cannot forecast the effects of social comparison, as well as changes in aspirations and hedonic adaptation (the tendency to return to previous levels of SWB after life events). If we continue to compare ourselves with others, it is very hard to get ahead, *relatively speaking.*

We thus often fail to anticipate the consequences of our decisions on future well-being – in particular, we tend to overestimate the effects of positive events and underestimate the effects of negative events. The prediction of one's emotional reaction (affect) to future events has been termed 'affective forecasting' (or hedonic forecasting). This is partly due to focalism (also known as *focusing illusion*; i.e., our tendency to focus on one aspect of life when we assess the impact of events on our future well-being). Couples who are expecting a child may focus on how much happiness holding a baby will bring them, but they tend to ignore that sleepless nights can be very detrimental to happiness, as well as relationships.

A well-known study asked people if they expected any changes in happiness if they moved to California (Schkade & Kahneman, 1998). Most respondents agreed that such a move would certainly increase their well-being because they focused on the pleasant weather. However, they did not consider other aspects, such as the high cost of housing and traffic jams which are also part-and-parcel of life in some parts of California – another example of how salient information can cloud our decision making.

To further illustrate this point, let us consider an example that most people expect to be the key to everlasting happiness: winning the lottery. Studies of lottery winners – which admittedly have fairly small sample sizes – show that these lucky folk are, on average, actually not happier in the long run than nonwinners (Brickman et al., 1978) (more than a few even claim that the win has ruined their life). Hedonic adaptation implies that lottery winners get quickly accustomed to their new-found wealth. And, that is not all. If the win is quite sizeable, they may buy a larger house in a fancier neighborhood, which means that they quickly change their peer group. They might now be a 'big frog' compared to their previous wealth but moving to a larger pond means they are suddenly surrounded by other, even bigger, frogs; therefore, their absolute, objective financial status may have improved but their *relative*, subjective status may have gotten worse (see text box). As the old saying goes, "be wary of what you wish for".

As economist Robert Frank expressed very aptly in his 1985 book, *Choosing the Right Pond: Human Behavior and the Quest for Status*, there

---

BIG FROG IN A SMALL POND

The Dutch Postcode Lottery (PCL) offers a unique opportunity to examine whether people are more likely to buy a car once a neighbor parks a shiny new BMW in front of their home. The Postcode Lottery randomly selects a postal code and distributes prizes to every lottery ticket buyer in that postal code. One of these prizes is a new BMW, which is worth considerably more than the cash prizes of EUR12,500 that the other ticket holders receive. Researchers surveyed households in winning postal codes six months after the draw and found that people who did not participate in the lottery and whose neighbors had won the new BMW were more likely to buy a car during the six months after the lottery than non-PCL participants who lived in postal codes that did not win the lottery (Kuhn et al., 2011).

This example shows in a very elegant way that most of us do, indeed, try to 'keep up with the Joneses'; contrary to what standard economic theory would predict, neighbors' consumption does matter.

is a difference between being a big frog in a small pond and a small frog in a big pond. Status, and the well-being we derive from it, because of the effects of social comparison, depends on the pond we choose. Overall, increasing aspirations, caused by social comparison and hedonic adaptation, can therefore easily counteract any short-term positive well-being impact a lottery win may bring.

MONEY, AFTER ALL, MAY NOT BUY HAPPINESS

Life is not all about money, and nor is subjective well-being. More happily for the financially (relatively) disadvantaged, many of the things that impact subjective well-being are less easy to quantify in monetary terms and, therefore, compare. For this reason, social comparison effects are less prevalent in life domains in which achievements are difficult to observe, including health and partnerships – where would you even start to compare the quality of your romantic relationship(s) with those of your friends? In these days of social media, we may know whether our friend has a new partner – and we may even know how attractive, successful, kind, and so on they are – but it is much more difficult to assess from this information whether they are happy (or even as happy as they say they are).

An important point here is that governments can nudge people in ways to enhance these financially intangible features of life where social comparison is less possible (e.g., social relationship, health, leisure). By this route, instead of envying we may well pity the fabulously wealthy individual who does not have the time to enjoy the 'simpler things in life' – or, at least, we can console ourselves in this belief and, thereby, make ourselves happier.

CONCLUSIONS

In this chapter, we have seen that a nudge, which is part of the toolkit of the behavioral policymaker, is often more effective than simply providing information, using incentives, or imposing regulation to change behavior, which in many instances (e.g., better health) are simply not viable options. For example, social incentives and precommitments can help to make people adhere to their goals and not to give in to temptations of immediate gratification. Along with other nudge-type models of behavior change, MINDSPACE is a convenient mnemonic to help policymakers design more effective policies based on behavioral insights, but we have also seen some of the conceptual problems with this approach. Despite these caveats, behavioral insights teams around the world now help governments design and evaluate behavioral policies. As the World Bank and the United Nations stress, as well as money in the bank, satisfaction, a sense of purpose, and flourishing are important components of the true wealth and health of the nation. If nothing else, nudge theory has encouraged us to think more rigorously about fundamental economic issues of choices and how best governments can promote the health and wealth of society, for the benefit of everyone.

FURTHER READING

Dolan, P., Hallsworth, M., Halpern, D., King, D., & Vlaev, I. (2010). *MINDSPACE: Influencing Behaviour Through Public Policy.* Institute for Government & the Cabinet Office. Retrieved from https://www.instituteforgovernment.org.uk/publications/mindspace

Infante, G., Lecouteux, G., & Sugden, R. (2016). Preference purification and the inner rational agent: A critique of the conventional wisdom of behavioural welfare economics. *Journal of Economic Methodology, 23,* 1–25.

Organisation for Co-operation and Development (OECD) (2017). *Behavioural insights and public policy: Lessons from around the world.* OECD Publishing

Thaler, R., & Sunstein, C. (2021). *Nudge: The final edition.* Allen Lane.

CHAPTER REFERENCES

Bates, L. (2022). *Fix the system, not the women.* Simon & Schuster.

Bertrand, M., Karlan, D., Mullainathan, S., Shafir, E., & Zinman, J. (2010). What's advertising content worth? Evidence from a consumer credit marketing field experiment. *The Quarterly Journal of Economics, 125,* 263–306. https://doi.org/10.1162/qjec.2010.125.1.263

Brickman, P., Coates, D., & Janoff-Bulman, R. (1978). Lottery winners and accident victims: Is happiness relative? *Journal of Personality and Social Psychology, 36,* 917–927. https://doi.org/10.1037//0022-3514.36.8.917

Brocas, I., Carrillo, J., & Dewatripont, M. (2004). Commitment devices under self-control problems: An overview. In I. Brocas, & J. Carrillo (Eds.), *The psychology of economic decisions. Volume 2: Reasons and choices* Oxford University Press.

Camerer, C., Issacharoff, S., Loewenstein, G., O'Donoghue, T., & Rabin, M. (2003). Regulation for conservatives: Behavioral economics and the case for "asymmetric paternalism." *University of Pennsylvania Law Review, 151*, 1211–1254. https://doi.org/10.2307/3312889

Chater, N., & Loewenstein, G. F. (2022). The i-frame and the s-frame: How focusing on individual-level solutions has led behavioral public policy astray. *SSRN Electronic Journal*. https://doi.org/10.2139/SSRN.4046264

Cialdini, R. B., Demaine, L. J., Sagarin, B. J., Barrett, D. W., Rhoads, K., & Winter, P. L. (2006). Managing social norms for persuasive impact. *Social Influence, 1*, 3–15. https://doi.org/10.1080/15534510500181459

Clark, A. E. (2003). Unemployment as a social norm: Psychological evidence from panel data. *Journal of Labor Economics, 21*, 323–351. https://doi.org/10.1086/345560

Dodsworth, L. (2021). *A state of fear: How the UK government weaponised fear during the Covid-19 pandemic.* Pinter & Martin.

Dolan, P., Hallsworth, M., Halpern, D., King, D., & Vlaev, I. (2010). *MINDSPACE: Influencing behaviour through public policy.* Institute for Government & the Cabinet Office. http://www.instituteforgovernment. org.uk/content/133/mindspace-influencing-behaviour-through-public-policy

Easterlin, R. A. (1974). Does economic growth improve the human lot? Some empirical evidence. In P. A. David, & M. W. Reder (Eds.), *Nations and households in economic growth: Essays in honour of Moses Abramovitz* (pp. 89–125). Academic Press.

Easterlin, R. A. (2001). Income and happiness: Towards a unified theory. *The Economic Journal, 111*, 465–484. https://doi.org/10.1111/1468-0297.00646

Easterlin, R. A. (2003). Explaining happiness. *Proceedings of the National Academy of Sciences of the United States of America, 100*, 11176–11183. https://doi.org/10.1073/pnas.1633144100

Easton, M. (2015, July 22). How politicians learned the power of the gentle nudge. *BBC News.* http://www.bbc.co.uk/news/magazine-33629019

Ferguson, E., Heckman, J. J., & Corr, P. (2011). Personality and economics: Overview and proposed framework. *Personality and Individual Differences, 51*, 201–209. https://doi.org/10.1016/J.PAID.2011.03.030

Festinger, L. (1954). A theory of social comparison processes. *Human Relations, 7*, 117–140. https://doi.org/10.1177/001872675400700202

Frank, R. H. (1985). *Choosing the right pond: Human behavior and the quest for status.* Oxford University Press.

Freud, S. (1904). *The psychopathology of everyday life (Zur Psychopathologie des Alltagslebens).* S. Karger.

Friedman, M. (1980). *Free to choose.* Harcourt.

Giné, X., Karlan, D., & Zinman, J. (2010). Put your money where your butt is: A commitment contract for smoking cessation. *American Economic Journal: Applied Economics*, *2*, 213–235. https://doi.org/10.1257/app.2.4.213

Hallsworth, M. (2022, August 2). Making sense of the "Do nudges work?" debate. *Behavioral Scientist*. https://behavioralscientist. org/making-sense-of-the-do-nudges-work-debate/

Harford, T. (2022, May 6). What nudge theory got wrong. Is behavioural public policy a distraction from finding systemic solutions? *Financial Times – FT Magazine*. https://www.ft.com/content/a23e808b-e293-4cc0-b077-9168cff135e4

Holland, R. W., Hendriks, M., & Aarts, H. (2005). Smells like clean spirit: Nonconscious effects of scent on cognition and behavior. *Psychological Science*, *16*, 689–693. https://doi.org/10.1111/j.1467-9280.2005.01597.x

House of Lords – Science and Technology Select Committee. (2011). *Behaviour Change*. The Stationery Office Limited.

Hume, D. (1738). *A treatise of human nature*. John Noon.

Infante, G., Lecouteux, G., & Sugden, R. (2016). Preference purification and the inner rational agent: A critique of the conventional wisdom of behavioural welfare economics. *Journal of Economic Methodology*, *23*, 1–25. https://doi.org/10.1080/1350178X.2015.1070527

Kimmel, S. E., Troxel, A. B., Loewenstein, G., Brensinger, C. M., Jaskowiak, J., Doshi, J. A., Laskin, M., & Volpp, K. (2012). Randomized trial of lottery-based incentives to improve warfarin adherence. *American Heart Journal*, *164*, 268–274. https://doi.org/10.1016/j.ahj.2012.05.005

Kuhn, P., Kooreman, P., Soetevent, A., & Kapteyn, A. (2011). The effects of lottery prizes on winners and their neighbors: Evidence from the Dutch Postcode Lottery. *The American Economic Review*, *101*, 2226–2247. https://doi.org/10.1257/aer.101.5.2226

Loewenstein, G., Krishnamurti, T., Kopsic, J., & McDonald, D. (2015). Does increased sexual frequency enhance happiness? *Journal of Economic Behavior & Organization*, *116*, 206–218. https://doi.org/10.1016/j. jebo.2015.04.021

Looney, J. J. (Ed.). (2005). *The Papers of Thomas Jefferson, Retirement Series, Volume 1 4 March 1809 to 15 November 1809*. Princeton University Press.

Maier, M., Bartoš, F., Stanley, T. D., Shanks, D. R., Harris, A. J. L., & Wagenmakers, E.-J. (2022). No evidence for nudging after adjusting for publication bias. *Proceedings of the National Academy of Sciences*, *119*. https://doi.org/10.1073/PNAS.2200300119

Mertens, S., Herberz, M., Hahnel, U. J. J., & Brosch, T. (2022). The effectiveness of nudging: A meta-analysis of choice architecture interventions across behavioral domains. *Proceedings of the National Academy of Sciences of the United States of America, 119*, e2107346118. https://doi.org/10.1073/PNAS.2107346118

Michie, S., van Stralen, M. M., & West, R. (2011). The behaviour change wheel: A new method for characterising and designing behaviour change interventions. *Implementation Science, 6*, 42. https://doi.org/10.1186/1748-5908-6-42

Milkman, K. L., Gromet, D., Ho, H., Kay, J. S., Lee, T. W., Pandiloski, P., … Duckworth, A. L. (2021). Megastudies improve the impact of applied behavioural science. *Nature, 600*, 478–483. https://doi.org/10.1038/s41586-021-04128-4

Norton, M. I. (2012, July 25). Inequality: The more money, the merrier? *New Scientist.* https://www.newscientist.com/article/mg21528752-300-inequality-the-more-money-the-merrier/

Ogilvy, D. (1963). *Confessions of an advertising man.* Atheneum.

Oliver, A. (2013). From nudging to budging: Using behavioural economics to inform public sector policy. *Journal of Social Policy, 42*, 685–700. https://doi.org/10.1017/S0047279413000299

Oliver, A. (2015). Nudging, shoving, and budging: Behavioual economic-informed policy. *Public Administration, 93*, 700–714. https://doi.org/10.1111/PADM.12165

Osman, M. (2022, July 29). Nudge theory doesn't work after all, says new evidence review – but it could still have a future. *The Conversation.* https://theconversation.com/nudge-theory-doesnt-work-after-all-says-new-evidence-review-but-it-could-still-have-a-future-187635

Raihani, N. J. (2013). Nudge politics: Efficacy and ethics. *Frontiers in Psychology, 4*, 972. https://doi.org/10.3389/FPSYG.2013.00972/BIBTEX

Reicher, S., Michie, S., & West, R. (2022). The UK government's "personal responsibility" policy for covid is hypocritical and unsustainable. *BMJ, 378*, o1903. https://doi.org/10.1136/BMJ.O1903

Schkade, D. A., & Kahneman, D. (1998). Does living in California make people happy? A focusing illusion in judgments of life satisfaction. *Psychological Science, 9*, 340–346. https://doi.org/10.1111/1467-9280.00066

Schmidt, K., Schuldt-Jensen, J., Aarestrup, S. C., Jensen, A. R., Skov, K. L., & Hansen, P. G. (2016). *Nudging smoke in airports: A case study in nudging as a method.* http://inudgeyou.com/wp-content/uploads/2017/08/OP-ENG-Nudging_Smoke_in_Airports.pdf

Sunstein, C. R., & Thaler, R. H. (2003). Libertarian paternalism is not an oxymoron. *The University of Chicago Law Review, 70*, 1159–1202.

Thaler, R. H. (2015). *Misbehaving: The making of behavioural economics.* Allen Lane.

Thaler, R. H., & Sunstein, C. R. (2003). Libertarian paternalism. *The American Economic Review*, *93*, 175–179. https://doi.org/10.1257/000282803321947001

Thaler, R. H., & Sunstein, C. R. (2008). *Nudge: Improving decisions about health, wealth, and happiness.* Yale University Press.

Thaler, R. H., & Sunstein, C. R. (2021). *Nudge: The final edition.* Penguin Books.

The Behavioural Insights Team. (2014). *EAST: Four simple ways to apply behavioural insights.* The Behavioural Insights Team. https://www.bi.team/publications/east-four-simple-ways-to-apply-behavioural-insights/

Tribe, J. (2016). *The economics of recreation, leisure and tourism* (5th ed.). Routledge.

Volpp, K. G., Loewenstein, G., Troxel, A. B., Doshi, J., Price, M., Laskin, M., & Kimmel, S. E. (2008). A test of financial incentives to improve warfarin adherence. *BMC Health Services Research*, *8*, 272. https://doi.org/10.1186/1472-6963-8-272

West, R., & Michie, S. (2020). A brief introduction to the COM-B Model of behaviour and the PRIME Theory of motivation. *Qeios.* https://doi.org/10.32388/WW04E6

Wilde, O. (1893). *Lady Windemere's fan: A play about a good woman* (16th ed.). Methuen & Co. Ltd.

Wilson, T. D., & Gilbert, D. T. (2005). Affective forecasting. *Current Directions in Psychological Science*, *14*, 131–134. https://doi.org/10.1111/j.0963-7214.2005.00355.x

Winkielman, P., Berridge, K. C., & Wilbarger, J. L. (2005). Unconscious affective reactions to masked happy versus angry faces influence consumption behavior and judgments of value. *Personality and Social Psychology Bulletin*, *31*, 121–135. https://doi.org/10.1177/0146167204271309

Wryobeck, J., & Chen, Y. (2003). Using priming techniques to facilitate health behaviours. *Clinical Psychologist*, *7*, 105–108. https://doi.org/10.1080/13284200410001707553

SELL! COMMERCIAL AND POLITICAL PERSUASION

Behavioral economic insights have been used in the private sector for many decades, though they have not been labeled as such – formerly, they went by such terms as 'motivation research', characterized as the 'hidden persuaders'. Advertisers have known about the power of framing to add psychological value to products, and other tricks from the behavioral economics tool kit have been used for a long time to great effect. Indeed, companies rarely just sell a product or service; rather they sell the idea and feeling of them: psychological value. The chapter discusses the clever use of psychological insights such as anchoring, framing, loss aversion, and decoy pricing – all aided by sophisticated behavioral science testing protocols. We discuss developments in the scientific understanding of persuasion that have led to a significant shift in strategies to communicate messages to influence consumers, as well as people more widely (e.g., government 'information campaigns'). Psychological insights are even being employed in political campaigns to sell ideas and policies. This concluding chapter ends with a discussion of the use of social media (e.g., Facebook) in such campaigns, and considers some of the ethical and moral issues entailed. Behavioral economics has strong upsides, but also concerning downsides.

DOI: 10.4324/9781003166900-7

INTRODUCTION

We saw in the previous chapter how behavioral economics is used by governments to nudge citizens to make better decisions to improve their health and wealth (e.g., pension savings), supposedly as *seen from their own point of view* – we also saw some of the conceptual problems with the whole nudge approach. Many of the same behavioral economic principles are employed in the commercial world to sell products and services – and increasingly, with attendant controversy, in the political world to sell ideas and influence over voters. Whether we are dealing with commercial data or political dogma, behavioral economics is perceived to be both relevant and effective.

In fact, long before the birth of the discipline of behavioral economics, there has been a large and lucrative industry devoted to exploiting psychological insights for commercial gain. These are the 'hidden persuaders' described by Vance Packard in his 1957 book of the same name and, more recently, depicted in the highly acclaimed television series of 1960/70s advertising, *Mad Men*. However, unlike this earlier, often psychodynamically inspired, *motivation research* – the name by which much of depth psychology was known in the advertising industry (see Smith, 1971) – modern-day consumer research is more concerned with the 'observable shallows': factors of persuasion that, although in full sight, are often overlooked.

If nothing else, the widescale adoption of behavioral economic principles and practices in the commercial world attests to the reality that this academic discipline has escaped the confines of the ivory tower. It is very much a science with variegated practical applications. In another important way, unlike much of the earlier motivation research, behavioral economics offers relatively simple and highly actionable proposals for persuasion; and, of no small importance, interventions that can be empirically tested to determine their (in)effectiveness – as discussed below, this is something that has long been practiced in direct response marketing campaigns, for well over 100 years, where advertisers would split-test, for example, different formats of coupons, or the same coupons placed in different newspapers/magazines. If we stand back, we might even say that advertising is one enormous social experiment, to uncover what does and does not work in the world of commercial persuasion. It has another fascinating side, too. It allows us a unique view of the nature of the everyday economic mind – the bread-and-butter of behavioral economics.

HIDDEN PERSUASION

The success of marketing, advertising, sales, and brand management depends critically on a proper understanding of the motivation of the consumer – without this understanding, they fail. Over the evolution of (un)successful campaigns, advertisers in particular have discovered that they rarely just sell a product or service – that is, their mere functionality. They know that to stand a chance of success, they need to sell ideas, aspirations, and the feelings that surround them – in other words, they sell something that is fundamentally *psychological*. No surprise there for the person in the street, perhaps; but something of an eye-opener for the mainstream neoclassically inclined economist. (For an economic analysis of advertising, see Bagwell, 2005.)

To understand a little more about the commercial economic mind, it is of some interest to note that mid-century American advertising was characterized by two major perspectives. One was based on identifying a Unique Selling Proposition (USP), conveying factual information, and building a strong brand reinforced by high volume media exposure – this was epitomized by David Ogilvy of Ogilvy & Mather (see Ogilvy, 1963, 1983). The other perspective took its inspiration from the, often, psychodynamically-inspired "depth boys" (notably Sigmund Freud; there were notable "girls" too, e.g., Anna Freud in the United Kingdom and Karen Horney in the United States) who sought to exploit the deeper and (often) darker forces of the mind – they believed in powerful unconscious motives, defense mechanisms, and general neurosis, driving behaviour in the general population. In the first episode of the highly popular TV show *Man Men*, this difference of perspective was dramatized by the main protagonist Don Draper throwing into the waste bin a report that suggested that the best way to advertise cigarettes is to tell consumers that cigarettes will kill them (playing on the Freudian notion of Thanatos, 'death instinct') – as the makers of Lucky Strike opined: "So we tell them that since you're going to die smoking anyway, you should die with us? That's crazy!". Of course, there have been intermediate positions, but in one form or another, all have stressed the psychological nature of advertising, and therefore the economic mind. Behavioral economics seems to offer what the advertising world has long hankered after: a scientifically grounded general approach acceptable by all.

Whatever variety or blend of approaches were adopted, long before the formalization of behavioral economics, the commercial world was in little doubt that the notion of the fact-seeking, rational *homo economicus* was, to put it mildly, less than ideal – and no doubt many businesses failed commercially by adopting this model. The successful enterprises knew that the typical consumer is not someone who knows what they always want (i.e., has stable preferences) and always knows how to maximize their utility by optimizing the available choices on offer to them. Indeed, it is evident that the commercial world gives such neoclassical economic notions scant regard, preferring instead to view consumer's wants and preferences as actively influenced and shaped, even created (e.g., the daily use of toothpaste over 100 years ago did not exist in the form we would recognize, or accept, today). Now, this perspective is perhaps inevitable when novel products and services are introduced to the market (who would have ever thought we desired smart mobile phones to keep us connected to every corner of the globe? We did not know until we were told!).

The motive to make money – and the Darwinian-like selection pressures of losing money – motivated and enabled the commercial world to become especially adept at devising psychological ploys to separate the consumer from their money – as Rory Sutherland of Ogilvy jokingly

EVALUATIVE CONDITIONING

A powerful and ubiquitous phenomenon in all areas of life is *evaluative conditioning*: this refers to a change in attitude toward some stimulus (it could be a product, service, or even a political idea). It can readily be applied to advertising and marketing. Evaluative conditioning reflects a change in the valence, positive vs negative, of a stimulus as a result of the pairing of that stimulus with another, positive or negative, stimulus, respectively. It is a form of classical (or Pavlovian) conditioning in which an initially neutral stimulus (e.g., light – technically known as the 'conditioned stimulus', CS) comes to take on the reinforcing properties of an innately rewarding (or punishing) stimulus (e.g., for Fido the dog, a piece of meat or a rebuke from its owner; technically known as the 'unconditioned stimulus', UCS). After a sufficient number of CS–UCS pairings, the CS acquires the power to elicit a response (the 'conditioned response'; the CR) which is similar to the response to the innate UCS (i.e., the 'unconditioned response'; the UCR).

By this procedure, in some form or another, evaluative conditioning can be employed to transfer emotional value to commercial products and services, where previously none existed. Think of George Clooney advertising coffee.

put it: "savings are only delayed expenditure". The job of the marketing expert is to discourage savings, to speed up the spending process.

It is little short of a wonder to behold: the commercial world is full of various types of creative agencies tasked with nothing more than finding better ways to portray even the most humdrum products and services as absolute necessities, comprising the essential requirements of the good life (think of the most recent iPhone). Of some wonder, too, it is not uncommon for senior executives to fly around the globe to get together to discuss how best to sell their brand of toilet roll, toothpaste, or toothpick. They know, of course, that they are not just selling a product; they are selling something much nobler, such as aspiration, status, and power. From subtle messages to more explicit associations of innately pleasant stimuli – so-called evaluative conditioning (see text box) – commercial bodies seek to influence the consumer in a myriad of ways, and all without much awareness, or even concern, on the part of the average consumer. These psychological ploys work best when the consumer does not feel they are being influenced, or at least manipulated – they may even enjoy the process (e.g., amusing advertisements or interacting with a personally optimized website).

THE BUTTERFLY EFFECT

In contrast to the typical ways neoclassical economics encourages us to think, small – and often seemingly irrelevant – things can have big effects, and they need not cost the earth. The behavioral science arm of the international advertising agency Ogilvy fully embraces behavioral economics (led by advertising guru Rory Sutherland, whom we already met above). They embrace what has become known as the 'butterfly effect' (see text box). The goal is to find small (preferably inexpensive) nudges that have a disproportionately large effect on behavior (Sutherland, 2014). Sutherland's (2019) aptly named book, *Alchemy*, presents the truly fascinating opportunities offered by behavioral economics to the advertising executive. (Rory's talks are available on the internet, and his creative thoughts are contained in his book, *The Wiki Man*; Sutherland, 2011.) It is also worth reading the 1963 entertaining book by the influential advertiser David Ogilvy, who established the company for which Rory works: *Confessions of an Advertising Man*; see also Ogilvy, 1983).

BUTTERFLY EFFECT

The idea of a butterfly flapping its wings in Brazil and causing a storm in Australia is based on chaos theory, which states that small (local) initial state changes can have large (global) effects. It was originally associated with weather systems but then got extended to other areas of science, including the behavioral variety. The basic idea is that the outcomes in nonlinear (complex) systems are sensitive to initial conditions, which, although small in magnitude, can exert big effects. Thus, a small contextual change – say a small nudge – may significantly affect people's decisions and longer-term downstream outcomes.

COMMERCIAL PREFERENCES

As an 'ad man' like the insightful, flamboyant, and irrepressible Rory Sutherland makes clear, if the consumer made perfect choices based on perfect information, under conditions of perfect trust, and possessed unlimited cognitive processing and will power, the advertising and marketing world would be populated by very poor people. We know it is not! And if, indeed, the typical consumer conforms to the neo-classical notion of *homo economicus*, then no one had the decency to tell this highly lucrative industry which must have been going about its business for so many years under a terrible misapprehension.

But, as we know, typically, the consumer *is* susceptible to the prac-tices and ploys of *Mad Men* (and women) – just look around your home to get a sense of this fact! Empirical data from the advertising industry tells us as much. In 2013, on behalf of the Institute of Practitioners in Advertising (IPA), two influential figures in the advertising industry, Les Binet and Peter Field, conducted an analysis of the most successful UK ad campaigns of the past 30 years. They found that "the most effec-tive advertisements of all are those with little or no rational content" – this conclusion flies in the face of one influential information-based theory of persuasive communication, as well as neoclassical economics more generally. These authors noted, too, that television remains the preferred emotional medium – even the smartest static advertisement is unlikely to make anyone grin, gasp, or weep. It does not really matter either if we are paying much attention: not only are they now targeted to the *specific* demographic watching a *specific* program on the many available *specific* TV channels, they are designed to seep through to our nonconscious (System 1) mind even when they are being played in the background. This channel of communication may actually make them *more* effective because it bypasses the editing facilities of the more cognitive and critical (System 2) mind. And whereas before, during an 'ad break', we may have taken the opportunity to leave the room to make a cup of tea, now we are more likely to be engaged with social media, and television advertisements play on this fact – in the not-too-distant future, the TV advert being shown will be synchronized with what we are at that moment experiencing on a social media platform (it is for such reasons that companies want us to sign-in via a single entry point, because this allows them to retrieve a mass of information which they can then use to tailor persuasive messages to influence us). Therefore, advertisers need only grab *some* of our attention for their message to land and their influence to be felt, and more often than not this is in purely emotional terms – something which even the most neoclassically inspired of us find difficult to ignore. This works best when the advertiser knows which of our psychological buttons they need to press. In all of this, something else is of importance: *mere exposure*. This psychological phenomenon is probably responsible for sustaining the advertising industry even when its creative juices have run rather dry.

Starting in the 1960s, work by Robert Zajonc demonstrated that people have a tendency to develop a definite preference for stimuli *merely* by virtue of being exposed to and, thereby, becoming familiar with them – this is the 'familiarity principle' (e.g., Zajonc, 1968). The mere exposure effect is robust and can be elicited by such stimuli as abstract geometric figures, paintings, faces, and sounds. In broader psychological terms, it may explain why we like being around familiar people – this effect is called 'glow of warmth', and it is likely to have an evolutionary origin: whereas a highly novel stimulus initially leads to a fear-avoidance reaction, this declines with repeated exposure when we come to learn that the stimulus is harmless and may well be useful. Advertising works to some extent through this very process. This is why exposure to adverts needs to be repeated. A single presentation of a high information advert – even assuming it were fully processed – is unlikely ever to be effective.

Another major advertising ploy relies upon the fact that we seek information and reassurance from other people – called *social proof*. There is even evidence that our facial muscles mimic automatically the facial expressions of other people (e.g., Prochazkova & Kret, 2017) and the configuration of our facial muscles then sends information to the brain which infers what emotional state we *ought* to be in (if you want a quick 'pick me up', just place a pencil between your lips to create a muscle smile!). Little of this knowledge, often built-up via industry folklore, has evaded the sharp advertising executive. We see their actions when, for example, we go to the cinema with the express intention not to eat the super-sized popcorn or drink the super-large drink, but once we see people doing this on the big screen, we often have a rapid change of heart and, then, mind – especially if we are in a group where others are eating and drinking (after all, who wants to be the odd one out?). Before long we are stuffed full of popcorn, hot dogs, and fizzy drinks, and we are left to wonder "how did *that* happen"? It was not by accident; it was by (behavioral) design.

This accumulation of knowledge of typical consumer behavior is all very interesting and, of course, of considerable commercial value. But, it has another important function to serve: it is of academic relevance. It reveals important facts about everyday economic life: how people make real decisions in real life. In this way, the commercial world may be seen as a big laboratory for the testing of behavioral economic ideas. This type of real-world research is quite different from the typical type conducted in academia. For one, the financial incentives to understand consumer motivation are huge in the commercial world, and if they fail, they run the very real risk of going out of business. In marked contrast, an academic behavioral economist can be wrong for many years without too much pecuniary disadvantage – indeed, during this time, they may well be promoted and esteemed by colleagues. These are underappreciated facts and have been neglected in academic circles, perhaps for an obvious reason, but also perhaps because of the notion among (too) many academics that commerce (worse still, 'trade') is a grubby profession and far too below their self-perceived exalted academic status. Very *homo psychologicus*!

Whatever one chooses to believe, there is little doubt that the *science* of behavioral economics is much enhanced by knowledge gained from *commercial* practices and ploys – what really works in the 'laboratory of everyday economic life'. The academic, Robert Cialdini, is a model of this approach: he worked alongside salespeople 'in the real world', getting his hands dirty at the sharp end of commercial persuasion. This led to his best-selling 2007 book, *Influence: The Psychology of Persuasion* which went on in various revisions to outstanding commercial success

The science of persuasion has been much enhanced by Cialdini's immersion in the "grubby" world of trade.

PERSONALITY AND INTERNET SHOPPING

Imagine a world in which internet shopping companies knew your gender, age, religious/political leanings, and personality, without asking you directly and without your knowledge. Well, they do already! At least, they can have a good guess based on the time of day/week you use the internet, and the considerable amount of personal information harvested from your social media data (e.g., Facebook 'likes').

As an example of the way the industry is moving, consider one London based company, VisualDNA – now part of the media research group, Neilsen. They have tested 100,000s of people on a personality test and then matched these personality data to how the same people navigate websites. They sell this information to companies who use it to predict the personality characteristics of browsers who they want to turn into buyers. But why would companies want to know the personalities of their potential customers? Well, to some extent, personality predicts preferences. For example, a highly extraverted person may want/need more of a social experience; an emotionally reactive person may want/need some proverbial 'hand-holding'; whereas someone low on agreeableness (i.e., tough-minded) may want/need to get in and out as quickly as possible. The upshot of this approach is that some companies are now using such behavioral technology to 'optimize' the shopping experience for specific personality types. This is one reason why some websites seem in tune with our personality while others grate on us. Depending on one's viewpoint, this is either a very clever use of behavioral science or rather sneaky – whichever, the intention is to turn browsers into buyers, and 'knowing your customer' is a great help to get the finger to press the 'Buy' button.

PSYCHOLOGICAL VALUE

As emphasized throughout this book, economics has long been concerned with the related notions of 'value' and 'utility', in relation to especially the optimization of the allocation of scarce resources to maximize them. How, though, should we define value and utility in behavioral economic terms? Well, we can start by distinguishing between *objective* ('real' tangible) value and *subjective* ('artificial' psychological) value. The latter, created by the marketing, advertising, and brand management world, has always been perceived as distinctly second best – even seemingly suspect. We should, however, note in passing that this distinction is not as clear-cut as it may seem, as discussed below. We can easily think of the objective value of a car, and the subjective 'badge' value of it: just think of the contrast between Jaguar and Skoda – yet sometimes what is under the bonnet is little different between low and high-end brands (e.g., Skoda is owned by Volkswagen and enjoys its technical strengths – for this reason, Skoda often appears at the top of car league tables). Yet, on the basis purely of 'badge' value, and the usual caveat of all else being equal, would you prefer to own a Skoda over a Jaguar? (It is true, though, contrarians might derive some idiosyncratic utility by violating this general rule, and some may feel uneasy driving around in a 'flashy big car'.) Once we decided on our car, we start to experience psychological value in the ridiculous; for example, a newly valeted car just seems to drive better!

Belief is important, too, in psychological value. For example, branded analgesics work better than generics (e.g., Hallam, 2015), not only in psychological but also in physical terms. (The distinction between the two is less clear-cut than implied by the names.) And fish and chips taste better when sitting on a harbor wall, looking out to sea. None of this is a magician's trick: *psychological* value is at the heart of what we perceive as 'value', of all kinds – there are many other instances of how perceived value is affected by what should be, in Richard Thaler's words, supposedly irrelevant factors (e.g., transaction value – see below).

Objective/tangible value is important, of course: faster trains are superior to slower ones, and cars that do not break down are always preferred to ones that do. However, if the cost of faster trains runs into the tens of billions of dollars/pounds and saves 20% travel time but the psychological cost is fewer tables on which to comfortably work, is this a sensible expenditure of scarce resources? For *many* billions less, technologically advanced trains could be built which are slower but which afford more opportunity for comfort and work: it is rather a matter of (re)framing. (And the saved money could be spent on other needs in society, e.g., hospitals – another example of opportunity cost.) This is especially true when many problems are not really problems of technology, but essentially of perception. The intriguing conclusion from such a consideration is that big solutions do not always require big capital investment; far better, cleverer and often much cheaper solutions might do the trick equally well – recall from Chapter 3 that in neoclassical terms, more is always better (e.g., more speed, saved time, etc. – often, though, to the neglect of any consideration of the alternatives and their psychological value, and also the entailed opportunity cost).

Recognition of the power of *perception* of value is one of the major insights of behavioral economics and the persuasive practices of the commercial world. But, as in the case of the reliability of cars, a minimum standard of objective value must be obtained before psychological value can be added to make things even better. Once this minimal level of acceptability has been achieved, the compelling idea is that most of the things we consume are infused with psychological value – although, when asked, we might find objective/tangible reasons for the subjective/psychological value experienced (e.g., Jaguar cars are technologically superior and more reliable than Skoda cars [the first author has had a number of Jaguars and knows too well this is not true – but they *seem* to drive better than a Skoda!]).

Appreciating the existence of psychological value means that we can exploit untapped potential to enhance the utility of the individual as well as to increase the general welfare of society, and potentially at comparatively low cost. If we accept the definition of economics as the optimal allocation of scarce resources, this psychological approach starts to look *very* rational.

In everyday life, we can all put these behavioral principles to good use. For example, we could apply consumer research published in the Journal of Wine Economics which shows that if we are told a certain wine is expensive, it will taste better (Goldstein et al., 2008) – this is psychological value, pure and simple. (Beyond a minimum threshold of acceptability, only a small percentage of true wine connoisseurs have much of a clue as to what is a good and less good wine.) In addition, lighting and music affect how we perceive the *same* wine, as indeed it can affect our experience of chocolate – soft notes (e.g., Adele's 'Hello') make dark chocolate taste creamier, whereas sharp violin notes make the *same* chocolate taste bitter (Reinoso Carvalho et al., 2017). And perhaps not surprisingly, the mood we happen to be in affects how we experience food. Knowing about behavioral science allows us to choice-architect our own lives to enhance psychological value. Also, we could use this knowledge to avoid falling – or should that be, *fooling*! – into behavioral economic pits. One example of these pitfalls is seen with the perceived value that is writ large in a class of goods that owes its name to Thorstein Veblen, whom we have encountered in Chapter 2: Veblen goods (see text box).

The thing to bear in mind is that there is a subtle interplay between tangible (objective) value and psychological (subjective) value. Returning to our car example, of course, those who can afford one would not buy a top-of-the-range Jaguar XJ if it did not have superb technological features (this is a *necessary* condition), but the psychological value comes from the brand (*sufficient* condition) which comprises total experienced *value*: not only does it have exceptional functionalities, it *drives* like a dream.

However, we must not run away with the idea of the apparently unlimited potential of psychological value. Framing is important, but it will never be an adequate substitute for tangible value. Basic needs must be met before psychological ones have much of a chance to add value. For example, a cold room or unreliable car is an objective fact, and no amount of reframing would create much of psychological value. But when the product/service is within the

VEBLEN GOODS

In Chapter 2, we saw the criticism of neoclassical economics by Thorstein Veblen and his argument that 'conspicuous consumption' – think of sipping champagne on a luxury yacht – serves an important *social* purpose but violates standard economic principles. A *Veblen good* is one for which demand increases as price increases. This is in opposition to the usual price and demand graphs of most products and services. Such *luxury brands* serve as status symbols and as a sign that resources can be spent on luxuries that have mostly psychological and social value – think of a Gucci handbag for $2,000 over a high street shop one for $40. It is in the very nature of a Veblen good that it is out of the price league of the *hoi polloi*. If nothing else does, Veblen goods attest to the fundamental psychological nature of *value* – and, perhaps, too, to the shallowness of many people's apparent economic preferences.

zone of tolerance, there is considerable scope for the manufacture of subjective value.

On a wider societal level, the creation of psychological value can lead to social leveling. As Andy Warhol observed in his 1975 book, *The Philosophy of Andy Warhol*:

> A Coke is a Coke and no amount of money can get you a better Coke than the one the bum on the corner is drinking. All the Cokes are the same and all the Cokes are good. Liz Taylor knows it, the President knows it, the bum knows it, and you know it.

Part of the American Dream is to enable all citizens to eat the same McDonald's burger, washed down with the same Coke, as the next person, be they a pauper or prince. As this example shows, psychological value can be created even when objective (tangible) value is not exceptionally high, but it does need to be consistent and reliable (we know what to expect and are not disappointed). This is one major psychological value of trusted brands (see below).

CLOCKS AND CLOUDS

The discussion so far in this chapter raises many issues of how to view the economic mind. We might add that the neoclassical economic approach is rather mechanistic. It does not easily accommodate the psychological value discussed above, nor the psychological opportunity costs (e.g., being on a faster train but in a less psychologically optimizing environment). As with a freshly washed car that just seems to drive better, there is leakage between objective and subjective value, and often the latter can provide a solution to the former, and almost always at a much lower cost – something that should be of special interest to the cost-benefit economist. As Rory Sutherland is fond of reminding us, this distinction reflects the differences between clocks and clouds – first put forward by world-famous philosopher, Karl Popper. Whereas clocks are mechanical, easily understood, and can be modeled in precise (mathematical) terms, clouds are altogether more mercurial and ill-defined, not lending themselves to precise mechanical solutions (Popper, 1966). So much of human judgment, decision making and behavior seem more like clouds, not clocks, and require a psychological solution. Some examples will suffice to make this point clear.

PSYCHOLOGICAL VALUE IN ECONOMICS

It should now be clear that mainstream neoclassically inspired economics has little time for such intangible entities such as psychological value, for how can they be measured, quantified, and modeled? It has even less time for those who attempt to 'conjure it out of thin air' (e.g., via advertising). Yet, the traditional (classical) notion of economic value a long time ago moved away from quantifying it with a metric (e.g., the number of man hours needed to make a good) to, what is essentially, a subjective notion which meant that the whole issue could be sidestepped by the assumption that value is what people assume it to be, and it is contained in the preferences they *reveal*. The neoclassical notion of value thus seems, essentially, to be *psychological*.

It is rather interesting to learn that the commercial notion of value as a central psychological construct is more in keeping with an older school of economics, associated with Ludwig von Mises (1881–1973) – an Austrian-American economist – who believed that the field of *praxeology*, which is the study of human action (what we would now call psychology), is the general field and that economics is only a sub-discipline (he defined economics as the practice of praxeology/psychology under conditions of scarcity, a rather pleasing definition of behavioral economics). This approach certainly is endorsed by the commercial world where *form* over *function* is important – as already emphasized, function (e.g., a technically sufficient car) is a necessary condition, but the psychological *form* is the sufficient one.

The major take-home message of the above discussion is that the commercial use of behavioral economics has been adding psychological value to products and services and, *par excellence*, shows that in human welfare, such value is important and should not be neglected in cost-benefit analyses – especially not now that subjective well-being is at the heart of the governmental social welfare agenda (see Chapter 6). What is especially valuable about the commercial use of behavioral economics is that we have the psychological technology to make people wealthier not by providing *more* choices (which can be just downright confusing, entailing the potential of disutility resulting from decision cost) but by encouraging and enabling them to make *better* choices. This may even allow us to jump off the hedonic treadmill and avoid the pernicious effects of social comparison (see Chapter 6) while at the same time enjoying the fruits of technological and commercial innovations: to become wealthier, healthier, and happier.

TECHNIQUES OF PERSUASION

Developments in the *scientific* understanding of persuasion have paralleled practices in the commercial world. In particular, there has been a notable shift in views regarding how best to communicate messages to influence the consumer, as well as citizens more widely (e.g., government information campaigns). To understand this field, it is necessary to know the difference between the 'information processing model' and the 'cognitive response model'.

Before the 1980s, most theories of persuasion stressed *systematic processing*, which assumed that changes in attitude depend on how the recipient of the message processes it – active and systematic processing of arguments being the important thing (e.g., Chaiken, 1980). The idea is that when attitudes, beliefs, and the like are changed, behavior invariably follows. This was all very logical and sensible sounding, but alas not very effective. Few studies supported this rational model: message reception (as measured by recall) tends not to correlate with attitude change and behavior.

Around about the late 1960s, an alternative, 'cognitive response model', was developed (Greenwald, 1968). This states that what is important about effective communication is not so much what is *said* but what is *heard*, and importantly the response it elicits – the same objective 'information' may be processed by people in different ways. More precisely, the cognitive response model assumes that for attitude change to occur it is not enough merely to receive and process the message; what matters are the thoughts ('cognitive responses') of the recipient which are elicited by the message. It assumes that listeners are active and relate messages to their own knowledge, experience, and *schemas* (i.e., cognitive structures that organize and assimilate new information). Existing cognitive responses are called into play, and it is these self-generated thoughts that mediate attitude change and actual behavior.

The world of advertising quickly caught on to this newer view – they had suspected as much for a long time. As seen above, the vast majority of commercial advertisements do not contain much of an 'argument' (indeed, there is a real poverty of information), yet they have the power to persuade and influence. They do not work through the 'central route': careful and thoughtful consideration of the arguments. Instead, they derive their influence from the 'peripheral route': emotional, with evaluative conditioning, mere exposure, and heuristic processing (e.g., "you can trust an expert"). What is now widely appreciated is that attitude, belief, etc. *follow* a change in behavior (however, induced) – we have already seen an example of this effect with *cognitive dissonance* in Chapter 6.

This is why today, there is typically an emotional invocation in advertisements, sometimes contained in some form of an ongoing storyline. A good example is seen in the classic television advertisement in the UK for Nescafé Gold Blend which contained more romance than coffee – as the lady coyly replies when asked by a dinner party guest whether she has met her new (and attractively charming) neighbor, "I've popped in for coffee" (the rest is left to the cognitive responses of the febrile, or salacious, imagination of the viewer!).

A/B TESTING: A METHOD OF EVALUATION

As with direct-response newspaper advertisements 100 years ago, campaigns can be scientifically evaluated. For example, the internet travel company Booking.com (www.booking.com) is an especially interesting example because it has invested heavily in, what is known as, A/B testing (see text box). By virtue of the fact that they have a large number of visitors to their website each day, it is reported that they run many such A/B trials every day of every week and that their system is automatically optimized when new features are shown to work (i.e., more people have pressed the 'buy' button on version A as compared with version B – these versions can be almost anything, for example, the position and size of a button on the page).

It is instructive to know that long before we had 'evidence-based medicine', based on randomized controlled trials (RCTs), the advertising world traced responses to evaluate effectiveness, often down to the single penny expended on the campaign. This fact is well described in a fabulous little book, *Scientific Advertising* (1923) by the acclaimed advertising guru, Claude Hopkins. David Ogilvy (1983) wrote, "Nobody should be allowed to have anything to do with advertising until he has read this book seven times. It changed the course of my

A/B TESTING

A/B testing – also known as 'split testing' – attempts to bring scientific methodology to marketing. It seeks to determine which factors work in communication campaigns by testing the effectiveness of two or more different variations of a message. This could consist of any set of differences: use of different words in a sales letter; colors, pictures, and shapes used on websites; the order of presenting material; what is shown on a website when loading (this can mimic loading a page); devices to 'close' the sale (e.g., *x* number of people are looking at the same product; limited period only); and so on – the list is endless. The goal is to determine what works best. All of us are part of large experiments of this type on a daily basis without even knowing it (see booking.com in text).

life". (It was one of the three books that all new recruits to Ogilvy's agency were required to digest; the other two being his partner's book on plain English and his own *Confessions of an Advertising Man.*)

As their employees are willing to disclose at behavioral science events (e.g., Nudgestock), Booking.com routinely uses a number of ploys to prevent the indecision shown by many website users: their goal is to convert browsers into buyers. How do they do this? One of us was recently looking to book a hotel in Warsaw. Not only were we reassured that they found the best price on the internet, after a few minutes they sent a pop-up message stating that the price was guaranteed only for ten minutes and that 6 other people were looking at the same room (whether these were Booking.com staff, we shall never know). All of this is intended to induce a state of apprehension and impulsiveness to avoid losing the apparent bargain (calling into play loss aversion; see Chapter 4). Helpfully, Booking.com allows the use of a debit/credit card to 'secure' the room, but no money is taken at this point – this exploits the ploy of imposing a psychological cost if the transaction is subsequently canceled, a 'loss of face' for reversing a decision, and psychological tension for not remaining consistent with oneself. Even when we know the intention of these ploys, they still work! (As a University credit card was needed to pay for this room, and thus there was a delay, the room that seemed so scarce an hour before was found still to be available much later – surprise, surprise!)

PSYCHOLOGICAL FACTORS IN CONSUMER DECISION MAKING

The way we go about forming judgments and making decisions seems to have deep roots in our evolutionary past, as we saw when discussing monkeynomics in Chapter 5. A splendidly readable book by the evolutionary psychologist, Geoffrey Miller, *Spent: Sexual, Evolution and Consumer Behavior* (2009), shows us in amusing detail how consumerism serves biological imperatives, especially signaling sexual *fitness* to potential mates – 'from mating to marketing', as the dust cover puts it. Of interest, too, Miller considers the role played by personality, which in Chapter 6 we saw has implications for economics. Miller believes that the display of expensive (Veblen) goods is an attempt to signal four main traits: conscientiousness, openness to experience, agreeableness, along with intelligence. Therefore, what might seem a foolish economic decision in the short run needs to be seen in the light of longer-term utility maximization, especially of a biological nature. These biologically rooted psychological factors are also reflected in the example of *transaction cost*, related to fairness, which we have already seen in the economic choices made by monkeys.

TRANSACTION COST

Imagine yourself lying on a beach on a very hot day. You still have some ice water, but now you have a fancy for an iced bottle of your favorite beer. A friend is going off to make a phone call and offers to bring back the beer for you. In this experiment, two conditions are presented: participants are told the beer is available only (a) from a fancy and expensive nearby hotel or (b) from a grubby and cheap corner shop (Thaler, 1983 – Thaler gives other examples). Your friend asks you how much you are *willing to pay* for it – and your friend informs you that they will buy the beer only if it costs as much or less than the price you are willing to pay; otherwise, they will come back empty handed. What price do you go for?

The tendency is for people to give a higher price for the fancy hotel version than the run-down version (medians: $2.65 and $1.50 respectively) – it is made clear to participants that the actual bottle of beer is identical in *all* respects. Now, from a neoclassical economics standpoint, this is a very strange decision indeed because it is the same beer in both cases. It is important to realize that (a) in both versions, the act of consumption is identical (e.g., chilled to the same degree) – drinking the beer on the beach; and (b) participants understand that they are not being asked a different question: "What price do you *expect* to have to pay"?

This rather unusual behavior is related to something called *transaction utility* – it cannot be *consumption utility* because the beers are identical at the point of drinking. It seems that we have a reference price for the two types of sales outlets and this affects our decision – even when we are not actually doing the transaction ourselves (if we had, we might get more pleasure from going to the fancy hotel and are, therefore, willing to pay a little more; or be compensated for having to go to a grubby shop).

Now, what do we think of this problem? Although nonrational from the standpoint of neoclassical economics, it is a commonplace phenomenon in the real world. Indeed, much of marketing is about manipulating perceptions of transaction utility, reflecting the effect of a reference price. Transaction utility seems to reflect social context and perceived *fairness* – according to Thaler who originated this concept in 1983, a fair price is said to reflect the seller's cost and a reasonable profit (obviously, a fancy hotel has much higher overheads than a corner shop). Once more, it is not all about money; the social context of the transaction is important, too.

THE EASE OF DECISION MAKING

There is a second form of transaction cost which relates to decision making. Making it easier for the consumer to come to a decision is one of the major functions of advertising and marketing – it disregards System 2 cognitively deliberate (reflective) thinking and seeks to exploit the vulnerabilities in System 1 automatic (reflexive) responding. We see this in shops with the positioning of goods, lighting, signage, and even the design of the floor tiles (to slow down customers), to nudge – bit-by-bit – the customer's buying decision (see text box). What most people perhaps do not realize is the extent of analysis used by larger retailers to influence their customers when in a store. Not only do they collect valuable information via loyalty cards – and increasingly online shopping (some major retailers have their own payment system app which also gathers further information) – they

ALTERING SPEED OF LOCOMOTION IN A SUPER-MARKET

In-store traffic flow, as moving around a shop is called in the world of consumer research, is a little researched topic, despite the fact that this is what we are doing 80% of the time when shopping. Work by Van den Bergh and colleagues (Van den Bergh et al., 2016) tested a number of floor patterns in a series of laboratory and field experiments. The results showed that customers walk faster with fewer 'progress markers' on the floor, but only if they have a goal in mind (e.g., to reach the hot food counter). The idea is that the number, nature, and salience of progress markers along the path to a physical location signal goal progress – cues in the environment influence our goal-directed behavior. This is of value to the shop because sometimes they will want customers to walk faster (e.g., entrance/exists) while at other times slower to allow them to browse (e.g., while at high value/profit shelves).

use scientific theories of biological (e.g., foraging) behavior. In fact, large retailers have highly detailed information on many millions of their customers, and they use truly sophisticated mathematical modeling that allows them to predict when customers are most likely to 'defect' from their usual brands and 'forage' for new ones – it is at this predicted point that retailers can target them with special offers to nudge the changing preference a little further down the path to purchase.

THE CUSTOMER JOURNEY

But even before we get inside the shop, the *customer journey* has begun. It starts with the initial thought of the shop (shaped by advertising, as well as previous experience); the entrance is made to look enticing, and the layout is designed to ease the physical journey around the store, or sometimes hamper it if the retailer wants the customer to slow down and browse – everyday items (e.g., bread) are often in the far corner, so a journey through the shop is required, and this allows more opportunity for in-store merchandising to influence often impulse, buying decisions. When it works well, the customer journey seems the most natural thing in the world, and few people feel in any way manipulated. As a result, most people leave the store with heavier bags and a lighter wallet/purse than expected when entering it: none of this is happenstance. And nor do such arrangements have to be terribly clever: the sign with tasty-looking fruit; the Grab and Go sign above the chiller display unit containing sandwiches, the two-for-one offers. In psychological terms, the typical supermarket allows the expression of basic (in a biological sense) instincts for hunting for food, drink, bargains, novelty, and so on. In its mundane way, shopping is both safe and exciting.

After leaving the store, we might then stop off for a coffee on our way home, where the barista might ask for our name which they write – often incorrectly – on *our* coffee cup. They are cleverly exploiting the phenomenon of 'sensation transfer' in which warm feelings we have about something (in this instance, our name) transfers to the contents of the cup. Something similar, 'Nudging by names', is widely used by supermarkets – giving brands a homely sounding name to instill, for example, a sense of quality or nostalgia (e.g., Hughes, 2011). (Major retailers have been criticized for this practice, as the source and means of production of the product often bear little resemblance to the psychological value generated.) Not only are we willing to pay more for such named products, but they taste better to us, too – calling something 'organic' elicits greater psychological value, but in blind taste tests most people cannot tell the difference. (Placing a few feathers in a box of eggs subtly implies healthy hens and hand-picking on the farm – the reality, alas, is likely to be *very* different.)

Despite the fact that our fridge is probably now bursting at the seams, we might decide to go out for a meal that evening with friends at a nearby restaurant. We think we can order what we like, but the choice architect has other ideas. Upon being seated, it is likely that the wine menu will be handed to one person, and more often than not this leads to the question: "white or red"? not usually, "does anyone want wine". It is natural and seemingly polite to reply "white" or "red". It is also likely that the wine list contains pages of foreign wines, many of which are hard to pronounce; but we are saved by the menu helpfully nudging us to the 'house wine' (which might be an inferior decoy; see below) and we decide to go for the slightly better Chilean Merlot which seems a good compromise. The fact that wine glasses are already on the table when we arrive sets the social norm that this is a restaurant where wine is taken with the meal. The interesting thing is that no one at the table realizes that their choices have been constrained from the moment they set foot in the restaurant. Few of us would want to dwell on this fact – after all, it might well spoil the meal (which probably consists of one of the limited number of 'Chef's Specials' helpfully pointed out by the waiter).

And this is not all when it comes to the psychological value of our restaurant experience. Research shows that if you order first in a restaurant, the food tastes better, as it does if it is served on heavy plates, but its taste is diminished if it is served on a red plate. The Oxford University Professor of Psychology, Charles Spence, believes that half of the pleasure we get from a meal comes from such psychological factors – these and many more examples are discussed in his 2014 book, coauthored with Betina Piqueras-Fiszman, *The Perfect Meal: The Multisensory Science of Food and Dining*. It includes such delightful insights that classical music played in the background induces a feeling of sophistication and diners spend as much as 10% more, and circular tables evoke greater feelings of pleasure. (Spence's 2017 book, *Gastrophysics: The New Science of Eating*, is also well worth a read.) Restaurants were never just about eating.

We might then stop off at a public house on the way home for a nightcap – and upon asking the bartender for gin and tonic, they might reply 'large or small', not 'small or large' – we now have 'large' in our semantic network which overshadows 'small', and it just seems the right thing to reply, "large, please". We can rest content that night that everyone had a good time – thanks in no small part to the behavioral choice architect.

BUYER'S REMORSE AND REGRET THEORY

An important feature of the consumer mind concerns the strong desire not to feel foolish – with any purchase this is a definite possibility. Buyer's remorse (or buyer's regret) is the negative emotional sense many consumers experience especially after a purchase – understandably, it is more likely with the purchase of an expensive item. This anticipatory negative emotion underlies consumer motivation. It is one of the reasons we tend to prefer the status quo and to go with the flow of others.

Although it is questionable whether a well-known consumer brand is significantly better (in objective value terms) than a lesser known one, most of us are willing to pay a higher price because, if nothing else, it gives us peace of mind – and there is utility in this state. If nothing else, we will be less likely to engage in regret and self-recrimination. The same is true of branded medicine. Many of us rush off to buy branded aspirin (e.g., Anadin) and ibuprofen (e.g., Nurofen) – often, they are branded as 'express', fast acting, and the like, and to confuse matters caffeine and other painkillers are sometimes added. Even if we had the knowledge, time, and effort to buy these things separately, and for a much lower cost, many of us would not. It is as if we have a desire to 'trust' branded products. Indeed, to the extent we hold such a belief, drugs may work, in part, by the placebo process, which is real enough, as shown by a review by Gupta and Verma (2013) of medical benefits in clinical trials.

As the advertising guru Rory Sutherland makes clear, brand management is all about reassuring the consumer that they have made the right choice and that they will not later regret it. He also makes the good point that our evolutionary past instilled in us the desire not so much to maximize in a neoclassical sense, but to *satisfice* in such a way as to avoid catastrophe. As any biologist will readily inform us, there are more ways to die than to survive, so risk aversion is a sensible strategy even though it means we may not maximize our *immediate* utility (at least as defined by expected utility theory; see Chapter 3) – of course, we may well be maximizing our subjective utility by taking uncertainty and risk out of the equation, and also perhaps our longer-term utility. All of this means that we have a very strong tendency to trust well-known brands – after all, if my flat screen trusted branded television turns out to be no good, I can hardly be blamed for making a foolish decision, but how different it would be with a brand no one has ever heard of – stupid me!

REACTANCE THEORY

There is something else about the consumer mind that is interesting to know. Few of us like to be told what to do. This knowledge can be used in marketing.

An effective ploy to achieve behavior change, including purchasing behavior, is to capitalize on the fact that, in all areas of life, persuasion is usually better than compulsion. This is what we know from the commercial world, where in any case compulsion is rarely an

A CIGARETTE BRAND TO DIE FOR

For a period of time in the 1990s, there appeared on the market a brand of cigarettes called *Death*. Given that cigarette companies could no longer avoid the connection between smoking and premature, and likely painful, death, entrepreneur B. J. Cunningham invested his life savings to build the Enlightened Tobacco Company to create and market this innovative brand. Living up to its name, Death Cigarettes disclosed its hazardous nature by having a skull and crossbones on the packaging – for those who yearned for the prospects of a little longer life, Death Lights was available. This brand especially appealed to the 'young underground punk rock' consumer market.

In an ironic twist of fate, the firm's trademark was successfully challenged by an alcohol company called Black Death. In a similar manner to many of those who consumed the product, the company met with an early demise. (The case study of Death cigarettes was described in O'Shaughnessy & O'Shaughnessy, 2004.)

option. Furthermore, individuals are influenced in reverse proportion to the force being applied – in a Newtonian mechanical-like fashion, there is an opposite force. There is even a term for this effect in social psychology: *reactance theory* (see Brehm, 1966). Specifically, externally imposed sanctions, for example by the government (e.g., taxation), can increase the attractiveness of the associated behavior (see text box) – this is another reason why a nudge might be better than a mandate. For some people, there is something especially alluring about forbidden fruit.

Reactance theory is the attempt to provide a psychological explanation of such seemingly perverse effects. It states that an aversive state is generated by restriction of an individual's freedom of choice over behavioral outcomes – it appeals especially to those of a personality disposition in the direction of sensation seeking and risk taking. As we have seen in previous chapters, such external pressure can lead to extrinsic motivation which can 'crowd out' intrinsic motivation. This might be another good psychological reason for not relying upon typical neoclassical economic incentives such as fines and taxes to achieve some desired end.

MONEY: PRICE AND PLOYS

The saying, "Not everything that counts can be counted, and not everything that can be counted counts", is (probably falsely) attributed to Albert Einstein – the fact that it is so attributed attests to the value people place on it (another example of the influence of the messenger effect). An earlier religiously motivated saying went: "Money is not what really counts, though it must be counted". Yet, despite the fact that much of the value we place on things in life (e.g., the love of a child) cannot sensibly be measured by the metric of money, few of us have the luxury of sailing through life without money being close to the forefront of our mind. Commercial enterprises exploit the psychology of money – this is brilliantly discussed in Adrian Furnham's 2014 book *The New Psychology of Money*. There is little doubt that financial products are especially prone to the biases inherent in judgment and decision making. For example, we get anchored to the minimum payment on our credit card, and for this reason, financial companies set deliberately low monthly minimum payments so we do not pay back the balance as fast as we might, thus increasing long-term repayments.

Other pricing ploys are routinely used, such as the ones we will now discuss.

ANCHORING EFFECTS

We have already witnessed the power of anchoring in Chapter 4; that is, the cognitive bias that leads us to be influenced by 'anchors' (reference points). For example, merely writing down the last two digits of our social security number influences the subsequent decision regarding how much we are willing to pay for everyday items. Related commercial anchoring ploys include highlighting the scarcity value of a good or service – "only a maximum of 12 cans of soup per customer". Building up psychological excitement and tension is usually good for business, itself a form of emotional anchoring.

Although such ploys can appear gross and tacky, suitably used they work their commercial charm – to employ North American vernacular, we just seem 'suckers' for them (despite the fact that few of us can be unaware of their purpose). Even professionals are prone to them. For example, it is reported that property agents place a higher value on a house if it comes with extensive documentation; and teachers anchor the marks of their students based on their previous grades. In Richard Thaler's words, these should all be 'supposedly irrelevant factors': they are far from being any such thing. Neoclassically-inclined economists are most assuredly getting a bald patch from scratching their heads.

FRAMING

As in so many other areas of economic life, framing is important. When Delta Airlines declared that customers who do not purchase their tickets online would be charged $2.00 extra, this led to an outcry from those who did not have internet access (e.g., Mehta, 1999). Reframed as a *saving* of $2.00 when booked online was altogether more acceptable – but *nothing* changed financially. When credit cards were first introduced, retailers wanted to surcharge customers for using them, but this was resisted by the finance industry because they knew that customers would be deterred. Instead, garages offered a 'discount' for cash. All of this is now in the distant past and today there is no differentiation in price and the credit card charge has been absorbed into the overall cost of doing business – this cost is now incurred by cash buyers, but as they are generally unaware of this fact, they do not see cause for complaint.

LOSS AVERSION

As seen elsewhere in this book, whether a transaction is framed as a loss or gain has important consequences – we love a $5 discount and hate a $5 surcharge, even though we end up paying the same for the product or service. Therefore, exactly the same *change* in price framed in different ways has a big psychological effect on how we think, feel, and behave. The powerful influence of loss aversion in marketing is shown in buyers' reactions to price changes to insurance policies: price increases have *twice* the effect on customer switching compared to price reductions of the same magnitude.

DECOY PRICING

The 'decoy pricing effect' is an especially effective ploy (see text box for an example). In the technical language of behavioral economics, it goes by the name of 'asymmetrically dominated choice' or 'asymmetric dominance effect' (e.g., Huber et al., 1982). The effect consists in the fact that our preference for one option relative to a second option is affected by the addition of a third (less attractive, perhaps more expensive) decoy option. With the addition of the decoy, customers are more likely to choose the more expensive of the first two options. So, if you go to the gas station and you have three choices of fuel (Standard, Premium, Super-Premium), more people will go for Premium than if they were presented with Standard and Premium alone. Well, what might be going on?

Example of the Decoy Effect

Somewhat appropriately, a good example of the decoy effect was seen with the marketing of *The Economist* publication. (This example was also described in Ariely, 2008.) In the United States, they offered three options:

1 Web Subscription – $59
2 Print Subscription – $125
3 Web and Print Subscription – $125

Option 1 ($59) appears reasonable. Option 1 ($125) seems a tad expensive just for the print version. But wait, Option 3 looks like a great deal: web and print versions, all for $125. Dan Ariely (2008) tested out these options with MIT students. His results were:

1 Web Subscription – $59 (16% of students)
2 Print Subscription – $125 (0 students)
3 Web and Print Subscription – $125 (84% of students)

Total revenue: $11,444
Well, maybe this does not have anything to do with the decoy option. To test this, next he removed the decoy option. This is what he found:

1 Web Subscription – $59 (68% of students)
2 Web and Print Subscription – $125 (32% of students)

Total revenue: $8,012
Of course, the cost of producing the print version would need to be factored into the final net profit of the different options.

Well, when making a choice between two options, things are rather difficult: Standard or Premium? Well, I do not really know! But, now with three options, it is likely not going to be the Super Premium, so I will opt for Premium. This is an example of where more choices make the decision-making process easier – and more lucrative for the retailer. It also plays into the behavioral notion that people can pay *less* by not going with the Super Premium option, as well as getting the Premium and not the perceived inferior Standard: now, that seems most satisfying. Under these circumstances, it takes a strong will to defend the decision to go for the Standard option. (Of course, not everyone is vulnerable to these ploys, but enough are to make them profitable.)

Decoy pricing is routinely used by large companies, and no less a company than Apple. There is a reason why many Apple products are sold in a pricing series; for example, iPhones can be purchased at different price points partly based on their storage capacities. The existence of the highest-price option with larger storage capacity makes the lower-price options in the line-up look like bargains although other brands might sell similar products at lower prices (comparison to other brands are obscured through Apple's unique, and highly distinctive branded design). The purpose of the decoy product is to make the other products in the company's product portfolio look more attractive. (This is important to Apple in production terms because they need to know in advance how many millions of their products they need to manufacture and ship.)

We can start to think about which psychological processes are driving the decoy pricing effect. To begin with, the fact that it exerts a 'force' on the consumer means they can go with the flow and use fewer cognitive, emotional, effort, and time resources in making a decision – this reduces the 'transaction cost'. In other words, it reduces psychological labor. In addition, there may be two additional effects at play: (1) the *attraction effect* and (2) the *compromise effect*.

ATTRACTION EFFECT

Going back to the decoy pricing of *The Economist* (see text box), the attraction effect is one of its main aspects: it is difficult to compare two options with very different attributes, but much easier to compare when they have very similar attributes. It is not easy to compare the print-only and web-only versions because they are so different, but it is much easier to compare them when they come in a bundle: with imperfect product information, consumers will tend to choose the bundle because it is the only product which provides complete information, and any resulting doubt and uncertainty are markedly reduced.

COMPROMISE EFFECT

People often prefer to avoid extremes – sometimes called 'extremeness aversion' – and they often prefer instead to compromise (there is also evidence that people do something similar when they fill in a lottery slip by avoiding numbers on the edges). This tendency gives rise to the 'middle' product being preferred. When we are presented with three product choices, we tend to think that the cheapest one is clearly inferior and the most expensive one is overpriced with nonessential features; therefore, the middle option just seems altogether more sensible. (As discussed above, Veblen goods violate this principle.) In addition, we might not want to be thought of either as a 'cheapskate' or someone who 'shows off', so the choice of the middle option is the safer, more socially desirable, option. It serves nicely to take the *dis*utility out of the decision.

THE CONSUMER HEDONIC TREADMILL

Now we know how commercial firms employ anchoring, framing, loss aversion, and decoy pricing to make purchases more attractive, will we still fall for them? Probably, yes. This might be because of the phenomenon of 'hedonic adaptation', also known as habituation (e.g., Frederick & Loewenstein, 1999). It refers to the fact that the pleasure, satisfaction, and utility we get from products and services tend to wane over time, sometimes quickly after the purchase, and we need another hedonic 'hit' (a new stimulus) to go back to the previous hedonic level. This demands that commercial products and services are novel and exciting and the 'new thing to have'. We see this writ large in fashion – last year's must-have coat is this year's *faux pas*.

We all experience hedonic adaptation: the new car is exciting for some time but then becomes a normal part of life, as we have adapted to seeing it sitting in the driveway – the first few scratches from the neighbor's cat may also serve to lessen our utility. Overall, the emotional impact of consumption tends to be short-lived. As we are not aware of the effects of hedonic adaptation, we tend to over-invest in acquiring new possessions and, thus, are prone to the commercial practices and ploys that capitalize on this tendency.

Hedonic adaptation is thought to occur because it allows us to retain the ability to react to novel stimuli, a useful trait for prehistoric (wo)man, but it is much less of use in modern society because it means that we need constantly to look for new sources of (apparent) happiness – once more we see the importance of biological factors in consumer psychology. The image of a hedonic treadmill, on which individuals need to keep walking just to stay in the same place, describes this effect quite nicely – the hamster on the running wheel is another instructive, if unflattering, image.

The hedonic treadmill supplies an account of why we tend to overestimate the impact of choices on our well-being: we are bad at forecasting how we will adapt (get used) to new products and services. We see this effect clearly in the case of positive and negative changes in life: winning the lottery or becoming disabled – in the case of bad events, this is something of a psychological blessing as we adapt to the displeasure ('disutility' in the economist's jargon) of such negative life events, although, it needs to be said, never quite as fully as to positive life events.

Daniel Kahneman has written extensively on the important role played by attention in our economic life. We are never quite as satisfied as when we are *thinking* of buying a new car, *planning* a wedding, and *looking forward* to the birth of a baby. But, once these things materialize, there is typically a drop in satisfaction: putting aside the problems associated with them, our attention (and, thus, pleasure seeking) is already off elsewhere. The whole point of advertising and marketing is to ensure that attention is directed to the acquisition of *new* products and services: in one – rather dismal – sense this means the neglect and withdrawal of affection for previously purchased ones. And, as so often, in relationships, too.

Quite a lot is now known about the hedonic treadmill. When surveys ask about well-being 5 years from now, respondents tend to take into account their current level of aspirations, which they use as an anchor to judge their future states (e.g., Easterlin, 2001). This tends to lead to an overestimation of their future well-being because it fails to take into sufficient account that aspirations do not remain constant – social comparison ensures that they do not (see Chapter 6).

DECISION UTILITY

A major point of behavioral economics is to show that people often misjudge the effects of choices on their well-being – assuming they can be said to have consistent preferences in the first place. As Daniel Kahneman would say, their *decision utility* – which describes how much satisfaction they assume their choices will bring them – does not necessarily match their *experienced utility* – which is the satisfaction they actually obtain from their choices (Kahneman et al., 1997). You may well think that a new car will make you very happy before you buy it, then only to realize later that the initial euphoria did not last as long as expected.

Returning to the issue of how to define and measure utility, the important point to note is that the revealed preferences approach considers only *decision utility*; but this is not seen as a problem by neoclassical economists because they argue that experienced utility cannot be measured and, in any event, is too abstract to be meaningful. However, this position is not accepted by all economists, and even fewer (if any) psychologists.

Now, can it really be the case that people have their own preferences; or are their preferences given to them by consumer society which they then try to satisfy? In any event, the neoclassical notion of reference independent preferences and choice is seriously undermined by behavioral economics research, generally and in the consumer world. Of course, this was the very point of such influential works as J. K. Galbraith's 1958 book *The Affluent Society* (see Chapter 2).

THE POWER OF SOCIAL MEDIA

So much of hidden persuasion is now on the internet. This has both positive and negative aspects. A BBC television Panorama program, first shown on 8th May, 2017, reported that 32 million people in the United Kingdom use Facebook, and 2 billion worldwide (MacIntyre, 2017). It can influence elections and is currently unregulated. Facebook's CEO Mark Zuckerberg declared: "What I care about is giving people the power to share, giving every person a voice so we can make the world more open and connected" (Zuckerberg, 2016). Whether this noble proclamation is the primary purpose of Facebook – and its $117.9 billion revenue in 2021 might suggest otherwise – users reveal more information about themselves than they are generally aware, which allows advertisers to produce targeted messages specifically tailored to groups of potential customers (or, even, voters) – much of this was revealed by Mark Zuckerberg's testimony before a Congressional Committee in 2018, as well as wider discussion of how Facebook data has been used by third parties (e.g., by using 'psychographic' techniques that map specifically designed persuasive messages to the personality profiles of the consumer or the voter).

Although Facebook's complex algorithms track our online lives, they are a closely guarded secret. Our online data are recorded and shared with advertisers. So, too, political advertisers can micro target communication to those who might be susceptible to respond favourably. Donald Trump's campaign team exploited this technology: they took the names and addresses of the electorate, sent them to Facebook, and back came detailed information on each person – these names were then put into an 'audience' (i.e., targeted group) and each audience was then exposed to specific political messages, tailored specifically (e.g., Beckett, 2017). Major political parties have dedicated Facebook staff on their campaign teams to maximize their political messages. To attract attention, campaigns do not shy away from using 'click bait', consisting of sensational and sometimes downright false stories ("fake news") to lure in audience – this has been a very hot topic since the late 2010s.

It is quite possible that the use of social media is decisive in political campaigns. This is seen in the once-in-a-generation UK Brexit Referendum in June 2016. Speaking at the Nudgestock conference in Folkestone (9 June 2017), Dominic Cummings, who was the Campaign Director of Vote Leave, revealed that his campaign team worked closely with Facebook to get information to target those of the electorate who were still undecided – those who were decided did not need much further encouragement and those who were opposed were probably beyond reach in any case and, therefore, could be ignored. Specific behavioral science principles were used. For example, one major slogan was 'Take back Control'. The key word is 'back' because it implies that something has been taken, even stolen. Cummings also revealed that he did not employ economists or market research pollsters because he thought they may have preconceived ideas; instead, he employed physicists who are trained to look at data in a very hard-headed scientific way and are less likely to engage in self-delusional thinking. He said he was impressed by the comment of the famous physicist, Richard Feynman,

> The first principle is that you must not fool yourself and you are the easiest person to fool.
>
> (cited in Feynman, 1985)

We may never know the extent of the influence of these campaigning ploys, but given that the Leave vote won by only a narrow margin it is possible they were crucial. In any event, the use of behavioral science tools in political campaigns is the focus of much controversy and debate in society – it is hard to see how it will not be for the foreseeable future.

It would be of value to society to know whether such political campaigns are effective in switching voters' intentions and actual behavior. There is a body of evidence that speaks directly to this question. In a systematic review of field experiments, Kalla and Broockman (2018) found hardly any evidence for an effect on voting intention, and there was only tentative evidence for the effectiveness of campaigns that contained three features: (a) the candidate assumed an unusually unpopular position; (b) heavy financial investment; and (c) it was possible to identify persuadable voters. Most forms of political campaigns do not conform to these features. However, this is not to say that such political campaigns do not work. As Kalla and Broockman point out, it is possible that such campaigns shift the focus of the political debate and this may influence what is deemed important in the mass media, which could affect voters – the effects may well be subtle, even 'butterfly' (see above).

Companies such as Facebook have a detailed understanding of our psychology and, also, of our network of friends – in fact, as we have witnessed in our academic profession, they are intent on recruiting the best behavioral scientists, often from permanent university positions. The information they harvest allows powerful predictions of our susceptibility to certain messages which can only increase in sophistication in the years to come. This behavioral technology will enable companies to predict with ever-increasing degrees of accuracy consumer preference and choice. Quite worryingly, the same algorithms allow the easy identification of gullible targets for misinformation and conspiracy theories, sometimes with tragic consequences. For example, misinformation about Covid-19 vaccines on platforms, such as Facebook and Twitter, likely contributed to vaccine hesitancy during the pandemic (e.g., Milmo, 2021). Indeed, the term "infodemic", first coined back in 2003 to describe "the rapid spread of information – both accurate and inaccurate – in the age of the internet and social media" (Merriam-Webster, 2022), gained new prominence during the Covid-19 pandemic. We cannot be sure of the resulting life-and-death consequences.

Commercially valuable information on our behavior, attention span, and even emotions can come from some unlikely sources. For example, a malfunctioning advertising display in a pizza shop in Oslo, Norway, revealed that it was, in fact, recording customer profiles: age, gender, attention time, and facial expression (e.g., Pettit, 2016). In another unusual case, a Wi-Fi-enabled sex aid was transmitting information back to the company. Following a court ruling, the Canadian firm Standard Innovation, agreed to pay CAN$4 million (about $3.1 million or £2.5 million with 2022 exchange rates) to members of the public who bought and used its We-Vibe products (e.g., Hern, 2017) (this firm had been collecting data and recording when customers used the sex toy, including information on the intensity of the vibration settings). Is nothing private anymore? This may well be to the long-term benefit of greater sexual satisfaction, but users were not made aware they would be sharing such intimate data. This example highlights the ethics, especially as regards informed consent of the practical applications of behavioural economics/science.

CONCLUSIONS

The *Mad Men* (and women) of the creative industries of advertising, brand management and marketing, and now increasingly highly targeted social media commercial activity, have never been much enamored of the notion that the consumer has stable and consistent preferences and responds only to 'information' in even an adequately rational way. Instead, they find greater commercial reward in assuming that needs, wants, wishes, and desires can be manufactured and that psychological value could be added to products and services, sometimes significantly exceeding objectively defined value. Studies of commercial practices and ploys provide important insights into real judgment, decision making, and behavior in everyday economic contexts – in a way, the commercial world is one big laboratory in which hypotheses about the human economic mind are tested daily.

We have attempted to show in this book the wide-ranging and important applications and implications of behavioral economics. It is a revolution still in progress and it is far too early to foresee its true long-term impact. We would be wise to be attentive to the downside as well as the upsides.

FURTHER READING

Cialdini, R. B. (2007). *Influence: The psychology of persuasion*. William Morrow.

Miller, G. (2009). *Spent: Sex, evolution and consumer behavior*. Viking.

Sutherland, R. (2011). *The Wiki Man*. Ogilvy.

REFERENCES

Ariely, D. (2008). *Predictably irrational: The hidden forces that shape our decisions*. Harper Collins.

Bagwell, K. (2005). *The economics of advertising*. Columbia University (Department of Economics Discussion Paper Series). file:///C:/Users/44740/Downloads/econ_0506_01%20(3).pdf

Beckett, L. (2017, October 9). Trump digital director says Facebook helped win the White House. *The Guardian*. https://www.theguardian.com/technology/2017/oct/08/trump-digital-director-brad-parscale-facebook-advertising

Binet, L., & Field, P. (2013). *The long and the short of it*. Institute of Practitioners in Advertising. [Summary: https://ipa.co.uk/media/5811/long_and_short_of_it_presentation_final.pdf]

Brehm, J. W. (1966). *A theory of psychological reactance*. Academic Press.

Chaiken, S. (1980). Heuristic versus systematic information processing and the use of source versus message cues in persuasion. *Journal of Personality and Social Psychology, 39*, 752–766. https://doi.org/10.1037/0022-3514.39.5.752

Cialdini, R. B. (2007). *Influence: The psychology of persuasion*. William Morrow & Co.

Easterlin, R. A. (2001). Income and happiness: Towards a unified theory. *The Economic Journal, 111*, 465–484. https://doi.org/10.1111/1468-0297.00646

Feynman, R. (1985). *"Surely you're joking, Mr. Feynman!": Adventures of a curious character*. W. W. Norton & Company.

Frederick, S., & Loewenstein, G. (1999). Hedonic adaptation. In D. Kahneman, E. Diener, & N. Schwarz (Eds.), *Well-being: The foundations of hedonic psychology* (pp. 302–329). Russell Sage Foundation.

Furnham, A. (2014). *The new psychology of money*. Routledge.

Galbraith, J. K. (1958). *The affluent society*. Houghton Mifflin Harcourt.

Goldstein, R., Almenberg, J., Dreber, A., Emerson, J. W., Herschkowitsch, A., & Katz, J. (2008). Do more expensive wines taste better? Evidence from a large sample of blind tastings. *Journal of Wine Economics, 3*, 1–9. https://doi.org/10.1017/S1931436100000523

Greenwald, A. G. (1968). Cognitive learning, cognitive response to persuasion, and attitude change. In A. G. Greenwald, T. C. Brock, & T. M. Ostrom (Eds.) *Psychological foundations of attitudes* (pp. 147–169). Academic Press.

Gupta, U., & Verma, M. (2013). Placebo in clinical trials. *Perspectives in Clinical Research*, *4*, 49. https://doi.org/10.4103/2229-3485.106383

Hallam, L. (2015, December 18). Why do people choose expensive branded drugs over cheap generics? *The Conversation*. https://theconversation.com/why-do-people-choose-expensive-branded-drugs-over-cheap-generics-52461

Hern, A. (2017, March 14). Vibrator maker ordered to pay out C$4m for tracking users' sexual activity. *The Guardian*. https://www.theguardian.com/technology/2017/mar/14/we-vibe-vibrator-tracking-users-sexual-habits

Hopkins, C. C. (1923). *Scientific advertising*. Createspace.

Huber, J., Payne, J. W., & Puto, C. (1982). Adding asymmetrically dominated alternatives: Violations of regularity and the similarity hypothesis. *Journal of Consumer Research*, *9*, 90–98. https://doi.org/10.1086/208899

Hughes, A. (2011, November 29). Nudged towards homebrand by our supermarkets; but is it really a choice? *The Conversation*. https://theconversation.com/nudged-towards-homebrand-by-our-supermarkets-but-is-it-really-a-choice-4430

Kahneman, D., Wakker, P. P., & Sarin, R. (1997). Back to Bentham? Explorations of experienced utility. *Quarterly Journal of Economics*, *112*, 375–405. https://doi.org/10.2307/2951240

Kalla, J. L., & Broockman, D. E. (2018). The minimal persuasive effects of campaign contact in general elections: Evidence from 49 field experiments. *American Political Science Review*, *112*, 148–166. https://doi.org/10.1017/S0003055417000363

MacIntyre, D. (2017, May 8). What Facebook knows about you. *BBC Panorama*. http://www.bbc.co.uk/programmes/b08qgbc3

Mehta, S. (1999, January 14). Delta adds fee to tickets not bought online. *Los Angeles Times*. http://articles.latimes.com/1999/jan/14/business/fi-63289

Merriam-Webster. (2022). *Words we're watching: "Infodemic."* Merriam-Webster. https://www.merriam-webster.com/words-at-play/words-were-watching-infodemic-meaning

Miller, G. (2009). *Spent: Sex, evolution, and consumer behavior*. Viking.

Milmo, D. (2021, November 2). Facebook failing to protect users from Covid misinformation, says monitor. *The Guardian*. https://www.theguardian.com/technology/2021/nov/02/facebook-failing-to-protect-users-from-covid-misinformation-says-monitor

O'Shaughnessy, J., & O'Shaughnessy, N. J. (2004). *Persuasion in advertising.* Routledge.

Ogilvy, D. (1963). *Confessions of an advertising man.* Atheneum.

Ogilvy, D. (1983). *Ogilvy on advertising.* John Wiley and Sons.

Packard, V. (1957). *The hidden persuaders.* D. McKay Co.

Pettit, H. (2016, May 11). Creepy pizza sign is caught using a hidden camera to scan customers for their facial expressions and gender. *Mail Online.* http://www.dailymail.co.uk/sciencetech/article-4495782/Pizza-sign-caught-using-hidden-camera-scan-customers.html

Popper, K. (1966). *Of clouds and clocks: An approach to the problem of rationality and the freedom of man (The Arthur Holly Compton memorial lecture).* Washington University.

Prochazkova, E., & Kret, M. E. (2017). Connecting minds and sharing emotions through mimicry: A neurocognitive model of emotional contagion. *Neuroscience & Biobehavioral Reviews, 80,* 99–114. https://doi.org/10.1016/J.NEUBIOREV.2017.05.013

Reinoso Carvalho, F., Wang, Q. (Janice), van Ee, R., Persoone, D., & Spence, C. (2017). "Smooth operator": Music modulates the perceived creaminess, sweetness, and bitterness of chocolate. *Appetite, 108,* 383–390. https://doi.org/10.1016/j.appet.2016.10.026

Smith, G. H. (1971). *Motivation research in advertising and marketing.* Greenwood Press.

Spence, C. (2017). *Gastrophysics: The new science of eating.* Viking.

Spence, C., & Piqueras-Fiszman, B. (2014). *The perfect meal: The multisensory science of food and dining.* John Wiley and Sons.

Sutherland, R. (2011). *The Wiki man.* Ogilvy.

Sutherland, R. (2014). *Rory Sutherland: How to be butterfly hunters (video).* https://www.ogilvy.com/topics/behavioural-economics-topics/6-seconds-of-great-advice-from-rory-sutherland/

Sutherland, R. (2019). *Alchemy: The surprising power of ideas that don't make sense.* WH Allen.

Thaler, R. (1983). Transaction utility theory. *Advances in Consumer Research, 10,* 229–232.

Van den Bergh, B., Heuvinck, N., Schellekens, G. A. C., & Vermeir, I. (2016). Altering speed of locomotion. *Journal of Consumer Research, 43,* 407–428. https://doi.org/10.1093/jcr/ucw031

Warhol, A. (1975). *The philosophy of Andy Warhol.* Harcourt.

Zajonc, R. B. (1968). Attitudinal effects of mere exposure. *Journal of Personality and Social Psychology, 9,* 1–27. https://doi.org/10.1037/h0025848

Zuckerberg, M. (2016, November 17). In Conversation With Mark Zuckerberg. *Techonomy.Com.* http://techonomy.com/conf/te16/videos-conversations-with-2/in-conversation-with-mark-zuckerberg/

GLOSSARY

A/B testing (split testing). A form of controlled experiment, often used in marketing, in which the effectiveness of two (or more) versions of a message is tested (e.g., letters, websites, ads). The response (e.g., in sales) to the two A/B versions is then examined to determine which version works best.

Affect. The expression of feelings or emotions; one's emotional state.

Affect heuristic. A mental shortcut that allows people to react to novel stimuli quickly by relying on their emotional response (their 'gut feeling').

Affective forecasting (hedonic forecasting). The prediction of one's emotional reaction (affect) to future events.

Allais paradox. A choice problem described by Maurice Allais in 1953, which was one of the first to demonstrate experimentally that actual observed choices are not always consistent with one of the major criteria of rationality (i.e., expected utility theory).

Ambiguity aversion (uncertainty aversion). The propensity to prefer risk (where the probabilities of outcomes occurring are known) over uncertainty (where these are not known).

Anchoring. A cognitive bias that describes people's tendency to rely too heavily on 'anchors' (e.g., selected pieces of information) when making decisions. This is often the first piece of information that is received and, thus, it has more influence than it might deserve.

Anchoring and adjustment heuristic. The tendency to base estimates (or decisions) on a familiar value or readily available number, and then shift up or down from that 'anchor' to arrive at a final estimate/decision.

Animal spirits. Term coined by John Maynard Keynes in 1936 to describe that economic decisions are much influenced by psychological factors (instincts and emotions), which, among other things, drive 'consumer confidence'.

Attraction effect. The observation that adding an irrelevant, possibly inferior, alternative to a choice set increases the attractiveness of the original choices (see also Decoy effect/asymmetric dominance).

Authority bias. We are overly influenced by who communicates the message; this is seen in trusting actors in a white coat selling a medical product, and demonstrated starkly in Stanley Milgram's series of classic studies on obedience to authority.

Autokinetic effect (autokinesis). The illusory, apparent movement of a stationary light in a dark environment. The light seems to move because of a lack of visual reference points in the environment.

Availability heuristic. A mental shortcut that relies on examples that immediately come to mind when forming judgments. When an unlikely or infrequent event comes to mind easily, we tend to overestimate the probability of its occurrence.

Axioms. Statements that are regarded as accepted assumptions, established truths – they are used as the foundations of a logical structure and are employed widely in formal economic reasoning and modeling.

Base rate fallacy (base rate neglect, base rate bias). The tendency to estimate the probability of an event based on specific, possibly irrelevant, rather than general (base rate) information.

Bayesian updating (Bayesian reasoning/inference). Based on Bayes' theorem; probabilities of an outcome occurring are updated as more information is obtained.

Benign paternalism. An alternative idea to the *Libertarian paternalism* of nudge theory. Benign paternalism holds that people's preferences are not psychologically free; instead, it argues that people's choice behavior should be nudged to achieve the best long-term interests for them, even if they would prefer different decision to serve their short-term interests. Benign paternalism does no rely upon the assumption of *preference purification* to maximize the utility of the economic agent as seen from their point of view (see also Preference purification).

Bias (cognitive bias). A systematic error in thinking or deviation from rationality which affects judgments and decision making.

Big-5 personality traits (five-factor model). A widely examined theory of personality which describes five basic dimensions of personality: openness to experience, conscientiousness, extraversion, agreeableness, and neuroticism.

Bounded rationality. Term first coined by Herbert Simon. It describes the idea that people have to make decisions under constraints, such as limitations of knowledge, time, and thinking capacity, which affect the ability to process information in an optimal (fully rational) manner.

Buyer's remorse (or buyer's regret). The sense of regret that may occur after a (usually expensive or unnecessary) purchase.

Choice architecture. Term first coined in 2008 by Thaler and Sunstein, which describes the careful design of how options are presented to people in order to influence their choices.

Classical economics. A school of economic thought that was dominant in the 18th and 19th centuries, developed by Adam Smith, Jeremy Bentham, Thomas Malthus, and David Ricardo, among others.

Cognitive dissonance. The psychological stress associated with a state in which attitudes, beliefs, and behaviors are in conflict. As a consequence, people readily change thoughts, attitudes, and beliefs to maintain consistency with their behavior.

Cognitive response model. A model which assumes that it is not the reception of arguments that mediates attitude change, but rather that attitude change is mediated by the thoughts (cognitive responses) which recipients generate as they receive and reflect upon communications.

Commitment. Being dedicated to a cause or other people. People seek to be consistent with public promises, and to reciprocate favors.

Commitment device. A strategy chosen in the present to restrict future behavior in order to adhere to long-term goals, which may otherwise not be reached because of lack of will power or present bias. Commitment devices come in many different forms, for example, study groups or pre-purchasing tickets for an event on a certain day to avoid procrastination.

Common prior assumption. An important assumption in Bayesian reasoning, which presumes that if people have access to the same information they will come to the same subjective probabilities. This implies that differences in judgments, beliefs, and opinions only reflect differences in information.

Comparative cost advantage. First defined by David Ricardo, it describes the idea that each country should produce goods for which it has lower 'opportunity costs' than other countries (this is different from absolute cost advantage, which exists when a country can produce goods at the lowest absolute cost). With the international trade of these goods and services, there is benefit to the whole world stemming from the most efficient allocation of scarce resources.

Compatibility effect. First defined by Slovic et al., it describes the phenomenon that attributes of a stimulus carry more weight when they are compatible with the output. For example, when the value of a gamble is expressed in terms of money, people find it easier to use this aspect of the gamble to set the value of the gamble.

Completeness (axiom of order). The assumption regarding preferences in neoclassical economics that states that a consistent set of preferences can be arranged in an ordering system.

Compliance. One of the broad categories of social influence. It describes behavior change following requests from others (implicit or explicit) but does not imply attitude change.

Compromise effect. The observation that consumers often prefer the middle option in a choice set as a result of wanting to avoid extremes.

Confirmation bias. The tendency to recall old information and interpret new information as evidence for supporting existing opinions and beliefs.

Conjunction fallacy (the Linda problem). When people are asked to compare the probabilities of a conjunction (two specific conditions) and one of its conjuncts, they sometimes judge the occurrence of both conditions at the same time to be more probable than just one of them, but logically this cannot be the case.

Consequentialism. The doctrine that actions, policies, rules, and so on should be judged on the basis of their consequences; that is, the utility they yield.

Consistency. People try to act in a consistent way; this means that they can be induced to behave in a certain way, e.g., allowing a small 'speed kills' sign on their front lawn and, in consequence, in order to remain consistent, they are more likely to agree to a much larger sign because they see now see themselves as a civic-minded citizen.

Conspicuous consumption. Term coined by Thorstein Veblen which describes the public display of spending money on (luxury) goods and services to enhance social status and power.

Conversion. The internalization of others' beliefs, thinking, and behavior (social norms become internalized). In contrast to compliance, conversion implies a change in attitudes, not just behavior.

Decision utility. The utility (satisfaction) people assume a specific choice will bring them.

Decoy pricing effect (asymmetrically dominated choice, asymmetric dominance effect). Describes the effect that consumers tend to change their preferences between two options when a third option is added. This third option is typically clearly more desirable (dominant) than one of the original options, but less desirable than the other one (asymmetric). Typically, this third option (the decoy) is priced close to the original high-price option, but it is less desirable. It is, however, clearly a better option (dominant) than the original low-price option. Consumers will then often purchase the original expensive option because the decoy option changed their perception of the relative merits of the original options.

Defaults. A pre-set option the decision maker will receive if no decision is made. An important tool for the choice architect.

Demand (law of demand). A law described in microeconomics which states that price and quantity demanded are inversely related: as the price of a good (or service) increases, demand will decrease and vice versa (all other things being equal). (For a violation, see Veblen good.)

Dilution effect. The effect that obtaining additional information can reduce stereotyping, possibly by affecting reliance on the representativeness heuristic.

Discounting (delay discounting, time discounting). The way in which people discount (devalue) rewards which are not immediately available. The value of the future reward decreases alongside the delay. The specific manner in which people discount is described by the discount *function*.

Dominant strategy. In game theory, the dominant strategy for a player is the strategy that produces the best payoff for that player regardless of the strategies employed by other players.

Dual-processing theory. A theory in cognitive psychology which explains how information is processed in individuals in two different ways: 1. a fast, superficial, unconscious mode (System 1), and 2. a slow, effortful, controlled, systematic reasoning model, which can give rise to conscious experience (System 2).

Efficient market hypothesis. An investment theory which assumes that the price of stock market shares reflects all relevant, available information. It should, therefore, not be possible to 'beat the market' in the long run.

Ego. A theoretical construct describing people's response to their internal workings. Behavior change can be facilitated by recognizing that people often act in ways to make them feel better about themselves.

Ellsberg paradox. A paradox in decision theory that demonstrates people's tendency to prefer a bet with a known probability (a sign of ambiguity aversion).

Endowment effect (divestiture aversion). The finding that we value things we own more than the things we do not own.

Equity premium puzzle. Describes the anomalous observation that the observed returns on stocks over the past century are much higher than returns on government bonds, implying that the stock market is required to pay an equity risk premium to attract risk-averse investors.

Evaluation heuristics. Mental shortcuts involving choices.

Evaluative conditioning. The change in perceived value of a neutral (conditioned) stimulus when it is paired with a positive or negative (unconditioned) stimulus.

Expected utility theory. A theory of decision making under risk or uncertainty, which states that rational decision makers will choose the option with the highest expected utility.

Expected value (expectation). The expected value of X is the weighted average of all the values that X can take. To calculate the expected value of X, each possible outcome of X is multiplied by the probability of the outcome occurring, and all these values are then summed. In a gamble, it is the anticipated value of the bet.

Experienced utility. The utility (satisfaction) that choices actually bring.

Exponential discounting. A specific form of the discount function (see Discounting), in which discount rates are constant over time (contrast with hyperbolic discounting).

Externalities. The consequence of an economic activity (i.e., consuming or producing a good) which affects a third party negatively or positively without this being reflected in market price (e.g., a factory pollutes a river but does not have to pay for cleaning it up).

Extremeness aversion (extreme aversion bias). The tendency to avoid extremes.

Focalism (focusing illusion). The tendency to focus on one aspect of life when individuals assess the impact of events on their future well-being.

Framing. The process of defining the context in which choices are presented.

Framing effect. A cognitive bias which describes that the form in which content and information are presented is highly relevant for decision making (for example, presenting a choice as a discount or surcharge in a shop).

Free market. An economic system in which prices are determined by competition between private firms without government interference.

Gambler's fallacy (Monte Carlo fallacy). The mistaken belief that past events affect the probability of future outcomes (e.g., when tossing a coin, a series of heads will be followed by tails). This reflects the tendency to expect outcomes to even out over the short run.

Game theory (economic games). The formal study of conflict and cooperation using mathematical models in which players make decisions while taking into account the decisions of other players.

Hedonic adaptation (habituation, hedonic treadmill). The tendency to revert quickly to previous levels of well-being after experiencing positive or negative life events. Adaptation can be complete (i.e., return to the same level of well-being) or incomplete.

Heuristics. Mental shortcuts that are automatic and intuitive and do not require conscious thought. They were initially described by Tversky and Kahneman in 1974.

Homo economicus (ECON). A term used to describe an economic actor who is assumed to be consistently rational, self-interested and utility-maximizing.

Homo psychologicus. A term used to describe an economic actor whose decisions are subject to systemic errors (biases and heuristics). The term is defined in opposition to homo economicus.

Hot–cold empathy gap. A cognitive bias which reflects the fact that people underestimate the influences of visceral drives on their attitudes, preferences, and behaviors. For example, they underestimate the effect of being hungry (hot state) when they have to make decisions when they are not hungry (cold state).

Hyperbolic discounting. A specific form of the discount function (see Discounting), in which discount rates are not constant over time. Discount rates are steep for earlier delay periods and smaller for longer delay periods.

Illusory correlations. The tendency to perceive a relationship between two variables when, in fact, none exists. They occur when two separate variables are paired together in such a way that overestimates their frequency.

Impartial spectator. Described by Adam Smith and defined in terms of the idealized person we wish to please in our dealings with other people (it is a form of conscience).

Inequality aversion (inequity aversion). People generally have a preference for fairness; a resistance to inequitable outcomes.

Insensitivity to sample size. A cognitive bias that occurs when people do not take the size of the sample into consideration when making judgments about the probability of an outcome occurring – smaller samples are less informative than larger samples.

Intertemporal choice. The study of choices that people make at various points in time, whereby current choices may affect available future options. Choices indicate how we value consumption today compared to future consumption.

Intrinsic motivation. Behavior is driven by internal motivation; doing something for its own sake.

Invisible hand. Described by Adam Smith in his 1776 book, *The Wealth of Nations*. An unobservable market force that helps reach and maintain equilibrium between demand and supply in a free market.

Judgment heuristics. Mental shortcuts involving making judgments.

Latent preferences. Hidden preferences which are not directly observed and may be inferred by revealed preferences in choice behavior.

Law of diminishing marginal utility. A concept in economics which states that the additional utility (benefit) gained from consuming an extra unit of a good decreases with each additional unit that is consumed (all other things being equal). In other words, the consumption of the first unit of a good yields more utility than the consumption of the second unit of a good, and so on.

Law of diminishing returns. A concept in economics which states that the additional output gained from adding an extra unit of a variable production factor decreases with each additional unit that is added (if all other production factors are held constant).

Libertarian paternalism. The idea that choices and behavior can and should, be influenced while maintaining people's freedom to choose. Such liberty-preserving nudges need to allow people to opt out. (See Benign paternalism.)

Loss aversion. "Losses loom larger than gains" (Kahneman & Tversky, 1979); the tendency to prefer avoiding losses relative to achieving gains of the same magnitude.

Macroeconomics. The branch of economics that studies the aggregate economy and general economic factors, such as inflation, economic growth, or the unemployment rate.

Mainstream economics. See Neoclassical economics.

Marginalism. The study of marginal theories in economics, which emphasize how much extra (marginal) output is gained by incremental additions of one unit of input (concepts cover opportunity costs and marginal utility, among others).

Marginal utility. The extra utility gained from consuming one additional unit.

Market equilibrium. State of the economy in which demand is equal to supply. The market-clearing price is the price at which the quantity that consumers demand and the quantity that firms are willing to supply are the same.

Matching law. A law which states that people will match their behavior/response to the relative rate of reinforcement.

Mental accounting. A term describing the tendency to allocate money to separate mental accounts based on individual criteria.

Mere exposure effect (familiarity principle). The tendency to develop a preference for things or people that are familiar.

Microeconomics. The branch of economics that studies single factors and the behavior of individuals (consumers) and firms.

Money illusion. The tendency to think of income/wealth in terms of the face value (the nominal value; e.g., $1) rather than in terms of its purchasing power (the real value which takes inflation into account).

Myopic loss aversion theory. Described by Benartzi and Thaler to explain the equity premium puzzle; it refers to a short-term view on investments which is characterized by a high sensitivity to losses.

Nash equilibrium. Named after Nobel Prize recipient John Nash, it is a concept in game theory which defines the best solution in non-cooperative games involving two or more players. It is the outcome of the game in which changing strategy would not lead to a better pay-off for one player while taking into account the best strategies of other players.

Neoclassical economics (mainstream, traditional). Current dominant approach in economics, which assumes that rational economic agents seek to maximize utility (consumers) or profits (firms), as well as a number of other axioms.

Normative economics. A perspective in economics that focuses on how people *should* behave and what the outcome of public policies *ought* to be; contrary to positive economics, it is value-based and subjective.

Nudge theory (nudge). An aspect of choice architecture that influences behavior in a non-coercive way; a nudge is said to be liberty-preserving and does not involve regulation or bans; it must be easy to opt out of the behavior, if it is not desired.

Opportunity cost. The value of the best foregone alternative when one option is chosen.

Optimization. The most effective use of available resources, choosing the best available option given budget constraints.

Peak-end rule. Experiences are not remembered in the same way; we tend to remember the most intense (peak) moments as well as the concluding moments (e.g., we prefer a longer, cumulatively more painful, dental treatment to a shorter one that contains a higher peak moment of pain).

Positive economics (descriptive economics). A perspective in economics that focuses on how people actually behave and economic facts; contrary to normative economics, it is fact-based and objective.

Praxeology. An old name for the science of human action (what we now call psychology).

Preference purification. The reconstruction of what the individual would have chosen in the absence of reasoning imperfections; the idea is that contaminated revealed preferences need to be 'purified' to get at true (latent) preferences.

Preference reversal. A situation in which preferences change between alternatives options; this could be due to a change in context, framing, the method of eliciting the preference or the point in time at which the outcome of the choice will be realized, among other reasons.

Present bias. The tendency to prefer immediate rewards over delayed rewards.

Price elasticity of demand. A measure which indicates how responsive (elastic) demand is to changes in price (i.e., to what extent demand increases/decreases after a price decrease/increase).

Priming. A nonconscious memory effect in which exposure to a stimulus affects how people react to another stimulus. The brain networks are activated by an initial 'prime' which then affect subsequent ('primed') behavior.

Prisoner's Dilemma. A scenario in which two players have to decide separately whether to cooperate or defect (i.e., 'rat out' their partner in crime). The common feature of Prisoner's Dilemma games is that the ideal outcome is achieved when both players cooperate; however, each player's dominant strategy is to cheat and, thus the Nash equilibrium is that both defect (see Nash equilibrium).

Procedure invariance. Preferences should be stable irrespective of how they are elicited.

Procedural learning. The nonconscious acquisition of a new skill through repeating actions.

Prominence effect. Prominent options are more likely to be chosen.

Prospect theory. Developed by Kahneman and Tversky in 1979; a theory that describes decision making under risk.

Psychological value. In marketing, the customer-perceived value of a product that often exceeds the functional or monetary value by making the consumer feel better (i.e., subjective utility).

Randomized controlled trial (RCT). A type of experiment in which participants are randomly allocated to either a control or treatment group in order to test the effect of the treatment.

Rationality. In neoclassical economics, rational consumers maximize their utility and rational firms maximize their profit. Rational behavior follows axioms (assumptions), including completeness, among others.

Rational choice theory. A framework for modeling economic behavior; it is assumed that rational agents will choose the best options to maximize their utility, given their constraints.

Reactance theory. A theory which describes that people often do the opposite of what rules and regulations mandate if they feel that their freedom to choose is being curtailed; more generally, they do not like being told what to do.

Reciprocal altruism. Doing something for other people with the expectation that this altruistic act will be reciprocated in the future ("you scratch my back, and I will scratch yours").

Reference dependence. Outcomes are evaluated relative to a reference point; an important aspect of prospect theory.

Reflection effect. Opposite risk preferences for gambles, depending on whether the potential outcome is a gain or loss (e.g., people tend to show risk-seeking behavior to avoid losses but risk-averse behavior to secure gains).

Relative utility. An individual's well-being relative to that of relevant others; as opposed to absolute utility, which does not imply a comparison with other people.

Repeated games (iterative strategy games). In game theory, a game in which the same base game is repeated over several rounds.

Representativeness heuristic. A mental shortcut which people use when estimating the probability that an event or object belongs to a certain class, by looking at how representative that event/object seems to be of that class – this can lead to base rate neglect.

Revealed preferences. An economic theory which posits that the best way to measure preferences is to observe actual choice behavior; the theory assumes that actual choices (e.g., purchases) reveal latent preferences.

Rhyme as reason. Similar sounds, sights, etc. are encoded more readily; when using words, a rhyme is better remembered and may be seen as more persuasive (this is why commercial forms of communication often use them, e.g., "naughty but nice" – in the court case of O. J. Simpson, "If the glove doesn't fit, you must acquit" is thought by some to have been decisive in the not guilty verdict).

Risk. The probability of an outcome occurring is known.

Risk aversion. The tendency to avoid risks among gambles with the same expected value: risk-averse individuals will always prefer the gamble with the lowest level of risk. Sure bets might even be preferred over risky options with higher expected values.

Salience. An aspect of a stimulus that is prominent or draws attention in some way; people's attention is drawn to what is novel and seems relevant and, therefore, processed more.

Satisficing. A portmanteau of 'suffice' and 'satisfying' introduced by Herbert Simon in 1956; it describes the tendency of individuals to make decisions that are not optimal as defined in mathematical terms, but that are good enough to provide a sufficient degree of happiness (i.e., utility).

Say's law (the law of markets). Described by Jean-Baptiste Say in 1803, which states that supply (or production) creates its own demand.

Scarcity value. Psychological value is higher for goods that are, or seem to be, in short supply.

Sensation transfer. The process in which warm feelings we have about something (e.g., our name) transfers to another object (e.g., the Starbucks cup).

Social comparison. Proposed by Leon Festinger in 1954, people's tendency to compare themselves to their peers in order to evaluate themselves.

Social influence. Refers to changes in attitudes, beliefs, opinions, values, and behavior as a result of exposure to other people's attitudes, beliefs, opinions, values, and behavior.

Social norms. The accepted (though unwritten and usually not articulated) rules of behavior in a society (that may change over time); we are heavily influenced by what we think other people expect of us.

Social preferences (interdependent preferences, other-regarding preferences). Individuals who exhibit social preferences take th utility/payoff of other people into account in their own decision-making process (e.g., altruism, fairness, envy, reciprocity).

Social proof (informational social influence). An individual's tendency to seek information and reassurance from other people (a type of conformity); we look to others for guidance on social behavior.

Spiteful behavior. In game theory, spiteful players are willing to forego a benefit in order to punish another player.

Status quo bias. A preference for the familiar, current state of affairs.

Sunk costs. A cost that has already been incurred and cannot be recovered; contrary to prospective costs which have not yet been incurred and will depend on the choice made.

Supply (law of supply). A law described in microeconomics which states that as the price of a good (or service) increases, the quantity that firms are willing to supply of that good will increase and vice versa (all other things being equal).

Supposedly irrelevant factors (SIFs). Term coined by Richard Thaler which refers to factors that are supposedly irrelevant in the thinking of a rational person – however, in reality, these factors do influence decisions.

System 1 (implicit/procedural). One of the two kinds of information processing described in dual-processing theory. At the moment of execution, all cognition and behaviors are controlled by System 1, which is reflexive, fast, automatic, biased, intuitive, emotional, habitual, nonconscious, and prepotent. System 1 is said to be responsible for the biases and errors that define behavioral economics.

System 2 (explicit/declarative). One of the two kinds of information processing described in dual-processing theory. System 2 is reflective, slow, controlled, and effortful and can be conscious. It is thought that System 2 operates only when there is a definite choice to be made and System 1 cannot arrive at a solution. System 2 is usually thought to have the capacity to be more rational than System 1.

Systematic processing. The assumption that attitude change is mediated by the message recipient's detailed processing of the (informational) arguments.

Transaction cost. The costs incurred in the process of buying or selling a good or service.

Uncertainty. The probability of the outcome occurring is not known.

Utilitarianism. A doctrine established by Jeremy Bentham that advances the idea that the greatest happiness of the greatest number should be the foundation of morals and legislation; it is based on the assumption that our decision making and behaviors are motivated by the pursuit of pleasure (utility) and the avoidance of pain and displeasure (disutility).

Utility. The enjoyment, benefit, or value that a consumer obtains from a good, service, etc.

Utility function. A utility function orders and measures preferences over a set of goods and services.

Veblen good. A good for which demand increases as price increases, which is a violation of the law of demand (see Demand); Veblen goods are usually positional goods or status symbols.

von Neumann-Morgenstern utility theorem. A theorem in decision theory which forms the basis for expected utility theory; it shows that rational decision makers who have to choose between several risky options (i.e., with known probabilities) will maximize the expected value of these choices.

INDEX

Printed in the United States
by Baker & Taylor Publisher Services